Modern
5

Disneyland
1985–1995

Sim City
1995–2001

Starchitecture
2001–present

day Casino
rah's) 1972

The International
(Westgate) 1969

Grand (Bally's) 1973

Treasure Island 1993

The Mirage 1989

The Excalibur 1990

Luxor 1993

MGM Grand 1993

Stratosphere 1996

Venetian 1999

Bellagio 1998

Paris Las Vegas 1999
Aladdin (Planet Hollywood) 2001

Monte Carlo 1996
New York New York 1997

Mandalay Bay 1999

Palazzo 2010

Encore 2008
Wynn 2005

The Cosmopolitan 2010
Project CityCenter 2009

THE STRIP

THE STRIP

LAS VEGAS AND THE ARCHITECTURE OF THE AMERICAN DREAM

Stefan Al

The MIT Press   Cambridge, Massachusetts   London, England

This book was set in Minion and Univers by the MIT Press.
Printed and bound in the United States of America.

Library of Congress Cataloging-in-Publication Data is available.
ISBN: 978-0-262-03574-3

10   9   8   7   6   5   4   3   2   1

Contents

Acknowledgments

This book began on Thanksgiving of 2005, my first visit to Las Vegas, as a paper for Ananya Roy's class. Thanks to her and my chair Nezar AlSayyad, as well as committee members Michael Southworth and Greig Crysler, it became a dissertation. Ultimately, with great thanks to Roger Conover and the MIT Press, including copy editor Gillian Beaumont, it turned into this publication.

In Las Vegas, I owe the ever-helpful Su Kim Chung and Delores Brownlee from UNLV Special Collections, David G. Schwartz of the Center for Gaming Research, Dennis McBride of the Nevada State Museum, and Lebene Aidam-Ohene of Clark County Planning. At the University of Pennsylvania, I am deeply indebted to Marilyn Jordan Taylor, Eugenie Birch, John Landis, Tom Daniels, Erick Guerra, Francesca Ammon, David Brownlee, and especially to William Whitaker, curator of the Architectural Archives. I would like to extend my appreciation to the Trustees of the University of Pennsylvania for providing a subvention to print in color. Venturi and Scott Brown's *Learning from Las Vegas*, Alan Hess's *Viva Las Vegas*, and Charles Barnard's *The Magic Sign* were an inspiration, as well as the Vegas analyses of journalists and critics such as Paul Goldberger. I thank the Las Vegas News Bureau photographers for their sensational photos, and the resorts for allowing me to use their images.

Many have sifted through the manuscript. I benefited from my academic peers including Jennifer Day, Sophie Sturup, William Riggs, and with a special mention of Pietro Calogero. My creative writing group, spearheaded by wordsmith Sue Hollister Barr, comprised Steven Tate, Katie McElhenney, Mike Reilly, Amaya Swanson, Haisi Hu, Tom Piccolo, and Diya Gangopadhyay. Cathryne Lonahata, Duane DeWitt, and Jenya Godina generously read and edited chapters.

Finally, I thank Rebecca Jin, Vera Al, and Janneke van Kuijzen, for their love and support.

Figure Credits

Adam Nowek, author's private collection (5.6, 6.7)

Author's private collection (3.4)

Barbara Kraft, Wynn Resorts (7.2)

Charles Barnard private collection (3.11)

Las Vegas News Bureau (1.5, 2.3, 2.4, 2.7, 2.9, 2.11, 2.14, 3.15, 3.16, 3.18, 3.21, 5.2, 5.9, 5.11, 5.12, 6.4, 6.8, 6.10, 7.6, 7.7)

MGM Resorts (7.3, 7.5)

Ned Paynter Collection/FSDA (4.7)

Neon Museum, Charles Barnard Collection (3.20, 4.6)

Nevada State Museum, Las Vegas (1.6, 1.7, 2.5, 2.6, 2.10)

Raymond Winters, Las Vegas Chamber of Commerce, David Rumsey Historical Map Collection (1.1)

UNLV Special Collections (1.3, 1.4, 2.1, 2.8, 2.13, 3.6, 3.7, 3.17, 4.5, 5.1, 5.4, 5.5, 5.7, 5.8, 6.2, 6.3, 6.8, 6.9)

UNLV Special Collections, Bill Willard Collection (4.8)

UNLV Special Collections, Homer A. Rissman Collection (4.2)

UNLV Special Collections, Manis Collection (1.2, 1.8, 2.2, 3.1)

UNLV Special Collections, Martin Stern, Jr. Collection (3.10, 4.1, 4.3, 4.4, 4.9)

UNLV Special Collections, Union Pacific Railroad Photo Collection (2.12)

UNLV Special Collections, YESCO Collection (3.2, 3.3)

Venturi, Scott Brown Collection, The Architectural Archives, University of Pennsylvania (3.8, 3.9, 3.12, 3.13, 3.14)

Introduction: Las Vegas as America

Las Vegas exists because it is a perfect reflection of America. … It represents all the things people in every city in America like. Here they can get it in one gulp.[1]

—Steve Wynn, casino tycoon

Conventional wisdom holds that Las Vegas is deviant and the Strip a display of architectural freaks. But a closer look shows that the city is more representative of American architectural trends than we would like to admit. Since its beginning, Vegas developers have surfed waves of social, cultural and economic change to build casinos so compelling that they actually drew vacationers to the Mojave Desert. From exploiting Disneyland to the atom bomb to the sexual revolution to "green" building, the Strip mirrored America as a whole.

Las Vegas was a ghost town a century ago, but forty-two million people visited the desert city in 2015—ten million more than Paris. Today, Vegas is more influential than ever as a model for urban development. Macau reclaimed hundreds of acres of the South China Sea, only to build a Las Vegas-style Strip. Even Singapore, a nation known for outlawing chewing gum, built its new flagship business district around a Las Vegas-style casino. In 2007, the Brand Ranking survey saw Las Vegas rise to America's number two brand, behind only Google.

Yet architects have largely refused to take the city seriously—even though the time it *was* taken seriously, it had a major impact on the profession. Robert Venturi and Denise Scott Brown's seminal *Learning from Las Vegas* helped overthrow modernism, an architectural style that for decades reigned supreme, and invent postmodernism, which would influence architects worldwide.

This book tells the two parallel stories behind Las Vegas's evolution. The first narrates how Las Vegas developers continuously worked to improve the so-called consumer "Mousetrap." The protagonists include an eclectic cast of all-American characters: "Bugsy" Siegel, the founder of "Murder Inc.," whose obsession over his lavish casino cost him millions and drove him to death; American billionaire Howard Hughes, who masterminded a string of casino takeovers while holed up in the same hotel room for years; and business magnate Sheldon Adelson, who painstakingly reproduced Venice in the desert, but with monuments of gilded Styrofoam instead of stone.

The second thread positions Las Vegas at the forefront of broader societal trends: before the first astronaut headed into space, a Las Vegas casino incorporated a two-ton planet into its façade, then surrounded it with a sputnik. But the city also magnifies trends. When the Disney Corporation became the world's largest entertainment conglomerate, Steve Wynn opened the Mirage with an erupting volcano, and his competitor Bill Bennett promptly responded with a thirty-story toy castle, complete with a fire-spitting dragon. Wynn followed with a pirate village and scorching frigates; Bennett with a hollow pyramid and a ten-story laser-eyed Sphinx. Casino mogul Kirk Kerkorian entered the game with a lion built across from the Sphinx, with Dorothy, the Scarecrow, and the Tin Man walking beneath its chin.

The city is so attuned to change that perfectly sound buildings have been regularly torn down to make room for new structures. The ten-story lion was demolished after only three years, and Dorothy and the Tin Man were sent down the gray asphalt road of the Strip. Not lingering in nostalgia, developers would destroy their previous creations for the next new thing, earning Las Vegas the title "Implosion Capital of the World."

The story of Las Vegas is the story of capitalist development at large. "Creative Destruction is the essential fact about capitalism,"[2] claimed economist Joseph Schumpeter in 1942; coincidentally, a year after the Las Vegas Strip was founded. The ferocious competition and vast budgets for buildings created extraordinary design experimentation: a glass pyramid large enough to stack nine jumbo jets, and a hydraulic octopus hurtling showgirls, powered by nuclear weapons technology. Just after the invention of color television, Las Vegas developers dazzled audiences with neon screens displaying electronic messages as wide as two football fields. But on the dark side of the city's neon-electric creations lie hydroelectric river barricades, coal-hungry bulldozers and scorching ovens, and depleted natural resources. Hidden from the Strip's phantasmagoria of fountains, dewy lawns, and Olympic-sized pools rest dry groundwater wells and a diminishing Colorado River.

Las Vegas underscores America's entrepreneurial spirit to the extreme. A story of both waste and innovation, of failure and triumph, this book shows how a city tuned to the convulsions of the commodity economy and the fickleness of desire grew from a little desert town into one of the world's most visited cities. Although the city started as an exception to the Puritanical values of mid-twentieth-century America, it has become a major innovator in today's "experience economy."[3] From self-invention to cutthroat competition to risky "casino capitalism,"[4] Las Vegas is a microcosm of America.

1

Wild West (1941–1946)

Visitors are attracted because we publicize this as "STILL A FRONTIER TOWN," and are disappointed when they arrive and do not find the cowboys, prospectors and general Western atmosphere.[1]

—Las Vegas Chamber of Commerce

People aren't interested in the sober West, only the wild West.[2]

—Bill Moore, architect of the Last Frontier casino

In the early 1940s, scantily clad cowgirls drove a stagecoach stuffed with guests to a ranch where the owner, wearing a cowboy hat, greeted his visitors with "Howdy Pardner." Coach wheel "chandeliers" and cattle brands hung from the ceiling. Only a stone's throw away stood a Western fort and a mining village featuring a Pioche Pacific Railroad steam train and papier-mâché versions of Flat Rack Jack, Sheriff Bill McGee, and a Chinese man, "Sit-too-Long."

There were more glaring incongruities in this frontier construction: glittering pools, manicured lawns, and a gas station. Even the Western windmill rising on the skyline was far from a sign of frontier deprivation: its neon blades swirling to attract the motorist, it was merely a cover for ice-machine air-conditioning.

Standing along a pothole-filled road that was not yet known as "The Strip," Las Vegas's first two casino complexes were camouflaged in the theme of the Wild West. The image had been unabashedly invented at a time when the frontier days were long gone, and in a city that had no cowboy history. Nevertheless, the image had an important purpose. The backdrop dressed up a vital resource to the city in the barren Mojave Desert: regulations.

Las Vegas harnessed the statewide legalization of what was considered dubious in other places, including gambling. As Puritanical governments around the United States saw casinos as dens of sin, Las Vegans presented their games of chance as laissez-faire "frontier" activities, while exploiting a nationwide nostalgia for the Old West. The Western image was an even more appropriate symbolical fit for the Strip, lying in the middle of the empty desert, just outside of the city and its taxation laws.

During the Wild West phase of the Strip, casino developers banked on the profitable conflation of "Western" regulation and image. But as they pampered their "cowboy" gamblers with modern comfort and Wild West fantasy, Las Vegas started as a strange paradox.

THE LOOMING GHOST TOWN

From early on, Las Vegas struggled to find itself.

On the basis of its location, climate, or resources alone, it had no reason to exist in the first place. It lies isolated, hundreds of miles away from major cities, on all sides cut off by lunar-like mountain ranges. Summer days can heat up to a furnace-like 115 degrees Fahrenheit (46° C). The only species fit to live in the barren, dusty, and rocky Mojave Desert are creosote bushes and chuckwallas.

Fortunately, a few artesian wells nourished some grassy areas. They functioned as an oasis for travelers crossing the Mojave Desert, explaining the first recorded settlement in the early nineteenth century. In 1829, Spanish Mexican explorers of the Antonia Armijo army, most likely guided by Ute or Paiute Indians, named the area "Las Vegas," Spanish for "the meadows."

This moist patch first became a home for questionable activities. In the early 1840s, Bill Williams, a Baptist minister who had become a mountain man and cannibal, used it as a base for his band of Indian horse thieves. Williams also worked as a guide for the U.S. government taking armies across the desert, and was known to introduce hungry soldiers to eating "the long pig," a euphemism for Homo sapiens. "In starving times," an acquaintance of the preacher said, "don't walk ahead of Bill Williams."[3]

In 1844, the wells were given a military purpose with the first recorded structure: a secret fort, built by explorer John C. Fremont to prepare for the war with Mexico. The war was won, the fort never permanently inhabited, but Fremont's lasting influence on Las Vegas was putting it on the map.

Fremont's map inspired Mormons to settle in Utah. They built a 150-square-foot adobe fort meant to refuge travelers along the "Mormon Corridor." Meanwhile, they used it as a base to baptize local Paiute Indians who, unappreciative, raided the fort's crops and animals. After three years, Mormon leadership gave up on the fort, and on Las Vegas, which one missionary described as the land the "Lord had forgotten"[4] (there are many who would still describe it this way).

"It is easy to foresee that it will never become considerable,"[5] two French cartographers wrote of Las Vegas in 1861. But that year a large gold strike was reported in

Chapter 1

El Dorado Canyon. The Mormon fort was acquired by a group of men, and changed ownership a number of times, until Montana Senator William Clark purchased it in 1902. Clark wanted to make Las Vegas a "water stop" for locomotive boiler replenishing, servicing his proposed rail line from Salt Lake City to Los Angeles. Before the train rolled in, the Senator had already auctioned off all lots of the 110-acre "Clark's Las Vegas Townsite" on May 15, 1905, the day that became the founding date of Las Vegas. It was the promise of material wealth that finally led to the founding of the city.

Las Vegas was born as a classic Western railroad town, one of many water stops along new railways that evolved into settlements. The mines and train brought customers for the speakeasies, brothels, and "sawdust joints," small uncarpeted casinos with sawdust on the floor to soak up beer and tobacco spit. Even the layout of the city was very uniform. To more easily sell off Las Vegas's lots, they were equal in size and laid out in a grid—a city layout dating back thousands of years, even before the Roman military camp.

But it would have been equally normal for Las Vegas to return to dust. In 1919, the mines ran out of ore. Three years later, Las Vegas workers joined the Great Railroad Strike. In retaliation, the railroad company moved its repair centers out of town. Without the railroad jobs, Las Vegas could have shared the tragic but common fate of new cities in the West. These cities were founded on serious risk. Their bustle could stop as soon as their mines were stripped, only to render them ghost towns, left to decay.

Desperately looking for another industry, Las Vegans established a Chamber of Commerce, which marketed the city as a resort city, out of envy for Palm Springs, the Californian desert city that successfully attracted tourists. In the 1920s, a few resorts and a golf course were constructed, and a Las Vegas lobby managed to include the city in the United States's new highway system connecting Los Angeles to Salt Lake City—later known as the Los Angeles Highway, with a four-mile stretch that became the Las Vegas Strip.

But few people came.

DAMMING SIN

Who would have expected that the federal government, when it was at its most Puritanical, would not only come to help Las Vegas grow, but also indirectly mark it for a future of sin?

In 1928, the government announced the federal construction of the Boulder (later named Hoover) Dam. It planned to dam the Colorado River to create cheap hydroelectric power, and to create Lake Mead for a freshwater supply. Las Vegas would benefit from all of this and, more importantly, since it was the closest city to the site, the dam would bring an even more valuable resource: dam workers, looking to drink and gamble their paychecks away.

U.S. Secretary of the Interior Ray Lyman Wilbur—characterized by a reporter as "a very blue-nosed man"[6]—planned to visit the city to look for a suitable place to house the dam workers. But Las Vegas had become notorious for clubs, brothels, and speakeasies illegally providing alcohol during Prohibition. Las Vegas was willing to let this industry go in exchange for the workers. Residents temporarily closed all drinking, gambling and prostitution dens, even repainting buildings, to show it was a place suitable to work in.

Unfortunately, one of the Secretary's employees strayed, and was found with alcohol on his breath. The Secretary retaliated. Instead of housing the workers in Las Vegas, he chose to build from scratch the "model town" of Boulder City, federally controlled and without vice. "Instead of a boisterous frontier town," he said in his speech, "it is hoped that here simple homes, gardens with fruit and flowers, schools and playgrounds will make this a wholesome American community."[7]

Vegas merchants feared that their future was shattered. Nevertheless, by the spring of 1931, at least 42,000 unemployed workers came to Las Vegas hoping to find a job. At the abyss of the Great Depression, "the little desert town," wrote *Time*, "has been swelling and swelling like a toadstool."[8]

Having tried to conform to the rest of the nation, but failed, Las Vegas finally decided to embrace its rebellious self. Business owners reopened the clubs and developed casinos and showgirl theaters, teaming up with organized crime figures and Mormon financiers. Despite the decision that workers would not be housed in Las Vegas, the city benefited from mostly male visiting dam workers who came at weekends searching for alcohol, prostitutes, and gambling—all of which were banned in the vice-free worker city.

The intended separation of activities between Las Vegas and Boulder City resulted in each city supporting the other. Ironically, for the same reason that Prohibition had led to the rise of organized crime, the Puritanical attitude of federal authorities opened a space for Las Vegas to thrive. The city stepped into providing niche services that most people at the time considered unwholesome or morally questionable, but for which there was still a market. Having unsuccessfully gone through multiple identities—a base for horse thieves, a military fort, a Mormon stronghold, a railroad town, and its latest unsuccessful attempt to provide a "wholesome" place to house the workers—Las Vegas understood there was profit to be made by being Puritan America's "Other."

The "otherness" of Las Vegas was further institutionalized through a whole set of "libertarian" state regulations ranging from taxes to marriage, conducive for business. In 1931, Nevada legislators lowered the minimum residency requirement for out-of-state divorce petitioners from three months to six weeks. Since many states had very strict statutes on divorce, divorcees fled to Nevada, and in particular to Reno, well-known as a place to get "Reno-vated." Retaining a residency requirement was important, helping to fill hotels and guest ranches with divorcees.

That same year, the state legalized gambling, bringing about Nevada's eventual forty-five-year, countrywide monopoly on casinos. Despite the Great Depression, Las Vegas's resort industry grew. Divorcees passed time in guest ranches, while thousands of dam workers patronized the city's nascent casinos: for instance the 1932 Hotel Apache, the city's first hotel with an elevator and air-conditioning. State regulation, Nevada's unique "commodity," had a major impact on the city of Las Vegas, a city lacking other resources.

In the big picture, for the United States as a whole, by legalizing gambling only in remote Nevada it could be contained; for the same reason, the area would be a good site for nuclear detonations. Las Vegans realized their city's remote location had been turned into an advantage. And as they built more casinos, the city would become the focal point of a national experiment in the legislation of sin.

OUTLAWS OF THE MEADOWS

During Prohibition, Italian immigrant Tony Cornero was caught with more than 1,000 cases from Mexico that, he told reporters, he had imported "to keep 120 million people from being poisoned"[9] by drinking moonshine. After a two-year jail sentence, he founded an "insulation" company, which a federal authorities' raid revealed to be a whiskey-smuggling business.

From behind prison bars, Cornero decided to bring his penchant for illegitimate business to a place where the rules were skewed in his favor. He masterminded building a casino in Las Vegas. Tony and his brothers moved to the city, along with gambling operators around the nation who now found a place where they could run casinos legally. Las Vegas's authorities granted the brothers a gaming license, despite their criminal past.

It took an Italian immigrant to bring the Las Vegas "casino" back to its etymological roots. Casino originally meant "little house" in Italian, and referred to a small country villa, or a luxurious pavilion built for pleasure, typically in the grounds of large palaces, such as Villa Giulia in Rome, built by the Pope. These pavilions had a somewhat public function as places to listen to music, to dance, and to gamble. Tony Cornero built his Meadows in this more glorious tradition: a "carpet joint," with carpet on the floor, very different from existing Las Vegas casinos, which were like small "sawdust joints," which focused on gambling only, and had sawdust on the floor. He built a white adobe hacienda-style building with large churchlike doors leading to a high nave and a plush interior. It even had a cabaret, "Meadows Revue."

In a stroke of foresight, Cornero built right outside of the city, avoiding city taxes and zoning laws. After running from the law for years, he had finally managed to find the one place in the United States with the loosest of all regulations: outside of the influence of city hall in the lenient Clark County, within the "libertarian" state of Nevada. But even though he technically did not build inside Las Vegas, he still had the audacity to name his casino "The Meadows," after the English translation.

Las Vegas's first establishments needed to be in downtown for its steam-power boilers, but the advent of electricity enabled power transmission anywhere through a simple cable. Therefore Cornero could build along the busy Boulder Highway, so he could catch tourists from the Hoover Dam, their wholesome vacation taking a diversion. They would see Cornero's casino even before the ones in downtown, and they could park more easily, out in middle of the desert.

It was this location outside of city limits that allowed the Cornero brothers to exploit the more modern Italian meaning of casino, which also translates as *bordello*. With the church trying to outlaw prostitution in the city of Las Vegas, the brothers struck a deal: they would add a thirty-room hotel, and let it happen properly. They would have exclusive rights to prostitution.

But then the Syndicate's Charles "Lucky" Luciano and his associate, casino owner Meyer Lansky, wanted a piece of the action. Cornero declined. In 1932, his casino "accidentally" caught fire. The Las Vegas Fire Department refused to drive outside of city boundaries to put out the flames. What had seemed to be an advantageous location outside of the city had backfired: Cornero saw his casino go up in smoke. Nevertheless, he set the template of the strip casino complex: a luxury roadside casino-hotel, built outside of city limits.

After the fire, Cornero moved back to Los Angeles to return to the ocean, where he would once again bank on territorial regulations. In 1938, he established two casino boats, anchoring them in international waters, just outside of Santa Monica and Long Beach. In spite of that, in 1939 the coastguard tried to embark his boat. Cornero aimed fire hoses at the attackers, but after a nine-day siege on the *Rex*, known as "The Battle of Santa Monica Bay," he surrendered.

He explained: "I have to get a haircut and the only thing I haven't got aboard ship is a barber."[10]

VICE IN DISGUISE

Guy McAfee was a man of lucrative contradictions. He had combined a career as a Vice Squad captain of the Los Angeles Police Department with owning saloons and brothels during Prohibition, and a marriage to a high-end Hollywood madam. The reversible gambling tables of his Clover Club, Los Angeles's most profitable casino, were double-faced also, so he could conveniently deal with the raids he could accurately predict. Nicknamed "Overlord of the Gambling Tables," he created a scarcity he could cater to, by selectively enforcing the illegal.

In 1938, however, a new mayor was elected who declared war on illegal casinos. McAfee was forced to resign, and faced possible trial. He fled to Las Vegas and bought the Pair-O-Dice, the first casino along the Los Angeles Highway. Despite his checkered past, McAfee was allowed to operate the casino and quickly rose to become Las Vegas's first casino mogul, owning a handful of establishments. Las Vegans nicknamed him "the Captain."

Guy McAfee was a typical Las Vegas casino owner of that time. He and fellow gambling operators had run from places like Los Angeles that cracked down on gambling. But even though Las Vegas benefited from people like McAfee, experienced operators who brought their Los Angeles clientele, it also created a public relations problem.

The city became known as the "American Gomorrah." A headline in *Look* proclaimed: "Wild, Woolly and Wide-Open: That's Las Vegas, Nevada, Where Men are

Men and Sin is A Civic Virtue."[11] But Las Vegas's immoral reputation could potentially alienate mainstream visitors and business travelers, or the federal government, which had supported it, paying for the city's first convention center and public golf course.

Las Vegans, however, had an idea. In 1939, the year of the first turbojet flight, when Las Vegas downtown already had air conditioning, elevators, and paved streets, the Chamber of Commerce marketed the city as "Still a Frontier Town." It helped cloak the city's deviant behavior under the Frontier, a period of time that took Americans away from European institutions and ideas to more informal and individual ways of life, now recognized as "American." Gambling fit naturally into this frontier myth. Historian John Findlay later wrote: "Gambling and westering thrived on high expectations, risk taking, opportunism and movement."[12]

Las Vegas had dabbled with Western images as early as 1935, when it started its yearly Helldorado festival, a ploy to attract tourists. Business leaders wore Western movie costumes and residents participated in a daring "hoochie coochie dance" show and a "Whiskerino" contest, a challenge for men to grow the longest beard. It was such a success that the festival grew to include a beauty pageant, a professional rodeo, and a temporary theme park, the Helldorado Village.

1.1 In 1939, with planes flying into Las Vegas, the Chamber of Commerce marketed the city as "Still a Frontier Town," dedicating this map to the prospector, "who has built the West … in his quest of hidden treasures."

Las Vegas's festival was an unashamed clone of the Helldorado Days in Tombstone, Arizona, but Tombstone was an "authentic" Western town whose festival commemorated the famous thirty-second Gunfight at the O.K. Corral that established the deadly reputation of Marshal Wyatt Earp. Las Vegas, on the other hand, had very limited frontier roots. By the time the city was founded, in 1905, the American frontier period was already over—by fifteen years, according to the historian Frederick JacksonTurner, who claimed the frontier had closed by 1890. Other than one single ranch, there had barely been any cowboys in Las Vegas.

In 1940, the Helldorado Village was expanded with wooden sidewalks and twelve separate entertainment buildings, described by a reporter as a "six-acre replica of Las Vegas as it existed in the [18]80's, enclosed in a stockade as was used by early Western settlers in defense against the Indians"[13]—except that Las Vegas never did have such a settlement. "The Las Vegans plan to preserve this village as a permanent attraction for visitors who go to the Nevada city the year 'round," the reported noted. The village would constitute a lasting reminder of Las Vegas's fiction of the West.

Las Vegas capitalized on the popularity of the frontier period, fueled by Western movies such as *Cisco Kid*. The city even tapped into the dude ranch industry, a tourism sector dedicated to providing a "Western" frontier-style experience for well-to-do Easterners, called "dudes" or "tenderfoots," without the discomforts of the frontier days. In Las Vegas, however, the dude ranches became the perfect places to sit out the divorce residency requirement, since they provided for extended stays. The 1939 Boulderado dude ranch, for instance, catered less to "cowboys" than it did to "cowgirl" divorcees, in town for a "quickie" divorce.

The Western theme also appealed to patriots, especially in a time of anticommunist sentiment. In 1936, the First National Bank in Reno and the Nevada State Journal teamed up to distribute a booklet promoting the state: "The law-makers are cattlemen, miners, lawyers, business, and professional men, and there hasn't been the slightest whisper of radicalism from one of them."[14] Plus the image effectively cloaked the state's regressive income taxation as "western"—even though it was mainly rich Reno voters who were behind the regulations, many of them from Northern California.

All of it seemed to work. *Time* magazine wrote: "Nevada is a thinly populated State where easy divorce, open prostitution, licensed gambling, and legalized cock fighting are only the more luridly publicized manifestations of a free & easy, individualist spirit, deriving straight from the mining camp and cattle ranch."[15] Despite all this, in 1939 the Chamber felt the need to remind Las Vegans "to don their Western clothes." It stated: "Visitors … are disappointed when they arrive and do not find the cowboys, prospectors and general Western atmosphere."[16]

Nevertheless, the residents already played their part. "There is a considerable amount of Western posing in Reno and Las Vegas," an observer noted. "There are bellhops, orchestra players, lawyers and merchants who confidently wear 'Western' dude-ranch costume: cow[boy] boots, blue jeans, gray neckerchiefs, and Stetson hats."[17] Moreover, the city had a unique hooliganism, a reporter wrote: "A horse [is] a permissible means of entering a bar if you can get him through the door."[18]

Las Vegas casino operators also eagerly exploited the theme of the West, giving their casinos Western names such as Boulder and El Cortez. The theme fit into the escapist culture of Great Depression, was generally perceived as welcoming, and helped encourage "Western" daredevil-like risk-taking at the gambling tables.

Guy McAfee, a master of deception, happily played the Western card. In 1946, a decade after the California Gold Rush, he opened the Golden Nugget casino, built in the 1850s San Francisco Barbary Coast style. He imported antique Victorian woodwork for the interior, and hung it with gas globe chandeliers. As a final touch, he added "1905" to the Western neon sign: the founding date of Las Vegas, *not* of his casino.

Both "The Captain" McAfee and "Frontier Town" Las Vegas knew how to put up a phony front.

THE AIR-CONDITIONED COWBOY

The Las Vegas Strip was born on April 3, 1941, when Thomas Hull, a California hotel operator, opened El Rancho. It was the first casino complex on Highway 91, the dusty little potholed road stretching through the Mojave Desert, connecting Los Angeles to Las Vegas. Locals were beyond surprise. Two observers wrote later, "Two miles out! Middle of a desert! To promoters and builders in Vegas proper, the idea was insane."[19]

Even the lady who sold Hull the land was astonished. Legend has it that she offered it for free, since she thought it was "worthless." Nevertheless, Hull wrote a $57,000 check for 57 acres. A bargain, he thought, much cheaper than downtown, and outside city taxation limits.

Would this be another of Hull's failed business ventures? In 1913, he had first tried his luck with mining in Mexico, but in the midst of the Mexican Revolution he ran into Pancho Villa's army and had to walk 600 miles to get back to the border. He operated a movie theater, then a state-of-the-art industry, but it flopped.

Hull finally hit the jackpot in the hotel business. He had traded on his flying past when marketing San Francisco's Bellevue as a place for aviation heroes. Its success helped him to develop a luxury version of the motel, a new invention that rendered obsolete auto camps, which provided small cabins and public toilets to drivers. In 1925, the first "Mo-Tel," a portmanteau of "motor" and "hotel," gave drivers more hotel-like privacy and facilities all under a single roof, including a grocery market, a restaurant, and a private bathroom in each room. Hull called his version the "El Rancho," built a few in California, and planned to build one in Las Vegas.

Hull read in a highway engineering survey that almost one million cars traveled on the Los Angeles highway between Nevada and Southern California every year. Since his motels relied on passing automobilists, not downtown pedestrians, the highway location was perfect, despite being in the middle of the desert. In fact, Hull had had his eyes on Las Vegas ever since he had explored it three years earlier as a resort destination

1.2 Built in 1941 just outside the city, in the vast Mojave Desert, the El Rancho was Vegas's first self-contained casino complex with a swimming pool, entertainment, and lush landscaping.

with his architect, Wayne McAllister. He was commissioned to design "the Caliente of Nevada," a smaller version of Tijuana's Agua Caliente, the spectacular casino-resort that Mexico's President Cárdenas had turned into a state-run school after outlawing gambling.[20] But investors refused to take the risk. Now backed by a private loan from Texas, Hull resuscitated the idea.

But Hull, who was not a gambler, initially planned to build a motel only, just like the other El Ranchos, *without* a casino. During construction, his local friends said: "Why don't you build a casino building?"[21] The adding of the casino to the resort was an afterthought, merely a geographic add-on to a motel that happened to be built in Las Vegas.

McAllister also deviated from the El Rancho template elsewhere. While it was a luxury motel, it could not be perceived as too fancy, which would have turned off local patronage, accustomed to Western-themed places. An observer wrote of Las Vegas: "The mood is … 'Western,' lower middle class, proletarian even … people are … quite without pretension … their shirts open at the throat. … Old clothes and battered hats are common."[22]

Therefore, McAllister designed the interior in the local "Western" style. He hung wagon wheel chandeliers from the ceilings. He draped cowhide curtains from poles with cattle horns. In the lobby, he built a two-story stone chimney, a fake fireplace, mounting deer heads. "El Rancho Vegas is the physical expression of the warm hospitality that has been the tradition of our great Southwest since the days of the covered wagon," the publicity brochure stated. "Dress is informal. Bring your westerns."[23]

But the Western theme also led to some glaring contradictions. The nostalgic décor clashed with the ultramodern facilities of what was billed as "a truly modern hotel." McAllister built an "Old West" with a swimming pool, right next to the highway. Downtown casinos did not have the space for such facilities. It beckoned passing automobilists eager for a swim after a long, dusty, desert ride. "Instead of hiding its glittering swimming pool in some patio," noted the *Saturday Evening Post*, "they stuck it in their show window, smack on Route 91. It was a stroke of showmanship. No traveler can miss the pool, few can resist it."[24]

And the cowboys were quite the landscapers. Hull hired a staff of ten gardeners to maintain the lawn, fenced off by rough-hewn logs with crosshatch patterns typical of the Old West. He imported full-grown trees and rock waterfalls, soaking up to 10 million gallons of water per month from Las Vegas's groundwater wells—hardly a sign of frontier scarcity.

The Old West resort was also air-conditioned. Even the windmill, a key design element of the El Rancho chain since automobilists could see it from afar, did not actually pump water but held the air-conditioning equipment. And to make sure it could be seen at night, McAllister lined the blades with neon. "Stop at the Sign of the Windmill" became the motel's slogan. But Hull did not rely solely on his windmill to attract drivers; he convinced the local radio operator to move his station and tower to the resort,

1.3 A then skimpily dressed cowgirl holds a whip in front of the El Rancho, "A truly Modern Hotel" rife with "'Old West' hospitality."

with the proviso that the station must mention that it aired "from the fabulous grounds of the fabulous El Rancho Vegas," every twenty minutes.

The El Rancho, with its neon windmill looming over a mix of ranch and Spanish mission-style buildings, air-conditioned cowboy interior and radio tower included, was a giant paradox. But unlike other architects, McAllister was not hung up on achieving an integrated identity. A high-school dropout, he once bid for the design of the Agua Caliente. His plans called for an overall Spanish colonial revival-style building, adding baroque touches and Moorish elements, a Louis XIV room, and a Zigzag Moderne dining room. He tiled a 150-foot-tall power plant smokestack, encrusting it with ironwork, and turned it into a minaret. His client loved it.

Not bogged down by an architectural education that emphasized "honesty" of function and *Zeitgeist*, McAllister held a philosophy closer to the original Californian architects, the padres who built the Golden State's missions in the eighteenth century. They borrowed haphazardly from their memories and impressions of Europe, mixing Roman domes and arches with Spanish bell towers. While it was rife with contradictions, and surrounded by little but dry desert, the eclectic mix of El Rancho was nevertheless a huge success. "The place was jam-packed from opening night on," Garwood Van, the El Rancho bandleader, said. "Why? Highway 91 was so busted up that if you went over 40 miles per hour, you'd break an axle."[25]

McAllister had added just enough of the Old West. Even Hull got into the spirit, surprising tuxedo-wearing casino patrons on opening night by showing up in cowboy boots and a ten-gallon hat, drawling "Howdy Pardner." He also forced his staff to wear hand-embroidered Western outfits. "We wore guns; we were all cowboys,"[26] Guy Landis, the bass player, later said. Only the El Rancho Starlets, showgirls from Hollywood, relied on fewer clothes; one observer remembered them as "very pretty, with scantily-clad outfits and good figures."[27] Under the umbrella of the Western theme, the El Rancho somehow just managed to be the most novel, comfortable, and risqué of all.

The Western theme helped render this lavish and modern hotel less intimidating. The *Saturday Evening Post* observed: "The [El] Rancho somehow has managed to make the riveter, the carpenter and the truck driver at home in overalls in the same rooms with men and women in smart clothes, with an eloping Lana Turner posing for news photographs. … No resort is likely to succeed in Vegas that doesn't accomplish this democracy."[28] It would thus set the tone for the future Strip.

The El Rancho immediately enhanced the importance of that dusty, potholed road stretching through the barren Mojave Desert. Other hotel and casino developers would take a serious look at what Hull had built.

Even though the casino was an afterthought, Hull had invented the perfect casino complex. The large lot enabled him to include a whole range of facilities downtown casinos could only dream of, including a swimming pool, parking lots, a dining room, a coffee shop, a travel agency, badminton courts, and even riding stables with fifteen horses. With a range of resort facilities at their convenience, guests would never need to leave the premises. By including a hotel, Hull's casino had a captive audience.

Ironically, a man who had never gambled before had unintentionally built the Strip's first casino complex, and set the model for future developments: a self-contained and luxurious resort along a highway—where no one worried about using the right fork.

FRONTIER BATTLES

In 1941, R. E. Griffith from Texas, whose family owned hundreds of theaters, and his theater architect nephew, William Moore, wanted to build Hotel El Rancho in Deming, New Mexico. They heard of the developments in Las Vegas, and decided to make a brief stopover. "The opportunities were fabulous,"[29] Moore said. Even though Moore had already finished the drawings for the Deming hotel, the duo chose the lure of Las Vegas.

Guy McAfee sold them the Pair-O-Dice. He saw more prospects in downtown, where most of the casinos were. Driving up and down the Los Angeles Highway, he sarcastically nicknamed the gravel road "The Strip," after the Sunset Strip in Los Angeles.

"Mr. McAfee, for a solid month, walked around showing everybody a cashier's check for $35,000," an employee of Griffith remembered. "He caught a Texas sucker; he sold him that piece of land."[30]

Moore knew that it would be a challenge. "It did present a problem in that the opportunities, we felt, were quite some time in the future," he later said.[31] But Griffith and Moore were highly skilled promoters who helped the theater industry grow to the extent that many Americans would see a movie several times a week.

Griffith planned on calling his resort El Rancho, since he had built the El Rancho Hotel in Gallup, the first of a potential chain. But since the name El Rancho was already taken, he settled on the Last Frontier, with the slogan "The Early West in Modern Splendor." As at the El Rancho, it was cowboy comfort that was being offered, far from frontier deprivation.

The theater duo planned to upstage the nearby El Rancho in all aspects. They made the Last Frontier bigger, with more facilities, and chose a better location: south of the El Rancho, so drivers from Los Angeles would see it first. They built more parking spaces, planted more greenery, and dug a pool even closer to the highway. They also added more Western flavor. Moore said: "The Last Frontier was conceived to be as near Western as we could make it."[32]

Griffith and Moore organized roping contests, rodeos, and even moonlight horse rides from Moore's stable of thirty horses. A gift shop sold Mexican and Indian jewelry, saddles, and Western costumes. Stagecoaches picked up guests from the airport.

Theater architect Moore brought in Navajo Indian masonry artisans from New Mexico to build sandstone patios, floors, and fake fireplaces. He built ceilings from rough-hewn timber, antiqued to look old. He decorated the lobby with rifles and a moose head, the Trophy room with mountain lions, and the Horn room with 200 pairs of Texas longhorn steer horns, some of them as long as five feet. He used saddles to build bar stools, and wagon wheels to make chairs. "The beds had horns over them and there were cow horns everywhere," an observer later wrote. "The headboards looked

A NATURAL COLOR REPRODUCTION FROM KODACHROME

1.4 A postcard of sunbathing swimmers around the Last Frontier pool, sandwiched between horse-drawn carriages and the highway.

like big oxen yokes."[33] Moore even suspended wagon wheels from heavy chains and hung them with pony express lanterns, to build Western "chandeliers."

But Moore also had practical reasons for his custom-made "Western" furniture of salvaged materials. The United States had entered World War II, and many manufacturers ceased production to save materials for the war effort. In response to this scarcity, he and Griffith incorporated the existing Pair-O-Dice to become the casino. They bought the leaded glass entrance and bar of downtown's Arizona Club, known for prostitution. "It's a massive, hand-carved mahogany relic of the rip-roaring 90's," the Last Frontier publicist later boosted, "a landmark of San Francisco's Barbary Coast. Hauled overland by oxcart to Las Vegas, it gathered polish and bullet scars in the famous (or infamous) old Arizona Club."[34]

During Last Frontier construction, the War Production Board seized all their electronic materials and wires to build a new Army air base north of Las Vegas. The military also set up a magnesium plant (BMI) east of Las Vegas, with 10,000 military workers. But as the military took the Last Frontier materials, Moore decided to captivate the workers. He disguised the casino in the shape of a Western fort. Like an American flag bikini, he flipped immorality into patriotism.

Just as at the El Rancho, the Last Frontier's Western theme helped make the resort seem unassuming to local residents and military workers, despite its luxury. "The friendly Western hospitality of the Last Frontier greets you from the moment you enter the lobby," the publicity stated. The Colony Club, on the other hand, which opened the same year, was, according to a reporter, "as modernistic, as chi-chi, as sophisticated in decor as anything in New York." It failed. "One glimpse of the deep-napped carpets and Park Avenue swish of the Colony is calculated to give an honest BMI worker a virulent inferiority complex."

The Last Frontier, however, was an immediate success. While it was fundamentally the same as the El Rancho—a self-contained, Western-themed casino-resort—it was perceived as superior. "I can't tell you why it was different," a reporter later said, "but it seemed that the Last Frontier had a higher-type clientele than the El Rancho did."[35]

If El Rancho had set the model for the first casino-resort, the Last Frontier set the pace for competition, giving a taste of the resort wars that would soon rage on the Strip. "If El Rancho was splendid, the Last Frontier would be splendiferous," two commentators later wrote. "It has remained the theme of Las Vegas resort hotels ever since. The newest with the mostest."[36]

Finally, at the Last Frontier, Griffith created a relationship between Las Vegas and the movie industry that would shape the future of the town. He built the Leo Carillo Room, a bar in honor of "Pancho," the Cisco Kid's sidekick, with a large picture of Carillo in Western outfit, astride his horse. "Strip hotels ceaselessly identified themselves with film stars in their promotion,"[37] historian John Findlay later wrote. "Movie making and Las Vegas gambling were closely linked as industries devoted to mass-producing leisure that incorporated fantasy." In addition to their mutual resemblances, however, the resort and movie industries had an actual connection, since Griffith combined his career as a theater mogul with that of a resort operator.

And so the theater operators were terribly disappointed when, upon delivery of the Arizona Club's bullet-scarred bar, it had lost some of its drama. The previous owners of the bar had varnished it and plugged the bullet holes. Moore immediately had the bar "restored."

It was sandblasted and shot up with holes again.

FALSE FRONTS

William Moore eventually became general manager of the Last Frontier so he could keep tinkering with the property. A former designer, he knew how to present an appealing front. If rooms were empty, he would tell employees to park in front of the hotel and turn on lights.

In 1942, Moore wanted to build a chapel to get a slice of Las Vegas's wedding business. "Most of the wedding chapels," he said, "had the interior of a chapel or church, but the exteriors were usually an old home or a part of another structure of some kind."[38] His chapel needed to reflect the Last Frontier. He finally found a redwood Western church in California, dating back to the '49 Gold Rush days. Since all he required was a chapel, not a full-sized church, he needed to scale it down. But since only the nave was scaled down, the recognizable elements of the church, the bell tower and the steeply pitched gable roof, became more dominant. Paradoxically, scaling down the original Western church made it look more authentic. "It must be understood that values become condensed and enriched in miniature,"[39] the philosopher Gaston Bachelard wrote. The replica church, aptly called "the Little Church of the West," was Las Vegas's first attempt at the hyperreal.

1.5 A 1954 renovation of the Last Frontier forced the Little Church of the West, a miniature replica of a pioneer church in California, to relocate.

Moore then came across the Western collection of "Dobie Doc," a millionaire gambler and compulsive collector in Elko. Described by some as a kleptomaniac, Doc had absconded with the abandoned possessions from whole ghost towns, including schoolhouses, train cars, and even a worn-out bustle owned by a prominent madam. He crammed 900 tons of artifacts, some with questionable sources, into two warehouses.

Moore had an idea. He convinced Doc to use his collection for a new Western village at the Last Frontier. He hauled all of his goods from Elko. It included a gun collection with a 25-pound elephant gun, a nineteenth-century Chinese temple used by Chinese railroad workers, and an old wooden jail, with leg chains attached to walls, charred by the tragic failed escape of a prisoner who ended up burning himself. But the point of it all was not cultural preservation. "It was an advertising method in order to induce people to come to the hotel and stay there," Moore said. "Patronize the hotel, patronize the village."[40] His masterstroke was to place all these artifacts on display, for free. The village was a mousetrap.

Moore constructed the village less like a museum and more like a movie set—adding a bit of drama, an anachronism here and there, while thickening the plot. He reproduced Hollywood stereotypes. Life-size papier-mâché figures adorned the streets, a reporter noted, including "Flat Rack Jack, Rabbit Sam, Sheriff Bill McGee. ... The Chinaman, Sit-too-Long, has been doing just that—you'll find him out in back."[41] He displayed two complete 1800s Nevada trains, but he was not going to be confined to local trains alone. He added a replica of a San Francisco cable car to transport guests between the village and the hotel. Like a cowboy wearing an electric watch, he then lined his Western village with vintage cars.

Decades ahead of the now customary gift shop entrance to any museum, Moore also built shops including a "museum" selling everything from leather goods to Native American burial robes. One reporter noted the dilemma of "the problem of providing commercial shops, yet retaining the flavor of the old west."[42] Appropriately, Moore turned a trading post into a gift shop. But with the addition of a cactus shop and a modern health club, one could be excused for wondering whether the deadly sheriff Bill McGee liked to landscape his garden with succulent cacti, or enjoyed luxuriating in long steam baths.

Moore also wanted to include a gas station to attract passing automobilists. Since Texaco used a fire chief as advertising, he gave his architects the mandate to "design a structure using the [Western] period-type architecture that tied in with the old fire engine and tied in with Texaco's advertising."[43] They designed a Western fire station, including a bell tower displaying "Fire station, 1856." While the Old West Texaco gas station was a complete fiction, it was nevertheless sensitive to what a gas station would have looked like if cowboys had driven cars.

All of this made for good family photos. "BRING ALONG YOUR CAMERA!" the brochure exclaimed. "You'll want to take home a picture of yourself on our original prairie schooner—or maybe on the old locomotive or in our wedding coach. There are hundreds of fascinating scenes." To reel in families with children, Moore also added a merry-go-round and pony rides. His village had become a theme park.

1.6 A postcard of the "1856" Texaco gas station at the Last Frontier, c. 1942.

As the final touch to his Western village, in 1950 Moore added a second casino, the Silver Slipper, designed after the 1850s Barbary Coast style. But since many of the original saloons of that era no longer existed, architect Richard Stadelman studied Barbary Coast movie sets.

Ironically, the false fronts in the Hollywood movie sets were also typical of frontier towns. Historian Richard Erdoes later wrote of Western architecture: "The false fronts were pasted like sheets of cardboard to one-story log cabins or board shacks to give the impression of splendid two-story saloons. In character with the Westerner's proclivity for bragging, for trying to appear a little more than life-size, the false fronts gave the appearance of a stage set."[44] As Stadelman copied fake Western villages from Hollywood, he got to the essence of Western architecture, which was all about faking it.

With the Last Frontier Village, the Wild West phase of the Strip had reached its peak. Trying to exceed the El Rancho in terms of a Western theme, Moore condensed so much of the West on a single site that it could never be bettered. He created two lasting legacies on the Strip: a Western "church" that is the only structure of the Wild West phase that still exists today, and is now Las Vegas's most famous marriage chapel; and a full-fledged theme park, anticipating the themed casinos in Las Vegas and around the world.

1.7 A Last Frontier Village brochure depicts a child aiming a gun for a photo, while in the background, from a rooming-house window, a papier-mâché madam flaunts her leg.

The story of the Western phase of Las Vegas shows the importance of both legislation and architecture in establishing places. Legislation brought outlaws from other places to Las Vegas, where they could be legitimate. Architecture helped their establishments seem legitimate to outsiders, presenting casinos as Western strongholds.

Like its early residents, Guy McAfee, a police captain who ran illegal brothels, and Bill Williams, the Baptist preacher who was secretly a cannibal, Las Vegas knew how to fake it. The city found that identity could be invented, and very profitably. And whether the cowboy imagery was fake or not, the desolate desert surroundings of the Strip needed little imagination to make it work. It was a classic case of city branding—before this marketing discipline even existed.

As in the lawless times of the real old West, developers exploited activities that were considered immoral. Capitalizing on the lack of taxes and regulation outside of city limits, they undertook a highly risky conquest of the desert, knowing that the payoff could be great. Ironically, it was precisely this "Western" risk-taking attitude and lack of regulation that would undo the Western theme. In fierce competition with one another, as soon as developers found themes that appeared more profitable, they relentlessly dropped their nostalgia for the West. Architect Wayne McAllister, who designed the El Rancho in Western and Spanish mission style, explained: "Spanish was out and Los Angeles and Moderne was in, so contemporary was what we were doing."[45]

Free of interference by local preservation groups and beautification committees, developers built as they pleased to attract people from outside. Instead of urban planning committees, the Strip guided itself by opportunism. The El Rancho anchored the Strip's northern location, just outside of city limits. But one by one developers built further south, until the location outside the town became the town.

The El Rancho and the Last Frontier had a profound influence, beyond Las Vegas. The El Rancho pioneered the nation's casino-resort, a self-contained complex filled to the brim with recreational activities, with the casino at the center. The Last Frontier first used a theme to market the casino-resort, going as far to construct an entire theme park. "Almost all casino gaming in North America takes place in self-contained casino resorts," gaming historian David G. Schwartz argued. "And many of these resorts … use theming to attract customers and stimulate play."[46]

If the fake Western village would have gotten attention then, developers later resorted to global themes, building a pirate ship and an Egyptian Sphinx. And when Las Vegas developers came to build worldwide, they built Venetian canals as far away as Macau. Even from their humble beginnings, however, Las Vegas's casinos had global connections. An Italian immigrant, Tony Cornero, built Las Vegas's first entirely new casino, the Meadows. A Tijuana resort inspired the city's first casino-resort, El Rancho. And with customers driving in from other states, developers looked outward, keeping a close pulse on what was hot.

From a cowboy gas station to an out-of-scale Western church, the first architecture of the Strip embodied its dominant design philosophy: build a false front, as long as it is a spectacular one.

1.8 A Greyhound bus stands next to a horse-drawn coach at the Last Frontier Village; behind, a drive-in movie screen.

2

Sunbelt Modern (1946–1958)

You live in a luxury world where the fact of money seems beneath notice; a world of Olympic swimming pools, hanging gardens, waitresses beautiful as movie stars, marble baths and bars a block long, air conditioning, deep carpets, royal buffets and obsequious waiters offering free drinks. The illusion is created that we are all rich, that money means nothing.[1]

—Julian Halevy, 1958, The Nation

The goddamn biggest, fanciest gaming casino and hotel you bastards ever seen in your whole lives.[2]

—"Bugsy" Siegel, c. 1946, about his plans for the Flamingo

In 1947, Benjamin Siegel built the Flamingo with an Olympic pool with scalloped edges. Then the Desert Inn promptly built a bigger, keyhole-shaped pool. Thereupon the Sands retaliated with an even larger pool, the shape of a kidney. Then the New Frontier built a heated pool a with a subsurface glass-enclosed observation chamber, serving underwater cocktails. But the Tropicana topped them all, creating a half-moon-shaped pool that featured underwater Muzak.

By 1958, the Strip was lined with large bungalows with clean modern forms and glass façades looking over sparkling azure pools with shapes like V's and Z's. Compared to the fake wooden fronts and square pools of the 1940s cowboy town, the 1950s Strip had dramatically refined its architectural vocabulary.

The Strip during its Sunbelt modern phase reflected how American cities would be built around the car. Instead of downtown grids with small lots, which had shaped cities during the age of the train, postwar cities were increasingly structured around a strip, the urban form that belonged to the age of the automobile.

Las Vegas developers exploited the emerging American dream, the reason behind millions of Americans leaving Frostbelt cities for Sunbelt suburbia: a modern bungalow, a lawn, a pool, and fun in the sun. They borrowed from modern Sunbelt suburban architecture, including Los Angeles's modern drive-in coffee shops, Palm Springs's resorts, Miami's hotels, and Frank Lloyd Wright's ranch houses. They dropped the Wild West wagon wheels and buffalo heads for Cadillac-like grilles and tail-fin shapes.

Behind the modern resorts also lay a Sunbelt type of finance: the Mafia, headquartered in Miami. People like Meyer Lansky, armed with dirty money, scaled up the Wild West to Sunbelt modern. They built one resort after the other, transforming what was once a desolate desert patch into a four-mile, flourishing Strip. But as the competition intensified, the gangsters quickly escalated the suburban model, launching a race for the most sumptuous pools, the plushest interiors, and the most lavish lawns.

By the late 1950s, the Strip had become a catalog of modern suburban homes on steroids.

HOLLYWOOD WITHOUT SUNSET

In the early 1940s, Meyer Lansky drove Benjamin Siegel, his fellow co-founder of "Murder Inc.," the enforcement arm of the Mafia, from Los Angeles to Las Vegas. With temperatures going up to 120 degrees, the wires in his Cadillac melted. "There were times when I thought I would die in that desert," Lansky later said. "Vegas was a horrible place, really just a small oasis town."[3]

Lansky needed Siegel in Las Vegas to convert the local bookies to the Syndicate's wire service. Siegel, whose nickname "Bugsy"—though better not to his face—was bestowed on him because his infamous temper tended to "go bugs," quickly converted every horse parlor in Las Vegas, especially after killing two men. He used the profits to buy downtown's El Cortez casino in 1945. At the time, Lansky's empire already included casinos in Florida, New Orleans, and Cuba.

Lansky then eyed a construction site along the Los Angeles Highway, the Flamingo, an unfinished casino-resort owned by Billy Wilkerson, founder of the *Hollywood Reporter* and owner of a string of fashionable Los Angeles nightclubs. But Wilkerson was also a terrible gambling addict, thinking the only way out of his gambling addiction was to own a casino. He lost his construction budget on the craps table, and desperately accepted a $1 million investment from Harry Rothberg, Meyer Lansky's secret associate.

Lansky had grasped the potential of Wilkerson's glamorous Las Vegas project. Wilkerson had commissioned architect George Vernon Russell to depart from the Western saloon-casinos with the latest architectural style from Los Angeles, in hopes of attracting the high-end crowd of his Hollywood clubs. He designed a casino with sleek, thin horizontal lines and large panes of glass, the façade oriented toward traffic. It was

2.1 A postcard of the "Fabulous Flamingo Hotel" depicts its sharp roof, glass façade, and colorful neon pylon—in sharp contrast to the Western, sepia-toned casinos.

representative of the "Googie" architectural style, after the Googie coffee shop on the Sunset Strip.[4] Since the 1930s, Los Angeles had had the country's largest percentage of single-family home and car ownership. The city had become the experimental ground for new buildings catering to the car, including drive-in fast-food restaurants. These buildings appropriated their clean lines and curvaceous forms from automobiles, symbolizing the new era of the car.

At the same time, the Western theme was ubiquitous. "The celebration of the Western past has grown enormously,"[5] wrote Bernard DeVoto in *Harper's Magazine* in 1946. By the 1940s, more than one hundred communities held Pioneer Weeks and Frontier Days. It made sense for Wilkerson to ditch the West for a new, more exiting lifestyle, to which so many Americans aspired. His timing was perfect, with postwar Americans determined to enjoy peacetime.

Wilkerson, a well-traveled man of sophisticated tastes, planned to include in his Las Vegas resort a Parisian-style restaurant and a showroom modeled after Paris's Moulin Rouge. A tall metal sign, placed on a stack of thin fins that resembled a grille, would display the name to drivers: the Flamingo.

But what was named a Flamingo was really a Venus flytrap, a casino plant designed to sever gamblers from their money. Wilkerson dug deep into his dark addiction to figure out ways for gamblers to lose themselves in "the action." He chose a site further down the Strip, so that other casinos were out of sight. In the center of the resort he placed the casino, "the hub," so that everyone would have to pass it. Wilkerson planned to use the latest air-conditioning equipment to keep gamblers on a constant cool temperature. Knowing that it would be best that time should pass unnoticed, he banned windows and clocks; the lights were permanently dimmed. He commanded: "Never let them see daylight."[6]

Lansky knew that the "super-luxurious" Flamingo could bring in "the high rollers from all over the world." And he liked the desert location: "Once you got tourists there, after they had eaten and drunk all they could, there was only one thing left—to go gambling."[7] He put Siegel in charge of the Flamingo. But Siegel's expertise lay in murder and extortion alone, not in construction. "Siegel did not know a bidet from a Bordeaux,"[8] Wilkerson's business partner said. Not only did Siegel replace the architect, he also fired the interior designer in favor of his girlfriend Virginia Hill, a Mob courier. He flew in plumbers and carpenters, greased truckers for speed deliveries, and paid a premium on the black market for scarce building materials in postwar America. He built walls so thick that during a 1960s remodeling it took a giant wrecking ball three whole days to demolish a single wall. He ordered a separate plumbing and sewer line to each of the 105 hotel rooms, and designed a private penthouse with an escape hatch to a zigzagging maze of secret passageways.

Construction costs skyrocketed from a planned $1 million to $6 million, to the frustration of the Syndicate. Meanwhile, five days before the opening, "not a blade of grass was to be seen," a reporter noted.[9] In a violent transformation of the desert, Siegel brought in truckloads of topsoil, acres of green lawn, and fifteen types of trees, including rare cork trees from Spain. He even tried to import flamingoes for his "Gardens of Grandeur," but canceled his hundred-count order when he saw two of them die in the desert.[10]

The opening was a fiasco. The hotel rooms were not finished and the air-conditioning regularly broke down, so that the casino became scorching hot. Siegel himself deterred local visitors with his tyrannical enforcement of a new dress code, forcing the entire male staff to wear tuxedos, and requiring male guests to wear a jacket and tie. To a guest in a sports jacket, he snarled: "You trying to louse up a class joint?"[11]

The Flamingo closed four weeks later. While Siegel eventually managed to reopen the casino, making profits, the Syndicate "retired" him. He was shot twice in the side of his skull, the pressure of the bullet blowing his left eye out of its socket. Siegel was murdered in his girlfriend's Beverly Hills home, not in Las Vegas, in obedience to the "purity code" of not tainting the lucrative resort city in blood.

But the gruesome death of the handsome gangster was reported all over the news. Hollywood had filmed seven motion pictures at the Flamingo by 1955, and Siegel's mythologized death instantly inflated his role in the building of the Strip. Siegel, rather than Wilkerson, is typically considered the Flamingo's founder. He had become the world's most famous casino operator—posthumously, and falsely.

Nevertheless, the Flamingo became a tremendous success, bringing in $4 million profit in the first year alone—not even including the skim. It also brought in an entirely new, more profitable, demographic. "My father and his partners brought their fancy city manners and suits to town," remembered the daughter of one of Siegel's lieutenants. "Alligator shoes started to take the place of cowboy boots."[12] As the Flamingo succeeded, others followed. Gambling addict Wilkerson knew how to prioritize a casino, in contrast to the hoteliers who built the first resorts. Specializing in catering to sin, new gangster operators continued to ban windows and overspend on luxury casinos.

Meanwhile, the architectural style of the Old West bled to death. The Flamingo propelled the Strip into the present with a new image of luxury and modernity. Its pink upholstery and metal-glass façade stood out from the sepia tones and fake wooden fronts of the cowboy town.

Once the Wild West mold was broken, existing and new resorts followed suit. The El Rancho redecorated the interior of its Western cottages in a French provincial style. Even the Last Frontier, the resort that so epitomized the Wild West, had a revamp. "They had all this beautiful stonework," a reporter later noted. "They painted it over with pink paint."[13]

The Flamingo taught developers to retire architectural styles and Mafia managers quickly, when other more profitable ones existed.

BIRDS IN PARADISE

In 1946, Nevada Lieutenant Governor Cliff Jones and contractor Marion Hicks built the Thunderbird, the fourth casino-resort on the Strip. Jones, who was called "Big Juice" (an unusual name for a government official) because of the deals he made, allegedly also accepted financing by Meyer Lansky.

With the Flamingo raising the bar for design, Jones and Hicks could no longer go back to the wagon wheels. At the same time, they wanted to appeal to a more local clientele, who perceived the Flamingo as too expensive. They decided to strike a balance of "luxurious informality." Instead of a Flamingo, they built a more local Thunderbird, the symbol of the Navajo Indian tribe that appropriately stood for "happiness unlimited." Instead of cowboy murals and deer heads, they hung paintings of Indian warriors and war bonnets, and called the casino the "Pow Wow Room." In short, they went from cowboys to Indians.

To make the Thunderbird homier, they added not one but three fireplaces to the lobby. They wrote "Come as you are" on the beamed canopy at the entrance. While the canopy was clumsily integrated into the resort—contractor Hicks had cut corners by not hiring an architect—this was nonetheless a welcoming gesture for automobilists, and a Strip novelty. In architectural lingo called a *porte-cochère*, literally "carriage gate" in French, it was originally a portico structure that provided cover for horse and carriage passengers in nineteenth-century mansions. With the twentieth-century ubiquity of the automobile, it had increased in relevance, and quickly became a new staple of the casino complex.

2.2 Compared to the sole Flamingo down the street, the Thunderbird featured a duo of neon birds, one with its claws sunk in an observation tower.

Although the Thunderbird and the Flamingo signs both seemed neon birds of a feather, unlike the Flamingo's flat and square figure, the Thunderbird was more voluptuous. And in contrast to the monochrome Flamingo, the Thunderbird was colored all the hues of the rainbow. It also sat more prominently on the Strip, its claws sunk in a pedestal on top of a three-story observation tower painted turquoise, a then-popular color for Cadillac convertibles.

The Thunderbird led the pack of four already existing signs. "In looking at the strip at night one would see the Thunderbird, the Flamingo, the bright red Pegasus on the Mobil station, and the El Rancho Windmill," noted the *Endless Desert Trails and Historic Sights for Riders.*[14] Although the signs competed with one another, collectively they offered the automobile traveler an "unplanned showing of bold colors and marvelous symbols"—a modern form of bird- watching in Las Vegas.

2.3 The El Rancho windmill, and an arrow pointing to it, compete with the Thunderbird duo and the Mobil Pegasus.

In 1946, Mayor Ernie Cragin had tried to annex this strip of lights, which lay outside of city limits. He cited the following reason: "to secure badly needed additional revenue to save our city, streets, sewer system, and other vital services."[15] In response, Flamingo manager Gus Greenbaum organized hotel employees and fended off Cragin by establishing the unincorporated township of Paradise City, named after the Strip's first casino, the Pair-O-Dice. To cement the separation of the Strip from downtown, in 1949 Lieutenant Governor "Big Juice" conveniently passed a law that prevented the city from annexing an unincorporated township without the approval of the county commission.

No longer would the city of Las Vegas be able to collect any taxes, or regulate the Strip in any form. The city had lost the revenues of its most important fiscal asset: the casino-resort industry. As urban critic Mike Davis would write later, "This is a political geography diabolically conceived to separate tax resources from regional social needs."[16] A few decades later, this "splintering urbanism" would become typical of American cities.[17]

Lieutenant Governor Jones had given the Flamingo and his Thunderbird a permanent tax shelter.

CAPITALIZING THE STRIP

In 1950, Wilbur Clark, who worked his way up from craps dealer to casino owner, opened the Desert Inn, the fifth resort on the Strip. The Desert Inn, with three hundred employees the largest employer in the state, propelled the area previously known as lower-case "a strip" to upper-case "the Strip." But Clark did not capitalize the Strip by himself. He had run out of money building the Desert Inn, and gave away a majority interest to Cleveland Mafia boss Moe Dalitz.

"Drug money founded modern Las Vegas,"[18] two investigative journalists later wrote. Organized crime had plenty of money to spend, and to launder. The Mafia nonetheless benefited from operating behind a façade of respectable casino "owners," called "fronts"—to complete the deceit, Dalitz named the resort *Wilbur Clark's* Desert Inn.

This setup would become typical. "The big guessing game in Las Vegas is 'Who owns whom,'"[19] wrote the authors of the 1963 *The Green Felt Jungle*, an exposé of gangster-owned casinos.

Armed with Dalitz's dirty money, Clark built the Strip's first fountain and curved pool—in contrast to the existing rectangular-shaped, "square" pools, it was by all accounts "a key-hole shaped triumph."[20] He also built the first curvaceous sign, a neon saguaro cactus sign that appeared to grow from the roof. The Desert Inn was originally designed as a ranch house with broad sloping roofs; Clark placed a glass sky lounge smack on top of the building. He added small twinkling lights in the sky lounge's ceiling. "What gets me," a chorus girl pondered as she looked out at the desert moon, "is the way people sit in a room like this, with all the electric stars in the ceiling, when they could get the real thing outside."[21]

Clark then built Las Vegas's largest showroom to host the Mafia's favorite performer. "Wilbur Clark gave me my first job in Las Vegas," Frank Sinatra later recalled. "For six bucks you got a filet mignon dinner and me."

Clark knew how to get guests into his windowless casino, the state's largest. One employee observed: "You came into the lobby, you fell right into the casino. As a matter of fact, you had to look for the registration desk."[22] The new mantra, "When you build a hotel, the gambling has to be first,"[23] was expressed in all parts of the resort, leading to some unique features. Imagine an unknown drunk wandering into the Desert Inn's bar. On the hour, a spinning wheel points to his stool, unleashing Lady Luck, a nude figure on the wall, to rain a shower of silver dollars.

Yet this shower of cash almost came to an abrupt halt when the Kefauver Committee came to Las Vegas in 1950, cracking down on organized crime. Clark was summoned. A committee member asked him: "Before you got in bed with crooks … didn't you look

2.4 A woman holding a camera sits on a high diving board at the Desert Inn's keyhole-shaped pool, overlooked by a glass skybox and neon saguaro cactus.

into these birds at all?" Dalitz was asked about his Desert Inn investment, and how he made his first money rum-running. "If you people wouldn't have drunk it," he told the senator, on national television, "I wouldn't have bootlegged it."[24]

But Kefauver could not convict anyone in Las Vegas. And as he moved to other cities to prosecute gangsters, they moved to Las Vegas, the only place with legal gambling and an "open city," where different Mafia factions could freely enter without a turf war.

The Desert Inn would become the Mafia's main cash cow. One Last Frontier employee suggested tapping into this success. "We should build a tunnel," he said, "from the porch of the Last Frontier to the porch of the Desert Inn."[25] One silent partner, conspicuously absent, greatly profited from this. Three times a day, "Miami hotel men" would walk into the Desert Inn's counting room. "Three for us, one for the government, and two for Meyer,"[26] a lieutenant's daughter overheard.

After the "mules" carried the money to Miami, Lansky distributed the profits to partners internationally, or made deposits into Swiss accounts. The year of the Desert Inn's opening, he financed drug laboratories in Turkey, establishing a new heroin route through Marseilles. His Las Vegas casinos now financed "a vast new international network of narcotics," two investigative reporters later wrote, "and the profits from that drug traffic would come back in various forms to build modern Las Vegas."[27]

Lansky, the Mafia's unofficial Chief Financial Officer, had turned Las Vegas into a global financial capital. "Throughout the Fifties, that secret, indirect, revolving traffic between the Strip and Switzerland was one of the heaviest flows of international capital of the era, making Las Vegas a world center of finance long before many knew its name."[28]

"There's no such thing as a lucky gambler," Lansky once said. "The winners are those who control the game. All the rest are suckers."[29]

THE POSTWAR SAHARA

"There are five major hotel-casinos on the Strip," the *New Yorker* noted in 1950. "All are made up of wide-flung low buildings."[30] Club Bingo, opened in 1947 by Milton Prell, a former jewelry salesman who had operated a club in Montana, was an exception to that formula. It was just a little bingo parlor, even though it did not look especially small thanks to a bingo-board sign, three times the size of the building.

Knowing that his site was not living up to its full potential, Prell decided to raze the club and build a casino-resort. He chose a desert-themed name, "The Sahara," a nod to American veterans, many of whom had fought in Sub-Saharan Africa. He commissioned architect Ragnar Qvale, who had once been an actor, but ironically landed his first role as a Nazi officer the same day the Germans invaded his native Norway. The architect ensured the "much desired unity of design," a reporter wrote. "Qvale believes that … all décor, furnishings and other incidentals such as menus, uniforms, etc., should have a unifying theme."[31]

The Sahara had a 20-acre "Garden of Allah," with rare blossoms and shrubs, a few murals of African warriors, a small band of plaster camels and nomads, and the "Casbar

2.5 A postcard features two plaster camels and a nomad standing in front of the Sahara roadside sign and the then-largest pylon on the Strip.

Theater" (deliberately misspelled from casbah). The theme was not much more than a semantic nuance, a marketing technique that concealed the fact that the resorts were all remarkably similar.

Nevertheless, the Sahara was bound to succeed. World War II had put a temporary halt on the advance of consumerism, but when the United States demobilized, men returned from the war with money in their pockets, and women had entered the labor force, bringing income to the table. As this new wealthy American middle class emerged, Las Vegas gave them a way to spend their money. Meanwhile, the postwar growth of commercial aviation helped bring them in, thanks to the conversion of military transport carriers and bombers into commercial airplanes.

"Las Vegas is a creature of the postwar period,"[32] historian John Findlay later wrote. The Strip came to occupy a bizarre intersection of illegal flows of capital and the postwar conversion to consumerism. Mafia money built it, leisure-seeking Americans bought into it, and converted military airplanes brought them there.

The year the Sahara opened, President Truman signed a secret foreign policy statement to contain Soviet expansion. It tripled the United States defense budget—much of this flowing to defense plants in Las Vegas. Fueled by its growing military and resort industry, Las Vegas's population tripled from 8,422 in 1940 to 24,624 in 1950.

Meanwhile, the Strip also benefited from exploding populations throughout the Sun Belt states. Millions of Americans left the Frostbelt cities to enjoy warmer temperatures, lower taxes, and better job opportunities, thanks to Cold War defense spending. Moreover, changes in Social Security laws made it easier for Americans to retire, and in contrast to what people thought, the elderly actually liked distance between them and their extended families, and would go as far as Arizona to achieve it.

Government policies, including loan insurances and tax reductions on mortgages, encouraged these people to buy into suburban homes, rather than rent downtown apartments. Levittown, New York, built for returning servicemen and their families in 1947, set the prototype of this single-family home, a mass-produced version of Frank Lloyd Wright's ranch house. To attract these new suburbanites, the Sahara was neither in the shape of a caravan tent, nor decked with onion domes, but a large ranch house with broad sloping roofs and a brick pylon—just like the Desert Inn, in the modern ranch tradition.

The federal government had skewed transportation in favor of cars, at the cost of mass transit, by subsidizing highways. Cars had enabled suburban life, making remote areas like the Las Vegas Strip accessible. Returning the favor, suburban life made the car essential. More than eight million automobiles were produced in the year 1950 alone. It marked the point at which most factories had transitioned from producing war-related items to consumer goods.

Meanwhile, the Sahara exploited wartime nostalgia, paying Marlene Dietrich $90,000 for a three-week stint in 1953, knowing that many visitors had seen her at the Front. In postwar Las Vegas, Dietrich adapted her "nude" dress, which at the Front had only simulated transparency. "It has to be Folies Bergère," she commanded, "but elegant"[33]—which meant that this time the transparency was real, with rhinestones stopping just beneath her gauze-covered breasts, revealing flesh.

"There were always veterans," her manager Burt Bacharach remembered. "It was an emotional thing, but she never cried, except maybe inside when someone was in a wheelchair, or there was someone who had lost a leg."[34]

If anything symbolized the conversion from wartime to leisure economy, it was the Sahara: an oversized bungalow with an air-conditioned casino, two plaster camels, and Miss Dietrich wearing a "peek-a-boo" dress.

CASINO SUBURBANISM

In 1952, a new resort called the Sands helped turn the Strip into the new center of Las Vegas. What was only a dusty little road to downtown a decade ago had become, according to a *New York Times* writer, "a never-never land of exotic architecture, extravagant vegetation, flamboyant signery and frenetic diversion." Downtown, on the other hand, was "a fairly humdrum small-town main-drag."[35]

2.6 A postcard depicts a woman in a beige Cadillac arriving at the Sands's angular entrance pylons. The neon Sands letters float on a see-through grille in the background.

It was a classic case of core-periphery reversal between downtown and the Strip. Although the Strip started as a periphery, when resorts multiplied and clustered outside the city, it became a core. This recentering of Las Vegas preceded what would become a national trend. By the end of the 1950s, one-third of Americans lived in the suburbs. Ten years later, there were more people in suburbia than in cities. The Strip catered to this growing demographic, offering a suburban vacation of azure-blue pools, dewy lawns, and ample parking lots. Just as suburbanites preferred to shop in malls, rather than go to the city, on a visit to Las Vegas they preferred the parking-friendly Strip over crowded downtown.

At the Sands, "Tramobiles," golf carts on steroids, transported guests to the room wings over thin winding roads, laid out like a suburban tract. Architect Wayne McAllister designed a triangular canopy floating over the driveway. As a sign he built a large see-through grid featuring "Sands," by all accounts looking like a "chrome badge on a Cadillac grille."[36] His buildings, as he often said, were "influenced by the automobile, not the architect."[37] He had grown fluent in the latest car shapes from Detroit, developing an aesthetic inspired by car curves and chrome grilles.

If the status of cars lay in the grille patterns and color coatings, which Cadillac had started alternating to make cars look new every year even though the technology had not radically evolved, so was the newness of a suburban resort defined by key symbols. Resorts refined typical elements of suburban neighborhoods—pools, road signage, and bungalows—to establish the difference between buildings that were fundamentally the same. Not only had McAllister designed the nicest *porte-cochère* and façade, he designed a kidney-shaped pool that was the biggest to date, an observer wrote, "a thing of free flow design large enough to float a cruiser."[38]

The casinos' obsession for pools mirrored a new trend. Between 1950 and 1955 the number of swimming pools in the United States grew tenfold[39] and would explode that year, when banks gave out home improvement loans to build pools. But Las Vegas's casino improvements were financed by that other financial institution: the Mafia. Rumor had it that Sands owner Jake Freedman had partnered with Meyer Lansky.

Freedman initially did not even bother with a name up until construction, when a builder asked for it. "There's so much sand in this damned place that my socks are full of it! So, why don't we call it 'The Sand.'" The builder responded: "You can't just say 'The Sand.' You must use the plural, 'Sands.'"[40] Freedman's construction workers were quite the linguists. But the slogan of the resort, "A Place in the Sun"—a riff on Las Vegas's slogan "Fun in the Sun" and a blatant copy of the 1951 Elizabeth Taylor movie title *A Place in the Sun*—summed up the genius of Freedman's place. The Sands, as did Las Vegas, had disguised gambling, a practice that still carried a stigma, as a suburban vacation.

"We stress sunshine, good entertainment, and swimming,"[41] the Las Vegas Chamber of Commerce manager said, without making a single reference to gambling. To seep gambling into a suburban vacation, the Sands even built poolside slot machines and a floating craps table. A 1953 photo showing the croupiers and female gamblers in swimwear became the most famous of all "cheesecake shots," typically pictures of bikini-clad showgirls and celebrities posing at pools, used to promote Las Vegas. In 1954, the Sands's pool made it again into the nation's consciousness as the backdrop of a showgirl featured in *Life* magazine, the editor in awe of her "spread-eagled" jump into the pool.[42]

Just as the pool was a domestic tool to keep mom, dad, and the kids at home, back in Las Vegas it was one of a range of captivating recreations, including shows. By 1953, the Strip hosted so many shows that *Newsweek* called Las Vegas "The Entertainment Capital of the World." Stars happily abandoned Broadway for the desert city. "Why do we do it?" asked Tallulah Bankhead, who had left New York for the Sands, which was paying her $20,000 a week in 1953. "Dahling, for the loot, of course."[43]

If any resort had disguised the casino inside a glamorous suburban vacation it was the Sands, a "Place in the Sun." This strategy helped gambling, historian David G.

2.7 Croupiers, gamblers, and female bystanders, all in swimwear, stand around the Sands's floating craps table, in front of three poolside slot machines, 1954.

Schwartz argued later, "in its rebirth as a mainstream recreational activity."[44] Even lying by the pool, guests felt they were at the center of the action. "In Las Vegas all paging is done by loud-speaker," two observers wrote, "and it is not at all uncommon to hear 'Paging Mr. Walt Disney, paging Walt Disney' echoing for miles around."[45]

On April 5, 1955, at 4.59 p.m., the Last Frontier closed, and reopened as the New Frontier at 5.00 p.m. The casino threw out its Texas cattle horns, wagon wheels and cowboys for planets, asteroids, and astronauts. This two-million-dollar upgrade was called the "Big Switch."

"The Strip had gone ultramoderne and super-*magnifique*, and it was the Frontier's turn to be the newest with the mostest,"[46] noted travel writers Katharine Best and Katharine Hillyer. Its Western-themed interior looked dated. Even its performers underwhelmed—including Ronald Reagan, whose 1954 act with chimps drew such poor audiences that he vowed to pursue a political career instead.

The Big Switch was emblematic of the city's dynamic atmosphere. "There is never a moment, on the Strip, that façades aren't being lifted, casinos enlarged, cocktail lounges lengthened."[47] For instance, in 1953 the Flamingo upgraded its casino façade and built a "champagne tower," an eight-story cylinder decorated with sizzling neon bubbles.

But the Last Frontier remodeling was the most extreme upgrade so far. The woodsy Western front was thrown out in favor of modern brick and glass with a lengthy canopy projecting from it: a 126-foot-tall space frame lit so strongly, it bathed the entire façade in all colors of the rainbow.

"Las Vegas is unquestionably the new frontier of America,"[48] a reporter wrote on the opening day. The Strip was an exhibition of new technologically advanced lifestyles. The New Frontier even built a glass-enclosed observation chamber at the bottom of the pool so that non-swimming guests could watch floating friends. "Where else in all the world but Las Vegas," a local newspaper wrote, "could Mr. and Mrs. Joe Doakes, of Wichita, Kansas, enjoy cocktails under water?"[49]

In contrast to seeing visitors as "suckers" or "escapists," historian John Findlay asserted that Las Vegas "offered tourists the chance to sample exotica and innovations. … Visitors to Las Vegas could learn something about the future that seemed to be in store for postwar society."[50]

A view of an atom bomb was part of that. When the first nuclear bomb detonated in the Nevada Test site in 1951, the explosion could be seen from Las Vegas. With detonations broadcast the following year, "atomic fever" swept the nation. For Cold War Americans the bomb was a cause for celebration, before they knew about the detrimental impact of radiation on health. To attract tourists, casinos organized "atomic lunch boxes" so guests could picnic near the detonation. They arranged "dawn bomb parties," serving "atomic cocktails," equal parts vodka, brandy, and champagne. Lili St. Cyr, Las Vegas's most famous stripper, postponed her wedding three times so that it would coincide with a major blast, and after cutting her mushroom-cloud wedding cake she honeymooned near the atomic proving grounds.

But Las Vegans quickly grew disappointed with the bombs. A showgirl said: "It's all over so quickly it looks more like a flash bulb going off."[51] Nevertheless, one casino owner knew what needed to be done. "Bigger bombs, that's what we're waiting for."[52]

2.8 A 1955 *Fabulous Las Vegas Magazine* cover depicts the conversion of Western "Last Frontier" to Space Age "New Frontier," with the then-longest trylon and canopy.

2.9 In 1953, the Flamingo added a canopy with metal cylinders, and a neon-ringed "champagne tower."

But why wait for the government's Big Bomb when you can get rainbow-striped lights, craps under asteroids, and gin fizz underwater at the New Frontier.

SWAYING WATER

On April 19, 1955, a 38-pound "dancer" was scheduled to perform exclusively at the Royal Nevada, the eighth resort on the Strip, dazzling audiences with 50-foot jumps, in sync with waltz music.

At their debut at the 1952 West Berlin Industrial Exhibition, the Dancing Waters's revolving and swaying water jets were the first to re-create the gracefulness of ballet in a "dancing" fountain. In Las Vegas, they became the Royal Nevada's universally popular attraction. A reporter noted: "It is the only successful act in Las Vegas devoid of sex appeal."[53]

By automating the show, the Royal Nevada avoided paying salaries to celebrities. The only person on the payroll was Hans Hasslach, who "played" the fountain's 4,000 jet streams and 16 batteries of lights from a keyboard with 280 switches and levers.

But the year the Royal Nevada opened, Lake Mead, Las Vegas's freshwater supply, dropped almost 20 feet. "With the Lake at its lowest levels since 1938," a reporter noted, "Las Vegans are wondering about the 78 tons of water to be used each night by the 'Dancing Waters.'"[54] Hasslach responded that the Dancing Waters used "only" about 200,000 gallons per year, half the amount the Olympic pool wasted. Moreover, the Royal Nevada had vast swaths of green lawn, requiring tons of water. At least it did not have a championship golf course, like the Desert Inn, which had diverted water from other precincts to irrigate the 10,000 imported trees and the lawns of the fifty-one gated homes around the course—Las Vegas's first gated community, and the first permanent homes inside a casino complex.

The Royal Nevada's Dancing Waters, T-shaped pool, and green lawns were the Strip's latest reworking of the desert. The resort's theme was supposed to evoke Arthurian

2.10 A postcard shows greeters dressed as Indian chiefs posing at a Cadillac, backed by the Royal Nevada's Arthurian crown and neon fountain.

munificence, riding on the 1950s trend of historic fantasy movies, such as *Robin Hood*. Its carpets had patterns of spilling diamonds, emeralds and sapphires, while outside stood a tower topped with a gold-leaf crown, the size of a small car, and a neon sculpture representing a fountain.

But as the Royal Nevada opened with a historic fantasy, the stark reality was that resorts had to drill as deep as 300 feet for water, since groundwater levels had been dropping more than 4 feet per year.[55] That same year, 1955, Las Vegas was forced to draw water from Lake Mead, which got its water from the Colorado River. This 1,450-mile river seemed to be an infinite source of freshwater, supplying millions of thirsty Sunbelt suburbanites in the arid Southwest, including California, Arizona, and New Mexico. Like Las Vegas casinos, they dug swimming pools and irrigated desert land.

Back on the Strip, so much water had been poured onto the sand that few desert traces remained. "Handsome, yes; inviting, yes," a reporter wrote, "but little incongruities keep alerting you to where you are"[56]—like the scorching and shimmering desert heat rising above the dewy lawns.

THE MIAMI HOTEL MEN

Casa Blanca, a new Strip casino, could not get a license because the applicants included a Meyer Lansky associate. But a new hotel name, The Riviera, and a new group of partners, including Harpo and Gummo of the Marx Brothers comedy act, enabled the casino to open in 1955.

Miami architects France & Son introduced Miami Modern architecture, the flashier school of modernism, to the Las Vegas Strip. They gilded the concrete elevator shaft with gold buttons, and decked the lobby with mirrors and Italian marble. The hotel was inspired by Miami Beach's Fontainebleau hotel, a stone's throw away from the apartment of Meyer Lansky—who liked to walk his Shih Tzu down to the hotel and sit around the bow-tie-shaped pool.

The nine-story building radically transformed the city's skyline, breaking with the low-rise, bungalow-style tradition. Boasted as "A New High in the Las Vegas Sky," the tower dispelled the belief that the desert's high water tables and hard caliche soil could support only low-rise structures. But more importantly, the tower stood as a testament to the only substantial source of capital available to developers: Mafia money. Apart from the Bank of Las Vegas, headed by Mormon Parry Thomas,[57] banks refused to lend to casinos. Moreover, since the Nevada Gaming Control Board demanded that every casino stockowner be licensed, it blocked casino ownership of publicly traded companies, which can have an infinite number of constantly changing stockowners.

In 1956, Lansky's partner Ed Levison built the thirteen-story Fremont casino hotel in downtown. Architect Wayne McAllister, a proponent of the Los Angeles modernist style, built a tall slab decorated with sunscreens and beige and pink concrete panels. The building towered above downtown's shoebox-sized casinos, its modern look diminishing the woodsy Western-style saloons.

2.11 A tall slab extends from the sunscreen-decorated Fremont Hotel, while a bright mushroom cloud climbs upward, 1957.

The Fremont was Lansky's "clearing house," where his entire Las Vegas skim was collected, allegedly delivered in hotel bakery trucks, counted, and sent to Miami, where Lansky would divide the money among partners, or reinvest it in other businesses. "It was Mob money," a reporter wrote, "that bought the land and financed the hotels along the Miami Beach Gold Coast … that financed … the deserts of the Southwest, in Palm Springs and all across Southern California."[58] But in addition, these hotels were built according to the Mafia's aesthetic preferences: Sunbelt modernism, inspired by the Los Angeles modern clubs and Miami modern hotels the Mafiosi liked to frequent.

In 1957, Lansky asked Wayne McAllister to design the Habana Riviera, the world's largest casino, in Cuba, and complete construction within only six months. McAllister declined, but Igor B. Polevitzky, a Miami Modern architect, accepted. Lansky's axis of casinos now reached from Las Vegas all the way to Cuba, spreading Sunbelt modernism along with it.

In Cuba, where Lansky befriended President Fulgencio Batista and financed his casino by the state-run bank, he even dared to put himself on the payroll.

His official title: "kitchen director."

AMERICAN BABYLON

"You just aren't anybody in Las Vegas these days unless you're building a luxury-casino-hotel," the *New York Times* wrote in January 1955 about "The 'Sure Thing' Boom at Las Vegas." "If it's just another motel, without a casino or Broadway shows, you're practically a peasant. And if you're just *talking* about building a hotel, or trying to scrape together the financing, you're nobody. Everybody's doing that."[59]

In 1955, four new resorts opened. Each had a show, hundreds of rooms, and an Olympic-size pool. But skeptics worried that the market was getting saturated.

The first victim was the Moulin Rouge, which opened that year as Vegas's first desegregated resort. It was situated on the "Black Strip," a parallel strip with nightclubs and casinos, located in West Las Vegas, where most of the black population was forced to live, an area without paved streets, running water, or sewage lines.

African-Americans were banned from resorts in Las Vegas, called by some the "Mississippi of the West" for its discriminatory and segregationist practices. They were permitted to work in "back-of-house" jobs on the Strip, where they had limited contact with tourists. Ironically, the Royal Nevada's architect, African-American Paul Williams, was not allowed to enter the resort he had drawn up. Black performers were the exception, but even they were not allowed to stay at casinos. "The second we stepped off the stage," Sammy Davis Junior of the Rat Pack recalled, "we had to leave through the kitchen with the garbage."[60]

But the Moulin Rouge closed within six months, and would not reopen. The Royal Nevada would also permanently close. The Riviera declared bankruptcy. The Dunes, which opened a few days before the Moulin Rouge, also suffered, even though the owners had followed the casino formula then considered successful. Riding on a trend of

2.12 A man in a spotted shirt photographs the fiberglass Sultan standing atop the Dunes entrance canopy.

exotic motel names, including Suez and Baghdad, they chose an Arabian Nights theme, which one of the owners liked for its "Middle Eastern symbols and art motifs."[61] But the theme was also timely, at the peak of a decade of Oriental themes in movies including *Princess of the Nile* (1954), and at a time of increasing United States involvement in the Middle East to contain communism.

The owners built a large suburban bungalow, like all the other resorts, but with a blue-and-white-striped casino entrance sloped like a nomadic tent. At the back, they built a swimming pool in the shape of a V—a yet untried letter of the pool alphabet that was forming on the Las Vegas Strip. They also added a fountain with sea horses and a 150-foot-long reflection pool, to be used as an ice-skating rink in winter. On top of the building, they placed a three-story fiberglass Sultan, hands on hips, his cape falling from his shoulders, his plumed turban illumined by a car light. Designed by fiberglass sculptor Kermit Hawkins, who would later sculpt Kermit the Frog, the sign built on the successful tradition of figurative signs, such as the Silver Slipper, a revolving slipper the size of a small car, and the Pioneer Club's Vegas Vic, a six-story-tall cowpuncher smoking a cigarette, waving his hand, greeting visitors with a recording of "Howdy Pardner."

But despite the inviting décor, the smiling Sultan, and promise of ice-skating in the desert, few people came. *Life* reported with the cover headline: "Las Vegas—Is Boom Overextended?"

The Dunes eventually closed its casino and became a motel only, without a casino, which as a Strip enterprise is considered the equivalent of running a bar without alcohol. It highlighted that both the "sure thing" boom and the formula for a luxury suburban resort were over.

THE CATTLE SHOOT

"FLY FREE TO LAS VEGAS!" the advertisement had beckoned. Reporter Peter Wyden wrote: "So there we were aboard the Hacienda Hotel's private Constellation … a 'champagne flight' from Chicago to the little oasis in the Nevada desert."[62]

Wyden was one of eighty "package" tourists on their way to the Hacienda, the latest Strip resort. For $188, they got a return flight to Chicago, five hotel nights, four meals, a lifetime membership in the hotel's miniature "golf club," and a free flow of California bubbly.

"We ran out of water but not champagne."[63]

In 1956, the Hacienda pioneered a unique strategy. Owner Warren "Doc" Bayley knew that all resorts mostly fished from the same pool: upper-middle-class gamblers. Bayley went after budget travelers. His chain of low-cost Hacienda motels in California specialized in unusual perks for travelers on a shoestring, including bellboys and room service.

His architect, Homer Rissman, designed the Las Vegas Hacienda to be spaciously elegant, with a curved modern glass façade and a large vertical marquee. He economically laid out 266 rooms in six hotel wings, connected through "enclosed promenade

2.13 In front of the Hacienda's curving façade and tall pylon, guests aim for a "$5,000 Hole-in-One Jackpot."

gardens," allowing guests to go from wing to wing without going outdoors. He built a miniature golf course and a shallow, family-friendly bathing area within a Z-shaped pool. However, Rissman designed the interior as a "cattle shoot." Guests on the way to their rooms were forced through the casino, where ceilings were low to focus their attention on the games. He said: "Patrons had to pass the slots on the way to the toilets."[64]

Initially struggling to stay afloat, Bayley advertised the "Hacienda Holiday," the first all-inclusive vacation package. For $27.50 you got a bed, a bottle of champagne, $5 of casino chips, and a free flight on "Hacienda Airlines." This strategy was so successful that by 1961 the Hacienda fleet brought 140,000 visitors to McCarran airport, more than all the commercial airlines combined.

That same year, Wyden flew in: "The rooms were comfortable, the meals good, the drinks were served by girls in abbreviated, not-quite-transparent 'baby-doll' night-gowns." But he knew there was no such thing as a free lunch: "We had to elbow our way past slot machines and wheels of fortune to reach our rooms." He quickly realized that he and his fellow tourists had heard too many dealers' exhortations, and drunk too much champagne: "Most of us had come under the spell."

Even "saucer-eyed" eighteen-year-old Miss South Bend, Indiana, who won the trip in a Miss America contest playing Goldilocks, showed a remarkable character shift.

She said upon arrival: "When I think how I scrape to go to college and how people here throw hundred-dollar bills around …"[65] After five days of exposure to people pulling on slot machines, however, Miss South Bend lamented that Nevada did not allow teens to gamble.

Bayley's strategy for the Hacienda was such an overwhelming success that in 1962 his fleet included thirty airplanes. But that same year, the Civil Aeronautics Board ruled that Bayley was running a de facto airline without a proper license, and closed the Hacienda airlift down.

While the Hacienda's strategy looked promising for a while, developers had to go back to the drawing boards to engineer a casino complex that made both business and legal sense.

PEACOCK ALLEYS AND SUBURBIA

In 1957, the Tropicana took the Sunbelt modernist phase to the most luxurious level. It had the most beautiful pool, the most sculptural sign, and the most theatrical canopy curving out from a perfectly symmetrical façade like a French *moustache*.

"They ought to stress the resort part of Las Vegas a little more," said casino owner Phil Kastel, nicknamed "Dandy" for his silk suits and gold-tipped walking cane. "A man wants to gamble, he's gonna gamble, but there's no point putting a rope around his neck and saying, 'Here, gamble!'"[66]

Going against the tradition of forcing customers to walk through the casino, as in the Hacienda's "cattle shoot," Kastel built "peacock alleys," corridors bypassing the gambling floor, to ensure a more elegant atmosphere. He also innovated by placing the back-of-house—including the kitchen and employee facilities—on the lower floor. This meant that the visitor area could better resonate with the tranquil semitropical gardens and the pagoda-lined, moon-shaped pool. Unaware of any conflict, Kastel fronted his serene resort with a six-story flashing neon tulip, and bragged of the Tropicana's speaker system that even pumped Muzak underwater into the pool.

Where the Hacienda had tried to find new customers in the hayseed, the Tropicana went for high society. Built in 1957 at a cost of $15 million, three times more expensive than the Hacienda, it was dubbed by the *New York Times* Las Vegas's only world-class luxury resort.

But four weeks after the opening, Frank Costello, the Mafia's "Prime Minister," was shot and wounded outside his Central Park apartment. The police found a handwritten note listing "gross Casino Win as of 4-26-57 … $651,284," the exact amount of the Tropicana's take. Kastel's casino license was denied.

With the Tropicana's reputation tarnished, the Sunbelt modernist phase had come to an end. Many resorts struggled to stay afloat, partially because they had saturated the market with almost identical low-rise bungalow resorts with green lawns and large pools. By the late 1950s, the Strip had become the epitome of suburbanization.

2.14 The Tropicana's circular drive leads to a razor-sharp, upsweeping canopy stretching out 130 feet with down-lighting, followed by a mosaic-tiled entrance.

While the Strip pretended to be an escape from everyday life, it was really reflective of how American cities would be built around the car. Instead of downtown grids with small lots, which had shaped cities during the age of the train, postwar cities were increasingly structured around commercial strips, which, according to architect Reyner Banham, were "a linear stretched-out automotive downtown, the kind of town-making that is natural and native to the motor age."[67]

In its continuing effort to spell the entire alphabet in pool shapes, the Strip adumbrated the rapidly evolving consumer society. Easier access to credit allowed consumers to spend money on leisure. But while the 1950s saw the rise of the "affluent society," up to 25 percent of Americans still lived in poverty. While African-Americans were mainly excluded from home ownership in suburbs throughout the nation, their neighborhoods "redlined" by mortgage lenders, they were also banned from Las Vegas resorts—except in the kitchen or on stage.

By framing gambling within images of suburbia, casino developers embedded a practice considered immoral deep into the American dream, connecting it to images as benign as suburban ranch housing. Scientifically designed Muzak put customers in a relaxed mood, enhancing an atmosphere of consumption. Just as suburbanites were forced into the consumption of autos and household equipment, so did the suburbanization of gambling in Las Vegas help contain people within resort grounds, and entice them to gamble. As more suburbanites came, the Strip converted them into gamblers, one by one.

Moreover, as Las Vegas's images of pools and celebrities spread, they popularized suburbia too. Millions of television viewers saw Lucy move from Manhattan to suburban Connecticut in *I Love Lucy*. Back in Las Vegas, millions of tourists, many of whom had yet to make it to Connecticut, could experience a suburban life of luxurious pools, spacious lawns, and modern bungalows.

And then other gambling options disappeared in 1959, when Fidel Castro outlawed gambling in Cuba, broadcasting that he would rather execute gangsters than deport them. With casino crackdowns in Miami, the Mafia operators would place all their chips in Vegas.

But before that could happen, the Mafiosi had already paid for the modern suburban buildings of the Strip's Sunbelt phase. From the Sands's triangular canopy to the Tropicana's *moustache*, Las Vegas showcased the potential of the suburban bungalow. Moreover, the Flamingo's sizzling champagne tower and the Dunes's three-story fiberglass Sultan revealed the latent possibility of the garden gnome.

Back in 1956, "Dandy" Kastel of the Tropicana knew it was just the beginning: "They haven't scratched the surface here … the whole Strip'll be hotels in ten years. It'll be the playground of the whole United States."[68]

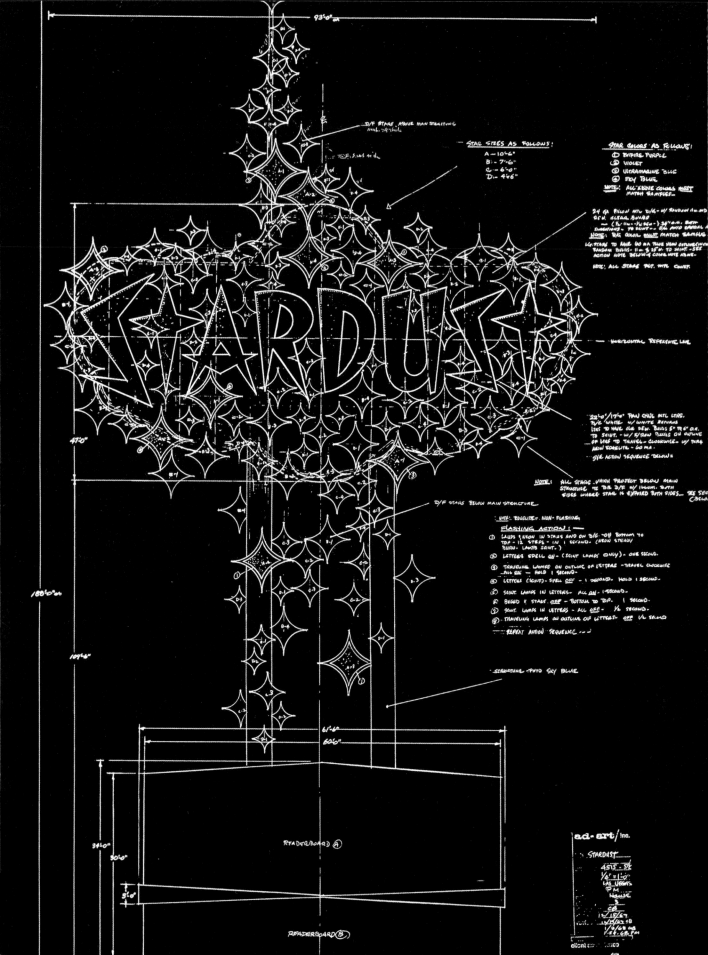

3

Pop City (1958—1969)

There was a jeweled city on the horizon, spires rising in the night, but the jewels were diadems of electric and the spires were the neon of signs ten stories high.[1]
—Norman Mailer, *An American Dream*

They said, "I want a big phallic symbol going up in the sky as far as you can make it."[2]
—Lee Klay, *Federal Sign and Signal Company*

Visitors to the 1960s Strip required no hallucinogenic drugs for a trip down the rabbit hole. It was as if all the light bulbs and fluorescents in the world had migrated to Las Vegas, where they had multiplied like rabbits. They crept up buildings until there was no surface left to occupy, formed gravity-defying structures rising far into the sky, and revealed our deepest desires in mounds of blinding light.

This was the "pop city age," the third metamorphosis of the Strip, set off by a new business strategy to target the mass market. Jet travel and the Interstate Highway System helped the middle class to travel cheaper and further. To get them all into their mouse-traps, Vegas developers expanded with gargantuan numbers of cheap hotel rooms and equally gargantuan signs. The flaming-red Dunes sign was as tall as a twenty-story building, the electric Thunderbird façade as long as two football fields. The Strip's new recipe for success became inextricably linked to the thousands of light bulbs and miles of neon—for in Las Vegas, neon was measured not by the foot but by the mile.[3]

Signs were no longer small objects attached to larger buildings but rather, in many cases, large objects attached to smaller buildings. Some were as tall as a skyscraper. Others were as long as a jumbo jet. Sometimes the building itself became a sign. So much had developers skewed the balance between buildings and signs that it seemed as if the entire city was a living Thomas Edison experiment. As a result of this emphasis, sign designers like Jack Larsen, who previously drew cartoons for Disney, became more influential than architects. These commercial artists mined images from all aspects of popular culture, from Hollywood blockbusters to toy stores. In contrast to architects' more austere concrete boxes, they gave the Strip a skyline of eccentric neon spires.

At the same time, interior design themes taken from popular culture became more immersive and risqué, such as the interior of Caesars Palace, where sexy tunic-clad "goddesses" fed guests bunches of grapes, among Roman columns and architraves. No idea was too over-the-top and truck drivers' pensions would pay for it all, thanks to Jimmy Hoffa's Teamster Pension Funds. Financed by the same class of people it tried to attract, Las Vegas was exempt from elite notions of taste.

So much had the city's architecture been inspired by popular culture, it delighted pop critic Tom Wolfe and architect Robert Venturi, who claimed that architects should *learn* from Las Vegas. Thanks to their influence, the Strip became a mandatory stop for architecture students, and Las Vegas was christened the paradigmatic pop city—its architecture to be emulated worldwide.

THE MASS-MARKET STRATEGY

Former bootlegger Tony Cornero, gave birth to the business model that kick-started the pop city age. In 1931, as we saw in chapter 1, he had built Vegas's first "carpet joint" while other gambling saloons were "carpeted" with sawdust. But the burning down of his casino a few months after the opening was symbolic of a casino career that was marked equally by innovation and tragedy.

Cornero knew that Las Vegas developers needed a new strategy. Almost all resorts competed for the same limited pool of high-end customers, and profits had diminished sharply.

From aboard his casino boat off the Santa Monica Pier, he learned that once the masses had been lured into his boat, they too rolled the dice and left cash behind. He brought his mass-market strategy to Las Vegas. Instead of a small casino for high rollers, Cornero built a big casino for low rollers. Instead of a few hundred rooms, he constructed a thousand—a new world record. Forsaking architectural elegance, Cornero built room wings with concrete tilt-up walls in the style of military barracks, perched atop a parking lot.

He did not hire an architect. Most probably, an engineer designed the buildings. He laid them out with maximum efficiency, cramming rooms into five parallel motel wings and using a construction method common to industrial buildings.[4] Instead of fussing about room views or landscaping, asphalt parking lots were placed in between the room wings, oriented to face the impossible-to-miss casino.

Demographic changes favored Cornero. Thanks to postwar prosperity, America's middle class was growing larger, buying cars and electronics. Cornero wanted to make these new consumers feel like a million bucks for only half the price of rooms at other resorts. He planned mass entertainments, including a large pool and a drive-in theater. His resort was to be called the Stardust.

He failed to fully execute his idea, however. He planned to sell $4 million worth of printed stock certificates, without bothering the Securities and Exchange Commission for approval. When the authorities shut Cornero down, he accepted money from Moe Dalitz, head of the Cleveland Syndicate. Dalitz's daily harassment about the loans ultimately took its toll. On July 31, 1955, during a craps game at the Desert Inn, Cornero collapsed and died, supposedly of a heart attack. The *Las Vegas Review-Journal* reported the following day that "He had crapped out."

Despite his premature demise, Cornero's business strategy shaped the Strip's pop city epoch and its architecture. His unspoken credo was simple: take something that could potentially appeal to the masses, then scale it up, preferably out of proportion.

COSMETIC ARCHITECTURE

A sign the length of a jumbo jet, containing 7,100 feet of neon tubing and 11,000 light bulbs, covered the Stardust's generic casino. It depicted a planetary system gravitating around a plastic globe, which stuck out exactly at the fold of the façade, positioned at maximum exposure and circled by a trailing "sputnik." Beams of light radiated from the earth into a sawtooth top, among flickering stars. On either side of the earth twinkled "Stardust" in massive Electra-jag font—the S alone contained 975 lamps.

The Stardust's stellar sign, its glow visible from three miles away, was a perfect expression of Cornero's business model. Since it affected only the surface of the building, not its substance, it was the antithesis of what was taught in schools of architecture—where the building's form is supposed to be expressive. But it was also much cheaper. This "cosmetic architecture," which at a relatively low cost achieved maximum visibility, defined and enabled the pop city age. It was a mass-marketing technique commensurate with the mass production of the Las Vegas vacation.

Did Tony Cornero, conceiver of the Stardust, plan the sign before he died? Or was it John Factor, the new front man of the casino?

John "the Barber" Factor was the black sheep half-brother of Max Factor, the makeup magnate. He trained as a hairdresser but made a career as a con artist. He fled his native England after a 1920s stock fraud, rigged the tables, and broke the bank at Monte Carlo. He then migrated to the United States and prevented extradition during trial by staging his own "kidnapping." John Factor, a master of misdirecting attention, knew how to put up an effective front.

At the moment of Cornero's demise, the Stardust was only 70 percent complete. Two years later, John Factor bought out the shareholders and resumed construction.

As massive as the sign was, it must have been an afterthought. With the Stardust nearing completion, Factor hired the Young Electric Sign Company (YESCO) to design the signage of the building, which had about as much personality as a warehouse—until Kermit Wayne came in. A graduate of the Chicago Art Institute, Wayne had painted

3.1 Amid a sea of tail-fin cars, the Stardust's circular sign fronts a starburst-plastered casino façade of plastic planets, neon rays, and a globe-circling Sputnik, 1958.

theatrical posters in Chicago and background scenes at MGM Studios. When the movie industry progressed to location shooting, making background painters obsolete, Wayne joined YESCO as a sign artist.

Instead of simply commissioning a designer for the Stardust, a competition was held. "The Stardust people had requested that YESCO provide them with a number of designs so they could choose," Wayne said. "We usually didn't do that—usually it was just one designer for a job."[5] This new process would provide the client with more options.

The task was daunting and without precedent. The Stardust had presented the competing designers with the largest canvas to date: 216 feet long and 37 feet high. Wayne decided to use a mixed-media approach: combining light bulbs and neon tubing with automobile-painted sheet metal and Plexiglas. "Neon" in Las Vegas meant not just fluorescent tubes but also incandescent lights, plastic, and fiberglass. Wayne had learned to use those materials on the job, not in art school. "We had to know what kinds of effects we could get with lights, how fiberglass could be used," he later said. "There wasn't any training for it. We just learned as we did it."[6]

Wayne stuck to a "Dingbat," a starburst motif in the tradition of Googie, the futuristic architectural style so typical of Los Angeles's drive-in coffee shops. But where classic starbursts were more modest—for instance, in the famous Welcome to Fabulous Las Vegas sign that featured a red star about the size of a person—Wayne's "Baroque" starburst covered the entire 216-foot-long sign; it was the Big Bang of all Dingbats. His hyperactive pair of stellar signs won. In contrast to his noteworthy signage, the rest of the Stardust casino complex was nondescript. There was no money spent on fancy landscaping, room views, or a circular drive like the one at the Tropicana. But $5 million cheaper to build, with almost four times more rooms, the Stardust got a lot more bang for its buck.

Wayne's Dingbat eclipsing the architecture was not simply the victory of surface over substance. The new formula worked out for everyone involved. The Stardust's efficiently laid out rooms, cross-financed by the casino, helped mass-produce the Strip vacation, making it affordable to middle-class tourists who were charged only $6 a night. Where else in the United States would they be able to get a decent room so cheap? At the same time, putting up a prominent and glamorous front allowed less expensive architecture at the back. While getting to the concrete room wings might have been a sobering process, Wayne's theatrical skills gave the middle class a celestial experience away from the everyday.

As a masterstroke, Wayne added a rocket, looking like an oversized firecracker, with which tourists could be photographed against the intergalactic sign. They now functioned as a Kodak moment, as a reporter noted, a "real traffic-stopper ... to be the most photographed items in the area."[7] Tourists would go home with a photograph immortalizing their bond with the Stardust brand.

Wayne's cosmetic cover-up had massive implications. Instead of spending money on sophisticated architecture, the Stardust proved that all you needed was the right sign.

And, with engineers to maximize the number of motel rooms and sign designers taking care of the façade, architects were rendered obsolete in this equation.

ATOMIC TIMES

With its internally lit earth, possibly the largest acrylic sphere constructed (16 feet in diameter, weighing over two tons), placed at the center of the universe, the Stardust hardly represented the Copernican model, but it was certainly indicative of the socio-cultural conditions of the time.

Outward-spreading rays pulsating from the earth, the Stardust sign alluded to the nearly daily dose of radiation in Nevada resulting from operation Hardtack II, which involved thirty-seven atomic tests within two months. The city's Chamber of Commerce even printed a special calendar with the times of the detonations and the places from which to watch them, so people could plan a holiday that included a nuclear explosion. The News Bureau had published the famous image of "Miss Atomic Bomb," depicting a showgirl with a cotton mushroom cloud attached to her bathing suit. In 1958, Clark County even incorporated a mushroom cloud in its official county seal.

Odd as this might seem today, Las Vegas in the 1950s banked on "atomic culture" and "nuclear optimism." This was before the Cuban missile crisis, when atomic associations in the cultural consciousness were not yet darkened by the looming specter of instantaneous annihilation, and radioactive fallout had not yet been linked to leukemia. Instead, nuclear weapons were seen as a force that would deter all warfare, while nuclear energy would advance people's lives with an unlimited power supply. It seemed inevitable that all Americans would soon drive cars powered by a small nuclear reactor, like the Ford Nucleon concept car.

The Stardust's two earth-circling "sputniks," elliptical neon lines that appeared to leave a light-bulb "trail," came a year after the Russians had revealed the Sputnik. The space race enthralled the world. Even car manufacturers designed automobiles with taillights mimicking space rockets, during the "tail-fin era" in car design.

While the Stardust's sign symbolized travel in space, its rooms at the back capitalized on new mobility back on the earth. In 1958, the year Stardust opened, the Boeing 707 made the first commercial flight in the United States, with jumbo success: it propelled the country into the "Jet Age," with more transatlantic passengers traveling by air than by boat. That same year Las Vegas became officially a metropolis, with more than 112,000 residents.[8] As the tourists came, so Las Vegas grew, almost as a direct function of carrier jet capacity.

Mobility down on the ground had also increased, thanks to the Federal Aid Highway Act of 1956, which authorized the Interstate Highway System, modeled after Germany's *Autobahn*. The network was originally intended as "defense highways": a quick way to move around weapons and troops, and secure the country. It turned out, however, that in Las Vegas the system mostly secured the Strip casinos. The new Interstate 15 highway, connecting Los Angeles to Salt Lake City, was placed right along the Strip.

Through its atomic aesthetic and its large-scale infrastructure, the Stardust placed itself right on the profitable collision point of the Cold War and the Jet Age. Anticipating *The Jetsons* by a few years, the Stardust epitomized and capitalized on new mobility, technological frontiers, and nuclear sightings. What better place to stay during your nuclear vacation than at the Stardust—Las Vegas's counter to the Soviet Sputnik—for only 6 dollars a day?

3D NEON

In contrast to the Strip, where at faster vehicular speed volumetric subtleties of signage would be lost, the slower pedestrian speed of downtown made three-dimensional neon worthwhile. There, sign designers built neon that was more spatially refined. Downtown signs became fully architectural.

The great instigator of it all was The Mint, a new 1957 casino whose signage was the product of a collaboration between sign designers Boernge and Wayne, and Las Vegas architects Zick and Sharp. They were given a bold mandate. Sharp said: "They said they wanted an unusual sign that could be seen all up and down Fremont."[9] Departing from the tradition of the vertical sign and the *porte-cochère* as separate structures attached to the building—an unconnected vertical and horizontal stroke—designers and architects connected the two into a single swoop. The Mint's sign started with an 85-foot-tall, 15-foot-wide "blade" on top, gracefully curved to form an eyebrow-shaped canopy, and finally terminated all the way down at the ground. It was a superb act of calligraphy.

White light bulbs covered the edge of the curvaceous "ribbon" on the fuchsia-pink façade. As the lights ran up and down the entrance, exploding into a 16-foot starburst on top, the Mint left the Glitter Gulch aghast, and even made the taller Las Vegas Club sign look flat.

With The Mint, neon had emerged from the vertical plane and entered the third dimension. Its three-dimensional curving sign defined the building architecturally. Sign and architecture were in an unusual symbiosis.

Street intersections, where signs could be seen from multiple angles, were particularly appropriate places for the volumetric neon shapes. The first such sign-corner was the sign-façade for the Golden Nugget in 1956, designed by Kermit Wayne. At the center of Wayne's sign was a "bullnose." But where in strict architectural terms a bullnose stands for a rounded, more finished edge, typically of a tile, Wayne's rounded the corner of the entire building with a 30-by-34-foot bulbous shape. It contained a golden nugget the size of a car. He then covered the remaining building with a sloping neon wall with a flowery Victorian-style border. The blue and yellow neon striped façade could fluctuate between yellow and blue, and if both were lit at the same time, it became a brilliant purple. Wayne had mixed colors like a neon alchemist.

Wayne's "bullnose" made noseless corners seem shallow. When The Mint expanded to a neighboring lot, YESCO designed another elliptical *porte-cochère* addition Wayne named "that eyebrow,"[10] deliberately abstaining from architectural terminology to describe his elliptical protruding arch that so beautifully rounded the corner. It led the

3.2 The Mint's curvilinear sign swept from a tall vertical "blade" into an "eyebrow" *porte-cochère*, 1957.

3.3 A Las Vegas Club photo-montage by Hermon Boernge features a woman holding a hamburger and a Coke, sitting on the casino's new 120-foot-tall sign. The smaller Pioneer Club sign is depicted on the right.

3.4 A postcard delineates the remodeled Horseshoe, now the "world's largest electric sign," blending Western-style letters and horseshoes with futuristic ribbed grilles and a concave bullnose.

neighboring Binion's Horseshoe Club to rethink the bare brick of the former Boulder Club, to which it had expanded. In 1961, eight miles of neon tubing were added—the building was classified as the world's largest neon sign. The design was a result of a unique arrangement between architects and sign designers, with designers producing the concrete ideas and architects serving as curators of the overall image. Wayne later said: "At the Horseshoe, the architect wanted two or three design ideas and then he combined them into one."[11]

Architects McAllister and Wagner had picked elements from a YESCO sign design competition and assembled them in a mishmash of neon Western and modern industrial forms. In contrast to the Nugget's convex bullnose, they placed a concave bullnose on the corner. It contained a screen of neon H's. Three sets of revolving H's and horseshoe shapes floated victoriously above the aqua neon-walled casino. This was cowboy futurism at its best.

The sign had come a long way in downtown Vegas. Initially a small flat part of the casino surface, it had come to dominate not just the overall image of the casino, but its overall shape. Fremont Street was no longer a Glitter Gulch but a free-flowing three-dimensional neon landscape with colors and forms too radical for their Bullnose and Eyebrow names.

3.5 A postcard shows the Golden Nugget's "bullnose," Lucky Casino's "nose," and Vegas Vic, from underneath a neon-swirled canopy.

POP CRITIC VISITS LAS VEGAS

Tom Wolfe was ecstatic at what he saw in Las Vegas. On a visit to YESCO's office, he noticed a model prepared for the Lucky Strike Casino sign. Two red curving faces came together into a narrow spine, as tall as a skyscraper. This incredible form fit perfectly into his expedition investigating "the new culture-makers" of "popular" society.

"I don't know … it's sort of a nose effect. Call it a nose,"[12] designer Hermon Boernge said of the shape of the narrow vertical face. Wolfe was amazed at the designer's description. "Okay, a nose, but it rises sixteen stories high above a two-story building," he wrote. "In Las Vegas no farseeing entrepreneur buys a sign to fit a building he owns. He rebuilds the building to support the biggest sign he can get up the money for and, if necessary, changes the name. The Lucky Strike Casino today is the Lucky Casino, which fits better when recorded in sixteen stories of flaming peach and incandescent yellow in the middle of the Mojave Desert."[13]

This "nose" represented a tipping point. Although it was only a remodeling of the Lucky Strike Casino, at 153 feet it was the tallest structure in Las Vegas. The shapes of the sign designers, claimed Wolfe, easily rivaled the modern forms of elite architects: "In the Young Electric Sign Co. era signs have become the architecture of Las Vegas, and the most whimsical, Yale seminar frenzied devices of the two late geniuses of Baroque Modern, Frank Lloyd Wright and Eero Saarinen, seem rather stuffy business, like a jest at a faculty meeting, compared to it."[14]

In contrast to these celebrated architects, the Las Vegas sign designers did not waste time theorizing their work. While the artists created a wholly original and new art vocabulary, "Las Vegas' sign-makers work so far out beyond the frontiers of conventional studio art they have no names themselves for the forms they create," Wolfe wrote of "America's first unconscious avant-garde." So the pop critic lent a hand by coining names for their shapes: "Boomerang Modern, Palette Curvilinear, Flash Gordon Ming-Alert Spiral, McDonald's Hamburger Parabola, Mint Casino Elliptical, Miami Beach Kidney."[15]

These vibrant new forms had emerged, according to Wolfe, because Las Vegas was unrestrained by "good taste." For Wolfe, Las Vegas embodied the new symbolic cultural high point of the people, an "American Monte Carlo," but without the distinction between "good" and "bad" taste: "At Monte Carlo … there are still Wrong Forks, Deficient Accents, Poor Tailoring, Gauche Displays, Nouveau Richness, Cultural Aridity—concepts unknown in Las Vegas."[16] And although the builders did not get critical acclaim, since they were of the "people" and not among the architectural elite, they knew how to appeal to the masses, and had a mass following: "Men [of YESCO] like Boernge, Kermit Wayne, Ben Mitchem and Jack Larsen, formerly an artist for Walt Disney, are the designer-sculptor geniuses of Las Vegas, but their motifs have been carried faithfully throughout the town by lesser men, for gasoline stations, motels, funeral parlors, churches, public buildings, flophouses and sauna baths."[17]

Since their popular style was repeated throughout the town, Las Vegas had become a highly consistent city—"and without the bother and bad humor of a City Council ordinance."[18] Paradoxically, absolute freedom had achieved uniformity in the skyline, not unlike zoning laws:

Las Vegas is the only town in the world whose skyline is made up neither of buildings, like New York, nor trees, like Wilbraham, Massachusetts, but signs. One can look at Las Vegas from a mile away on Route 91 and see no buildings, no trees, only signs. But such signs! They tower. They revolve, they oscillate, they soar in shapes before which the existing vocabulary of art history is helpless.[19]

Wolfe published his seminal essay in 1964, the same year as Elvis's *Viva Las Vegas*. And while Elvis added to the popularization of Las Vegas among the masses, Tom Wolfe popularized Las Vegas among the critics, who until then had snubbed the city.

Wolfe christened Las Vegas the paradigmatic pop city, and placed Lucky Strike's "Flash Gordon Ming Alert Spiral" firmly on the architectural map.

TEAMSTER TOWERS

Milton Schwartz, an architect from Chicago, remembered how he sat in his office as a trucker pulled up in front of his building, "unannounced with his big semi."[20] The man walked in and said: "I have something that may interest you." He threw the deed to the Dunes on his desk. "I just won this in a craps game on the highway."[21]

But the truth was that this man, James "Jake" Gottlieb, had just received a business loan from the pension fund of the Teamsters union, a union for truck drivers and warehouse workers. Gottlieb had gotten the loan from the union president, James "Jimmy" Hoffa. Hoffa owed favors to Chicago's organized crime, which had helped him to the presidency by "recruiting" voting members. Hoffa's fund, fueled by two-dollar monthly fees of truck drivers and warehouse workers, brought unprecedented amounts of capital to the Strip. From 1958 to 1977, the fund provided $240 million (about $2 billion in today's money) of low-interest loans to Las Vegas casino developers.

Gottlieb appointed Major Riddle, a former Al Capone associate who owned an Indiana trucking company, as Dunes president. In 1958, the pair got their first Teamster loan for the Dunes. Schwartz would fly up and down Las Vegas for the next few years to design a series of expansions, carrying his miniature drawing board and miniature 45- and 30-60-90 triangles onto the propeller plane, on seats one and two of first class— "Gottlieb would see to that."

The Teamster money was crucial in enlarging the Dunes's capacity in order to offset its operating costs. But adding a few new bungalow wings was no longer feasible, since lots had filled up. Milton Schwartz said: "The only way was to tear down one of the fifty-unit existing buildings and build this twenty-two-story building."[22] The two truckers commissioned Schwartz to design a tower that would double the number of hotel rooms in the resort. Balconies accentuated the "elongated diamond" plan shape, named the "Diamond of the Dunes." At more than 200 feet, it was the state's tallest structure and Las Vegas's most modern hotel.

Aided by pension funds, the Dunes would grow from 194 to 1,000 rooms, staffed by 1,800 employees, within ten years of its opening. As the wheels started turning, pension funds not only financed resort expansions but also helped build all four new resorts of the pop city age. Truckers' pensions, capital of the people, would build commensurate pop-culture architecture.

WEAPONS OF MASS STIMULATION

Jake Gottlieb, "an uneducated man" but with "understanding of human nature and people," gave his architect Milton Schwartz an unusual commission: a bar with strippers. Schwartz later said: "He wanted to bring all of his truck-driving friends from all over the nation into the Dunes Hotel."[23]

The architect needed to give it a twist, if he were not to waste his prestigious University of Illinois architecture education on designing a strip joint. "Let's do it artistically. … Let's have each of them carry an umbrella. … And then we'll put a gauze curtain around the umbrella." So girls were flown into Las Vegas, where they would walk *artistically*, gauzed *parapluie* held high, on top of the Dunes's bar. Schwartz remembered: "In no time at all we had every trucker in the United States stopping at the Dunes Hotel to see this show."[24]

Schwartz's artistic intervention helped to disguise seedy entertainment for which there was a large demand, but which was deemed immoral in America. It set the precedent for the mass-entertainment strategy of the pop city age. But what started with a few umbrellas quickly got out of hand.

In the face of expensive celebrity entertainers elsewhere, Major Riddle countered with a different philosophy: less is more—clothes, that is. He introduced the "Minsky's Follies," a Parisian revue, with the first bare-breasted showgirls on the Strip (the show also featured comedian Lou Costello, but his top remained on). The entertainment was presented under the extravagant tradition of Parisian plumes and feathers, as an exotic excuse for nudity.

An avalanche of French entertainment followed, starting with the Stardust's "Lido de Paris." It had a high-tech stage with an ice-skating rink, a rain curtain, a snow machine, a swimming tank, and six hydraulic lifts able to dive thirty feet deep into the ground. The stage enabled a bizarre medley of scenes, including the sinking of the *Titanic* and, most importantly, suspending the Bluebell Girls on two-foot-diameter disks above the audience. The stage's features were as important as the girls' 36-24-36 measurements, since they enabled the performers to get closer to the large audience.

Las Vegas had a new asset over other cities. Now visitors could come to the Strip to gamble, and attend a "French" revue to see a *derrière* or two. The Strip was on the frontier of the sexual revolution in the United States. And so when Brigitte Bardot's scandalous film *And God Created Woman* was released in the United States, heavily edited,

Harold Minsky told *Playboy*: "We have something people can't get on television."[25] And as the race to the bottom unfolded, more visitors came, and hotel towers rose to the top.

Tom Wolfe witnessed the height of this Francophilia, named the "French War": "The Tropicana fought back with the Folies Bergère, the New Frontier installed 'Paree Ooh La La,' the Hacienda reached for the puppets, 'Les Poupées de Paris,' and the Silver Slipper called in Lili St. Cyr, the stripper, which was going French after a fashion."[26] Wolfe also interviewed Major Riddle as he planned "Casino de Paris," a new five-million-dollar show: "The costumes alone will be fantastic. There'll be more than five hundred costumes and—well, they'll be fantastic."[27]

Schwartz and a renowned set designer, Sean Kenny, who created the spectacular set of *Blitz*, collaborated on an elaborate stage machine nicknamed "The Octopus." It had arms with hydraulic ramps that cantilevered fifty feet over the audience, enabling showgirls to walk down from the stage to approach the guests on the balconies. Twenty-foot-diameter flying-saucer disks were placed on the end of each arm, where the girls could dance. Meanwhile, elevators dropped girls down from the ceiling onto the stage, in the midst of smoke spewed by a dry ice machine. Wolfe described the whole mechanism:

As Riddle speaks, one gets a wonderful picture of sex riding the crest of the future. Whole tableaux of barebottomed Cosmonaughties will be hurtling around the Casino de Paris Room of the Dunes Hotel at fantastic speed in elliptical orbits, a flash of the sequined giblets here, a blur of the black-rimmed decal eyes there, a wink of the crotch here and there, until, with one vast Project Climax for our times, Sean Kenny ... presses the red button and the whole yahooing harem, shrieking ooh-la-la amid the din, exits in a mushroom cloud.[28]

Major Riddle bragged to Wolfe about how his Octopus incorporated "complicated machinery." "It moves all over the place and creates smoke and special effects. ... You can stage a bombardment with it. You'll think the whole theatre is blowing up," Riddle said. "They had to use the same mechanism that's in the Skybolt Missile to build it."[29]

The French War had forced the Dunes to dip into that dark source of technological innovation, the military arsenal. The Octopus was mobilized by technology from the decommissioned Douglas Skybolt, a ballistic missile with a nuclear warhead (the stage machine probably used its actuator device). As a result of the French War, Las Vegas was now also on the frontier of theater productions, influencing stages worldwide. Kenny found a new use for the Skybolt in his Las Vegas elevation of the bare breast. He later built another Octopus for the New London Theater, to swoop around performers of the musical *Cats*.[30]

IMMERSIVE DINING

In 1960, a tropical hut, two giant spears and a replica *Moai*, an Easter Island head, appeared on the Stardust parking lot. Banking on a nationwide trend of Tiki pop culture, when affordable air travel brought more Americans to tropical destinations, "Aku Aku" gave guests a Polynesian dining experience, complete with tropical foliage and flames. It kick-started another ingredient of the pop city casino complex: immersive restaurants with interiors so engrossing that the restaurant became a stage.

At the Dunes, Jake Gottlieb did not beat around the bush. "We've got to get rid of all these bums and we have to get the mink coat set in here," he told his architect. Schwartz remembered that this came as a surprise: "That's the way he put it! They were his friends. They were truck drivers and they were nice men." Since the Dunes had been running on full occupancy, the plan was to increase profit by going after the upper middle class. Gottlieb needed to wine and dine them: "I want the finest restaurant in America."[31]

On a reconnaissance trip that led him to the Beverly Hilton Hotel, Schwartz raided the maître d', Joaquin, "a bald-headed Spaniard who made a blue martini that I liked." In Mexico City's famed Villa Fontana, Schwartz found "Arturo Romero and His Magic Violins." To their surprise, they were brought to Las Vegas, signed for ten years, and placed on a revolving platform, where Schwartz spun the men around amid a waterfall, flaming sconces, and an aviary, among the tables of the Dunes's new steak restaurant.

The Sultan's Table was born, Las Vegas's first gourmet restaurant. Gottlieb then commissioned Schwartz to design a new seafood restaurant, the Dome of the Sea. Schwartz built a saucer-shaped building that appeared to float in a pool of water: "It looked like it came from outer space." But as a white skeleton of curvilinear ribbons suspended the sand-colored roof, while bubbling water shimmered light from underneath, the saucer appeared equally like a crustacean. (It was a classic case of form follows food—a seafood restaurant in the shape of a shell.)

While on the exterior the restaurant represented a clamshell abstractly, on the inside it did so literally. Schwartz collaborated with Sean Kenny on the interior. At the center of the dome, below the iridescent inner-shell-like vaulted ceiling, they floated a special performer. "I had chosen a woman with long, golden blonde hair," Schwartz said. "She was five-foot-six and played a harp, a golden harp, and I placed her in a seashell in the center of the restaurant that rolled around on a figure eight track in the water."[32]

The Dome of the Sea was a siren song of a dining experience, staking a claim on the Deep Sea theme—a popular science-fiction trope. The world became fascinated with the new oceanic discoveries of the late 1950s, when the first nuclear-powered submarine crossed under the Arctic ice cap, and Jacques Piccard descended to the deepest spot in the ocean. Hollywood exploited this deep-sea fascination with *Voyage to the Bottom of the Sea*; accordingly, the Dunes expanded its Arabian Nights desert theme with a bit of ocean and a mermaid stage prop.

The Dome of the Sea's level of immersion signaled a distinct departure from other restaurants. Previously, star performers had been the focal point. But Schwartz and Kenny encircled guests with wall projections of images of fish and seaweed, giving them a full 360-degree sea panorama. It made people full participants in the seascape. Schwartz remembered: "The people became part of the show."[33]

But with projections of fish and seaweed, the harp-playing mermaid riding her seashell incessantly in figure eights, all of this under an iridescent ceiling, the entire shell

DUNES HOTEL AND COUNTRY CLUB, LAS VEGAS, NEVADA

3.6 A Dome of the Sea postcard calls for the "seafaring traveler" to "submit" to the "seascape" of deep-sea projections, an iridescent inner-shell-like vaulted ceiling, and a harpist "Mermaid" whirling figure eights in a pool.

floating on a bubbling pool, it was an intense nautical experience: "We actually made people seasick with some of the underwater scenes!"[34] Yet this unintended side effect, unrelated to the *escargots*, was only a small price to pay to eat among the mink coats.

THE RAGING PILLAR

In 1964, the 30-foot fiberglass Sultan that stood so proudly on top of the Dunes was demoted to a turn-off signal next to the highway. The Sultan made way for the erection of a new Dunes sign: 181 feet tall, the largest freestanding electric sign in the world, as tall as the Leaning Tower of Pisa.

Exceeding the Flamingo's 80-foot-tall champagne cylinder (1953), the 126-foot trylon of New Frontier (1955), the 127-foot sign of the Sahara (1959), and even the downtown 153-foot Lucky Sign (1963), the Dunes took the sign race to another height. All of the first four were designed by YESCO; the Dunes sign, designed by Lee Klay of the Federal Sign Company, had represented the first challenge to their hegemony.

But casinos were not rated solely by the length of their signs in full erection. Among sign designers, the Dunes sign was respected for its "contained design and use of positive and negative space, the use of light to make it look taller than its 181 feet and the

3.7 A postcard features the flaming silhouette and brilliant diamond of the Dunes sign, eclipsing the hotel tower.

way it fills the area at which you are looking."[35] Klay had designed not a simple shaft but a figure made of two white pylons that rose up to form a bulbous shape evoking an onion dome—it held two-story-tall Dunes letters and a shimmering diamond. Besides being of an entirely different order of magnitude, the new Dunes sign made an appealing silhouette. Despite being a more abstract Arabic representation than the Sultan figure, it was a lot more in-your-face. Three miles of neon tubing and 7,200 electric lamps made it a significant upgrade of the Sultan's single headlight that shone into the night—to the pleasure of General Electric, who awarded it Sign of the Year. Architect Schwartz, however, attempted to prevent the looming icon from being constructed, since it would interfere with his carefully designed structures.[36] Yet Major Riddle, the Dunes president, who had earlier brought the bare-breasted Follies to the Strip, did not share the architect's austere conventions of taste.

The Dunes sign almost fully overshadowed the tower. In fact, it was practically a full-fledged building. One of its two gigantic support columns, each encased in thirty-ton slabs of concrete, housed a service elevator up to the top. Moreover, in contrast to the buildings that needed large upfront investments, Riddle was able to lease the $318,000 Dunes sign for thirty years, for $5,000 a month. This ingenious financial arrangement also enabled more control over the sign company's work, as they could design, build, and maintain it. The company designated three full-time service men to look after its light bulbs and neon, part of a permanent "neon patrol."

The Dunes's overwhelming sign made it clear to everyone that the tall freestanding pylon sign, placed along the road, was excellent at attracting attention from a distance. Once the Dunes's shaft was planted, new signs ascended like railway tracks set for the moon. But while the new Dunes sign was a fiery and effective symbol from afar, it eclipsed its immediate surroundings. It furiously painted Schwartz's white tower in firehouse red, in an incessant upward and downward motion. Patrons in the tower complained of trouble sleeping. Hotel management, forced to come up with a solution, covered the tower's windows with blackout curtains—far more sensible than softening the pillar's light.

THE BATTLE OF THE SPECTACULARS

Milton Prell gave up his early retirement for an opportunity he could not miss. He planned to revive the struggling Tally Ho, a Las Vegas Strip resort built by Edwin Lowe, inventor of the game Yahtzee, who had the outrageous idea of starting an "Olde English" themed country club (with gabled and half-timbered room wings) *without* a casino. It closed the same year.

In a record time of only ninety days Prell added a 500-seat theater, a 150-seat gourmet restaurant, and, essentially, the state's largest casino. He also discontinued the stodgy English motif in favor of an Arabian theme, tried and tested with the Sahara, the Dunes, the Algiers, and the El Morocco, all riffing on Middle Eastern deserts. From *The Book of One Thousand and One Nights*, Prell appropriately picked a folk tale about a poor young boy who rubs a lamp and whose wishes are granted by a genie—the Arabian equivalent of Lady Luck. And so the Tally Ho reincarnated as the Aladdin.

With these crucial adjustments made, how could Prell conceal the fact that his "new" casino complex was merely an infill of an existing project? How could he get around the theme of the existing Tudor-style room wings, which he left intact and nested into the new casino building, in order to avoid a pricey remodeling? He needed a sign.

Prell bought into a new widespread assumption on the Strip, established by the large Dunes pillar: tall totems bewitch the crowds. This explains the erection of four equally large signs in the mid-1960s. Prell's sign would be the second in the new "Golden Age" of signage in Las Vegas.[37]

So hot was the demand for signs that California design companies set up shop in Las Vegas. Whereas at first YESCO was the dominant sign business, now competition existed between three firms: YESCO (Young Electric Sign Company), Federal Sign Company, and Ad-Art. The competition was cutthroat, since sign designers got paid only after they landed the commission—unlike architects, who were paid to develop the design. Under these competitive conditions, with extremely large budgets, the neon sign reached its apogee, with sophisticated shapes and animation sequences.

Prell called for a competition between different design firms. He was only moderately impressed with YESCO's design, but a small "thumbnail" in the corner of the rendering had caught his eye.[38] This was Larsen Jr.'s design, a doodle that looked straight out of a Disney cartoon. Jack Larsen Sr., who had worked for Walt Disney Studios as an assistant animator on films such as *Pinocchio* and *Bambi*, decided to develop the design further. It was a whimsical figure. A string of hundreds of golden cylinders—secretly made out of beer cans—gradually curled up to a revolving three-sided whiteboard, holding a fountain spraying gold and floating a light-bulb-covered oil lamp. Three giant golden pylons scrolling up like Turkish slippers supported the structure.

The sign was up against the design of Ad-Art, a sign company from Northern California, which proposed a 200-foot-tall structure spewing a flame. While it was nowhere near as tall, Larsen Jr.'s design had a more elusive beauty. Because of its curvaceous figure, it was dubbed the "ice-cream chair."

But the biggest threat was Prell's architect, whose name is unknown. The architect wanted to see the sign design before owner Prell arrived. "God, I hate it," the architect said. "That's the ugliest thing I've ever seen in my life."[39]

The team decided to wait for Milton Prell. "This isn't what you want," the architect said as Prell walked in. Prell, however, was thrilled.

"Oh my God, where do I sign?"

"Milton, I knew you'd love it," said the architect, who was not going to lose his client over some aesthetic fixation.

The sign was the only exterior element revealing the Aladdin story—with the clarity of 40,000 light bulbs. Prell also commissioned YESCO to turn the casino's *porte-cochère* into a second neon sign. It jagged around individual neon letters of "Aladdin," written in an Eastern brush font, as a pop-culture interpretation of an Islamic dentate cornice. The importance of the signs was reflected in Prell's construction budget: out of a total $3 million remodeling, Prell spent $750,000 on the signs alone.

Larsen Jr.'s sign quickly became the poster child of the resort. It even made the cover of the 1968 March issue of *Architectural Forum*, photographed by Denise Scott Brown, a Yale architecture professor. "With pieces of Aladdin hauled into a gallery," noted one art critic in *Art in America*, "one could invent an artist worth marketing."[40] No words were wasted on the nondescript casino building, the sign's ugly stepsister in this modern Cinderella story.

While Aladdin was a more effeminate figure in the battle of the spectaculars, the Frontier's new pillar competed with its length: 184 feet tall, three feet taller than the Dunes. In the shape of a crucifix, it carried a heavy bar cantilevering far out on either side containing 16-foot-tall letters, and lit up a fierce red at night—X marks the spot.

But within all its masculinity there was a refined feature that had probably won Bill Clark, corporate art director of Ad-Art, the commission for the sign. He had invented a new logo for the casino, rebuilt with a new eight-story, 650-room complex. Having gone through multiple frontiers—from the "Last Frontier" of the Old West (1940s) to

3.8 The Aladdin sign, with its coil of golden beer cans and car-sized oil lamp, stands as a beacon of a generic casino building.

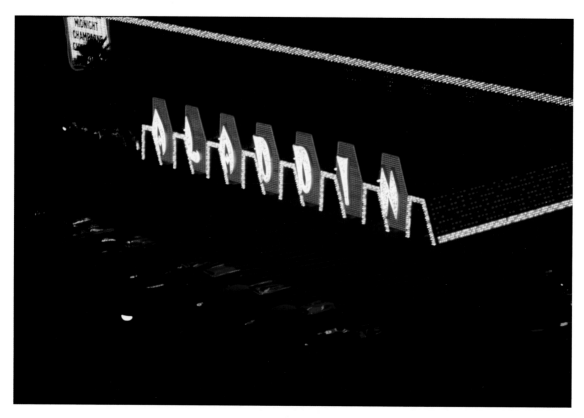

3.9 Aladdin's canopy, a neon version of an Islamic dentate cornice, paints the parking lot red.

the "New Frontier" of the space age (1950s)—it simply became "The Frontier," settling on the broadest coverage of the quintessential American myth.

Clark's F-logo was made up of shapes from a spades playing card. Blown up three stories tall, the logo would be placed on a 126-foot-long golden spine of stacked diamonds. All of this would revolve within an elongated arc structure, painted sky-blue so that it dissolved into the daylight. Clark had reinvented the Frontier as a game of chance.

With these "spectaculars" rising high, Stardust owner Moe Dalitz could not lag behind. He called for a competition, looking for a sign to "personify the Stardust mystique." Bill Clark struggled for another win, but when he gave the project to his staff, Paul Miller broke the "stalemate." He had reportedly scribbled his idea, a star cloud, with his Prisma pencil on a small 2.5-inch "rough" during a brown-bag lunch.[41] It was followed almost to the letter. A few months and half a million dollars later, it stood 188 feet, topping the Frontier as the newest, tallest freestanding sign in the world—its Stardust letters alone were two stories high.

3.10 In contrast to the smaller 1950s Desert Inn's sign stand the revolving 1960s Silver Slipper and the cantilevering Frontier, 1968.

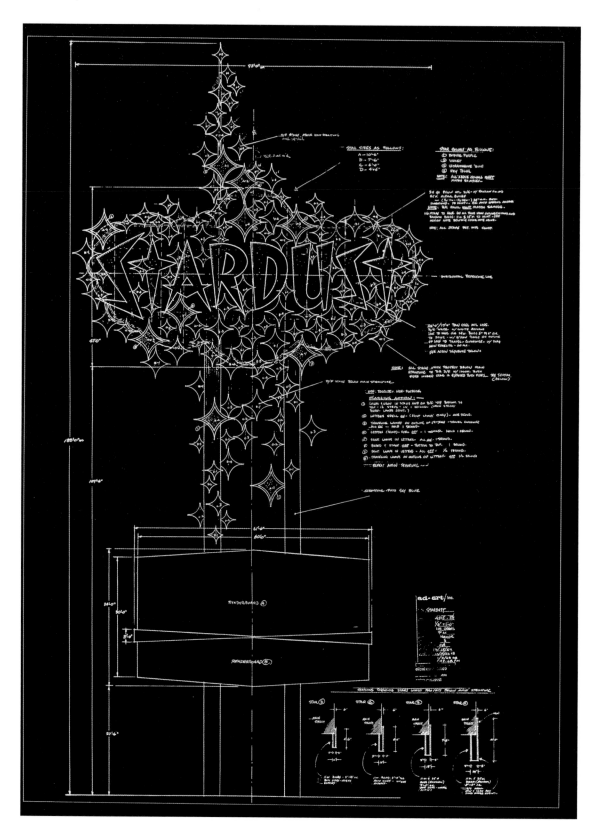

Its animation sequence included actions including "sweeps, washdowns and random scintillation."[42] At night, the cloud of scattered blue and magenta stars flickered. Meanwhile, the Stardust name glowed, after which shimmering stars appeared to drop like falling stardust. The two legs supporting the cloud were painted sky blue, so the cloud seemed to float during the day. The legs were not lit at night, so the cloud effect persisted. Appreciated by designers, the public, and art critics alike, the sign appeared on the cover of *Art in America* 1972. It was the only commercial sign bestowed that honor.

The Flamingo then called for an upgrade of its champagne tower, only a decade ago heralded by Tom Wolfe as a "smashing success … with neon rings in the shape of bubbles that fizzed all eight stories up into the desert sky all night long like an illuminated whisky-soda tumbler filled to the brim with pink champagne."[43] The once spectacular tower, now nicknamed "the silo," looked antiquated beside the new arrivals.

Once again, Bill Clark of Ad-Art won. He designed the world's tallest single-shaft sign, 130 feet tall and the shape of a plumed feather, with shades of pink, salmon, and blush. The plume would "fill upward" with light and "ripple" as a whole, concluding with a "fan out" of light and a letter sparkle. And once again, General Electric was thrilled with all this light business—a total of two miles of neon tubing and 6,000 light bulbs—awarding it the General Electric Sign Award.

With the Flamingo sign, the "Golden Age" of signage had come to an end. The Strip now outshone Ginza and Broadway. Stanford art history professor Albert Elsen noted: "Bold and big as the signs in Times Square are, they still lack the artistic sophistication and pizzazz of the Las Vegas mega-signs."[44]

The neon "spectacular" had come a long way in Las Vegas, evolving from "a pole and a box" to the world's tallest electric monuments. Although these signs had no other purpose than to shock and awe, they were deemed so important that a "lighting-up ceremony" was held for each new sign—a ritual in which typically the hotel president, the mayor, and a few showgirls climbed up it. But as impressive as the "spectaculars" were, they were an amplification of a simple credo. "In the sign business there's an expression that 'Lights attract the moths,'" Chuck Barnard, president of Ad-Art, said later. "People are attracted to glitter and lights."[45]

3.11 An Ad-Art blueprint for the 188-foot-long Stardust sign describes an eight-phase "Flashing Action" sequence that began with switching on all the lights, from bottom to top in 12 steps, in only one second.

3.12 At 130 feet, undulating neon tubes give a feathered look to the Flamingo's plume of salmon, blush, and pink, 1968.

Resorts, expanding with additional attractions, were presented with an aesthetic dilemma. The overall composition of the existing and newer structures, often a mish-mash of different-style buildings with unrelated heights, made for a visually incoherent front. How could resorts expand while maintaining a consistent and impressive identity?

Enter the Big Screen, a sign façade that enveloped not just one building but multiple unrelated structures into a single unifying swipe, and made for a highly noticeable front. They contained so many lights that when they were collectively animated, the overall impression was a supersized television set.

For a monthly lease of $19,000, Thunderbird got a 560-foot-long facelift. Ad-Art covered the hodge-podge of adobe-style and modernist buildings with massive teal blue and green metal panels. This was only the background to what would be the world's longest sign: a sheer wall of light bulbs, 37,000 points of light in total (about the same number as a low-definition television). Architect Reyner Banham wrote: "So the humble globe is to Las Vegas what the humble brick is to more conventional townscapes—the basic unit for building monuments."[46]

The simple light bulb had slowly gained dominance over neon, despite neon's brighter and deeper colors, since it was more controllable. "It can't do one or two things that a tube-light can, like drawing a neat outline round a giant cowpoke silhouetted five stories high," Banham wrote. "But it can do something which is beyond all tubes—it can glitter."[47] While one light bulb alone cannot do much, when thousands are placed together they can make patterns. "Yes, your friendly Edison-invented domestic globe," Banham continued, "may not strike you as a particularly glamorous light-source in itself, but when 2 or 3 million are gathered together it has a fantastic lot going for it."[48] They can "scint" (sparkle) or "chase" (make patterns in a particular direction). All this flickering in the darkness made the collective of light bulbs hard to ignore.

With eight miles of neon tubing, however, the new T-bird did not limit itself to sole-point lights. Neon was typically used to bring linear lines of movement, specifically for outlining figures or letters. In this case, neon outlined the 12-foot-high chiseled THUNDERBIRD letters.

Now that the T-Bird had upgraded its front, the Stardust's sign, which barely ten years earlier had elevated the sign race to cosmic proportions, needed a refresh. It was outgrown by a jumble of modernist expansions and a Tiki-style building. Competition, rather than planning codes, had forced the Stardust to unify its front.

Ray Larsen Jr. designed an electric screen the length of two football fields, consisting of a grid of units with different-sized and colored neon stars. By lighting similar-colored tubes at the same time, different patterns emerged that seem to move, lighting the façade from orange, red, blue and white, or any possible mix. Compared to T-Bird's simple dots, it made for a puzzling screen of neon stripes.

3.13 The new Stardust sign and animated electronic façade had recycled the globe and Electra-jag letters of the original 1958 sign-front, 1968.

Larsen repurposed some elements of the old sign, including the old globe, which he placed on a pole—not unlike the logo of the public broadcasting network, it was a fitting monument to the Television Age. In fact, television and Las Vegas had more than a symbolic connection: the same phosphor glowing inside people's living rooms—the cathode ray tubes of television—also lit up Las Vegas neon signs. As a result of intensive research on phosphor for use in color television, new phosphor colors were invented, which neon sign designers could add to their palette (by the 1960s, about two dozen colors were available).

And both television and Las Vegas animated phosphor to animate the crowds. Flickering screens in the midst of the dark, Banham had realized, easily grab attention:

3.14 The Thunderbird's new 560-foot-long sign-skin fronts the existing casino and even the hotel rooms, which now faced the sign's back, 1968.

[Las Vegas] wants something that can burn its way through the most bloodshot eyeball, tracer its way through the heaviest veil of fatigue or boredom. … The eye cannot ignore flashing or flickering lights; the brain, it seems, cannot but respond if the rhythm of the glass matches one of those buried rhythms of madness or hallucination—as Las Vegas may have known, by trial and error, long before psychedelic strobes.[49]

But as effective the Big Screen was, it had a drawback. For the sake of flickering and unification, the Thunderbird's big screen had also concealed portions of the hotel wings. Hotel rooms that previously provided a view of the Strip now faced the back of the electric sign.

The new rooms gave a close-up of the screen's guts of circuit boards and twenty-six miles of electric wire—it was a lot like peeking inside a television set. And with transformers going up to 15,000 volts per tube, the electric screen buzzed, while mechanical devices flashing the lights clicked. The Big Screen sparked almost as much as it sparkled, subjecting hotel guests to an unusual cacophony. While it might have annoyed them, for the management it had an unintended benefit: keeping gamblers awake and in the casino.

MILLION VOLT LIGHT AND SOUND CULTURE

Las Vegas was like an open-air laboratory experiment, with sign designers as uninhibited amateur scientists weaving tapestries of neon. It made other less technologically endowed places look like Luddites. Why did not other cities build electronic architecture, as in Las Vegas?

Architects were too repressed by "the traditions of architectonic culture, training, and taste," Banham claimed. Las Vegas's architecture was so far beyond the norm that it represented a paradigm shift: "a change from forms assembled in light to light assembled in forms."[50] Instead of being the stuff of bricks, Las Vegas's walls were made of energy. This architecture of "pure environmental power, manifested as colored light" was more "convincing" than conventional architecture: "the effectiveness with which space is defined is overwhelming, the creation of virtual volumes without apparent structure is endemic, the variety and ingenuity of the lighting techniques is encyclopaedic."[51] Banham titled his first article about Las Vegas, a review of Tom Wolfe's publication, a manifesto of technology: "Toward a Million Volt Light and Sound Culture."

The Strip showed the potential of "electrics-as-place," the British avant-garde architecture group Archigram argued: "Las Vegas suggests that a really powerful environment can be created simply by passing an electric current—in daytime the hardware is nothing."[52] Electricity had turned the desert into an exciting place. Archigram even used the city as inspiration for their speculative project the "Instant City," a touring assemblage of screens and sound systems that would wake up provincial towns with audiovisual bombardments. They made only one critical side comment regarding the lack of interactivity of Las Vegas's signs: "It is suggested the visitor himself could play with large areas of this lighting so that he makes it happen rather than gawk at it."[53]

Hunter S. Thompson was less thrilled with such a possibility, describing a new invention he saw at one of the casinos:

Stand in front of this fantastic machine, my friend, and for just 99$ your likeness will appear, two hundred feet tall, on a screen above downtown Las Vegas. Ninety-nine cents more for a voice message. "Say whatever you want, fella. They'll hear you, don't worry about that. Remember you'll be two hundred feet tall." Jesus Christ. I could see myself lying in bed in the Mint Hotel, half-asleep and staring idly out the window, when suddenly a vicious nazi drunkard appears two hundred feet tall in the midnight sky, screaming gibberish at the world: "Woodstock Uber Alles!"[54]

Tom Wolfe had also cautioned about the oppressive effects of technology on human beings. He described a gambler called Raymond, "a good example of the marvelous impact Las Vegas has on the senses,"[55] who was showing symptoms of "toxic schizophrenia" and kept droning: "HERNIA HERNIA HERNIA HERNIA HERNIA HERNIA HERNIA."

Like all visitors to the Strip, Raymond had been bombarded with a barrage of visual and audio components, starting with his drive into the city: "He had been rolling up and down the incredible electric-sign gauntlet of Las Vegas' Strip, U.S. Route 91, where the neon and the par lamps—bubbling, spiraling, rocketing, and exploding in sunbursts ten stories high—celebrate one-story casinos." Downtown, where all these signs condensed into one continuous façade of neon, was even more extreme. The juxtaposition of these various competing lighting sequences made Fremont Street look like a television, tuned to all channels at once.

Raymond had also been exposed to constant audio stimulation: "Muzak pervades Las Vegas from the time you walk into the airport upon landing to the last time you leave the casinos. It is piped out to the swimming pool. It is in the drugstores. It is as if there were a communal fear that someone, somewhere in Las Vegas, was going to be left with a totally vacant minute on his hands."[56] Add to that to the sound of slot machines, "churning up over and over again in eccentric series all over the place, like one of those random-sound radio symphonies by John Cage." This is why Wolfe titled his essay "Las Vegas (What?) Las Vegas (Can't Hear You! Too Noisy) Las Vegas!!!!"

Las Vegas, claimed Wolfe, "has succeeded in wiring an entire city with this electronic stimulation, day and night, out in the middle of the desert."[57] And while some stimuli were more low-tech, such as the humming of the card dealers, and "a stimulus that is both visual and sexual—the Las Vegas buttocks décolletage" (a sexually provocative dress for waitresses, exposing their backs), in the juxtaposition of these stimuli, "the casualties start piling up," including poor Raymond—who gets escorted out of the casino.

But one energy blackout or price hike, and all of Las Vegas's audiovisual architecture would vanish into the silent night. The Las Vegas walls of light were possible only because of that 660-foot-thick wall wreaking havoc on the Colorado River, the Hoover Dam, with its unstoppable supply of cheap hydroelectricity. In the early 1960s, Las Vegas per capita electrical consumption exceeded the national average by almost 300 percent, for only half the cost per kilowatt-hour.[58]

Light bulbs were particularly energy-inefficient because of their use of a metal filament, heated to thousands of degrees Fahrenheit, to generate light. This led to a dramatic heating up of the environment, particularly in downtown, because the concentration of lights was so intense. Normal Mailer wrote: "The Fremont was one electric blaze, the Golden Nugget another, the sky was dark, the streets were light, lighter than Broadway on New Year's Eve, the heat was a phenomenon. Was it ninety degrees at nine minutes to five, five in the morning now?"[59] Walking down Fremont Street felt like being a piece of toast browning on both sides, stuck in a toaster two stories tall.

Energy was also blown at cooling the desert. As early as the 1950s, Las Vegas led the nation in per capita air-conditioning sales.[60] But whereas in other deserts thick walls would have kept the cool air inside, Las Vegas's casinos opened their entire ground façades, so gamblers could more easily wander in. A cool blast of air-conditioning, an "air curtain," would seal off the desert heat, and in the process waste more energy. In 1959, the Lucky Strike Bingo Hall had the first air curtain in Las Vegas, which it deliberately advertised on its sign: "Walk Thru the *Air Curtain.*" A quintessential modern experience, it offered gamblers a shower of cool in the midst of desert and filament heat.

Las Vegas's sign, sound, and air-conditioning systems drew so much heavy voltage that they exhausted the city's supply from the Hoover Dam. In 1960, they built coal-burning plants in Southern Nevada, the first of which burned 1,050 tons a day. All this energy came at a heavy environmental cost. Bulldozers carved out natural environments in search of coal. Pumps sucked up water to supply the plants, which dropped drastically and polluted the water table. Chimneys filled the air with nitrogen oxides and arsenic emissions—as the neighboring Moapa Band of Paiutes found, their families suffering from unusually high rates of asthma, lung disease, and cancer.

While Las Vegas foreshadowed exciting architectural possibilities in its integration of technology, had it been imitated by other cities, apart from more casualties like Raymond, its hinterland required a makeover. Bulldozers, river barricades, and scorching ovens devastating local ecologies embossed the other side of the electric coin, invisible from the escapism in Las Vegas. On the front end of the electric supply chain, however, a unique profession emerged: neon sign patrollers, who drove around at night to spot broken lamps, like cable guys fixing a dead channel on a television set.

POPULUS ROMANUS

Jay Sarno started as a tile contractor and house-builder with his business partner, Stanley Mallin. He then received a number of Teamster loans to build hotels, thanks to an instant personal connection with Jimmy Hoffa—"Both were big, boisterous fellows,"[61] Mallin later said. Between 1965 and 1972, Sarno received an unprecedented total of $20.4 million in Teamster loans for the most lavish culmination of the pop city age, Caesars Palace.

All the way from driving up to the parking lot to throwing the dice in the casino, Caesars Palace provided the most immersive casino experience yet. Sarno was the first to design his casino as a conveyor belt of unique but interconnected experiences—a scripted narrative leading guests through an intoxicating euphoria of drinks, food, and gambling. He was the forefather of modern Las Vegas.

Sarno prided himself on being an atypical designer. He surprised a reporter with a rhetorical question: "Do I look like any designer you ever met?"

3.15 A guest poses with a fiberglass centurion at the base of Caesars's Roman-style roadside sign, 1970. The even larger Romans on the columns were later additions to the original 1966 sign.

So I don't look like a designer, but see that block outside there through the window, that design that covers the front of the building? That's the Sarno Block, I've had it patented and anybody wants to use it, they have to come to me! See this office? It's elliptical. An ellipse, in my opinion, is the friendliest shape. The new convention hall we're building will be my version of a Roman circus—elliptical.[62]

The oval was to dominate the entire resort. The Sarno Block was actually a large brick formed of two half-ovals which could be stacked to make a modern latticework screen. It made the resort's night façade glow evenly, smoothing over the chaos of dark and lit rooms behind it. "Over the years that I have been creating hotels, I've discovered that the oval is a magic shape … conducive to relaxation," Sarno said. Even the fourteen-story tower was crescent-shaped, making for a stately front—another function of the egg shape.

Sarno's oval inevitably impacted the casino space: "Because the casino is shaped in an oval, people tend to relax and play longer." Lit ribbons with a crystal chandelier at the center accentuated the dark dome, while false columns encircled the oviform space.

Before Sarno, casinos had low ceilings so people would focus on the games. In contrast, Sarno's high ceiling made for a dramatic space that displaced the attention to the experience of the space itself. This grand casino philosophy created a division among casino designers, one that persists today. Should a casino be a low-ceilinged dice den, or a spectacular space? Present-day research shows that gamblers spend equal amounts of money in both casino typologies, but that the "restorative effect" of the grand casino is greater: you feel less bad after losing money, since the space is so appealing.[63]

To this dramatic space Sarno added a narrative that further aggrandized the gambler's experience. He said, "A Roman-Greco motif was something new."[64] He chose only those aspects from Roman history that conformed to the popular imagination. "My approach is to guess what the public will like," he said during the opening. "It must be exciting and must give full pleasure."[65] Caesars Palace was pop Roman.

The first Roman sign visible from a distance was the roadside sign. Jack Larsen and Kermit Wayne had won the commission. Delving into architectural history, but not weighed down by its baggage, the pair took the most recognizable elements of a Roman temple—Ionic columns, a cornice, and an architrave—and inflated them to match competing signs. And for the art on the pediment they borrowed not from the Romans, but from the popular Roman illustrations drawn by American Dean Cornwell. It was postmodernism *avant la lettre.*[66]

A chance event led life-size colored Roman centurion statues to appear at the base of the sign. Wayne and Larsen drove to the local variety store to find scale figures of regular people. What they saw there was beyond their expectations: a 25-cent centurion figure, close to the correct scale. To Wayne's surprise, Sarno wanted the centurions built. The Romans would provide a so-called "picture gallery" to pedestrians (a growing group, as foot traffic between expanding resorts increasingly took hold). To arrest them with an uncanny effect, the centurions' overscaled proportion was kept. Wayne said: "They ended up having them made, about seven feet tall, in fiberglass."[67]

3.16 A replica of the Winged Goddess of Victory fronts Caesars Palace's driveway entrance, amid fountains and cypresses.

Sarno also innovated by incorporating the driveway into the theme. Typically, casinos had little more than a sign and a *porte-cochère* to ease the transition from the highway into the resort. Sarno set the main building 135 feet back from the Strip to accommodate a monumental driveway, lined with statues and fountains, leading to a pair of concave low-rise hotel wings lined with columns—an entrance borrowed from Versailles rather than Rome.

"He got arguments from everyone in town," remembered Sarno's wife years later. "It was too far back from the street. He'd go broke before you knew it."[68] So much did Sarno buck the tradition that even people in Las Vegas argued that he should not be doing this. But his driveway even became the focus of national attention. In the center stood eighteen fountains, spraying 350,000 gallons of water per minute. They were so big, reportedly the largest private fountains in the United States, that they obsessed daredevil motorcyclist Evel Knievel, who challenged Sarno that he could jump them. Knievel flew over the fountains, but fell short. He tumbled down the ramp, crashed into the Dunes parking lot, and spent twenty-nine days in a coma. Sarno's grandeur exceeded even Knievel's jumping capacity.

Sarno dotted his driveway with a $150,000 collection of facsimile sculptures, including the classic Winged Goddess of Victory. They were rescaled so they would each be a similar height. For instance, the colossal *David* was made to appear the same height as the much smaller *Bacchus*. A catalog explained the statues' history in museum-like fashion. And although they were replicas, Sarno arranged for their authentic fabrication. "The statuary that I used at Caesars was cut from the finest, purest, grade A Carrara marble from Florence," he said.[69] To Sarno it mattered that his sculptures were carved by Italians out of a Roman rock.

The cypresses lining the drive, however, were less inclined to obey Sarno's Roman zeal. They were dying in the desert. But Sarno "was not going to be thwarted by a couple of dozen recalcitrant trees," a reporter noted. "I don't worry, as they die off I'll just keep on replacing them," Sarno said of his cornucopia. "People say to me 'So why not have palm trees?' But I say that palms just don't have the *character* we want here."[70]

When Sarno was done with his driveway, it was so spectacular that it added to the experience of the theme: you could park your car among statues, fountains, and cypresses—just as the Romans did! It was symptomatic of the overall architectural strategy. "I believe very strongly that when you select a theme for a hotel, you ought to follow that theme in every aspect of the operation where it is possible to do so," interior designer Jo Harris later said.[71] Even the smallest patch of grass was somehow "Roman."

By "Roman," Sarno meant "Royal Roman Splendor," *not* Spartan. Hollywood movies had helped to associate ancient Rome with wealth, for instance *Cleopatra* (1963), which focused on the opulence of the late Roman republic.[72] Sarno further enhanced the Roman decadence in his own way. The buildings defining the plaza were modern and sleek, not Roman-style at all. He decorated the lobby with gold leaf and Brazilian rosewood. The pool at the rear was shaped like a centurion shield. Roman-chariot-shaped booths decorated the Circus Maximus theater, which had blue-painted walls to

IN CIRCUS MAXIMUS   THE BACCHANAL   CLEOPATRA'S BARGE

THE PIAZZA   THE GALLERIA   AH SO STEAK HOUSE

3.17 A brochure depicts Caesars Palace as a conveyor belt of unique experiences, from cocktails inside a moving Cleopatra's barge to dinner among Ionic-column-plastered walls and "goddesses" carrying wine casks.

create a more "authentic" open-air Roman Circus mood. Many suites were duplex, with spiral staircases, and had grand pianos and Jacuzzi bathtubs—stuff Romans would have had, argued Sarno, if they had lived in the twentieth century.

"We think of Nero in Hades, shaking his head in wonder and envy. Rome—his Rome, which he rebuilt with broad streets and splendid villas—was never a patch on Vegas,"[73] wrote a columnist for the *New Yorker*.

Sarno disguised this luxury palace behind populism. "Everybody is a Caesar," he used to say, meaning everyone could be like a king for just one day at Caesars Palace— everybody willing to pay $14 a night for the cheapest room, a lot more than the $9 a night average on the Strip. Sarno went as far to drop the punctuation mark in the name of his resort, Caesars Palace. "Without the apostrophe, it's the plural of a large group,"[74] he said. The paradox was that the popular imagery incorporated was so opulent, it was no longer aimed at the populace.

Unique services added to the personalized luxury experience. At the Bacchanal restaurant, waitresses—called "goddesses"—would introduce themselves to guests saying: "I am your slave," and responded to orders: "Yes, master," serving wine in narrow casks. They also gave "grape treatments," hand-feeding guests bunches of grapes. To evoke a Roman orgy, they would massage diners' backs and perform Middle Eastern belly dances—a dance so exotic that even the ancient Romans did not have it.

The $19 million resort, by far the most expensive Strip casino to date, opened with a lavish three-day party costing $1 million. Centurions hand-delivered and unrolled invitations, printed on faux parchment scrolls.

"We needed a guy like Jimmy," Sarno said during the opening of the Teamsters union president. "Only someone with his class, his integrity, could have added a little Greco-Roman class to Vegas."[75] Hoffa, however, was remarkably quiet, up to his ears in federal lawsuits, knowing he would go to jail soon. Yet Hoffa had helped bring to an end an eight-year hiatus of new resort construction since the Stardust. This long buildup led to the perfect culmination of all major trends of the pop city age, including a large freestanding sign like the Dunes, and a highly immersive interior like the Dome of the Sea (also oval-shaped), while adding a new feature: the micro-detail to the customer's overall experience, creating a new level of customer manipulation.

All this Roman decadence was union-financed by a truck drivers' pension fund, union-operated by "goddess" culinary workers, and built by a former tile contractor. In short, Caesars Palace was a resort of the people, by the people, and for the people—and particularly for *wealthy* people.

As the ultimate sign of Roman decadence, Sarno planned to implement an ancient form of excitement. Intrigued by the bacchanalia of Roman emperors, he filled the pool at the Bacchanal restaurant with piranhas. In a curious attempt to emulate a particular historic bacchanal, he wanted to sacrifice a baby piglet nightly—"to pick up the pace after the entrée service," according to a Bacchanal restaurant brochure. Luckily for the piglets, and for "animal lovers everywhere," the Health Department put an end to Sarno's Roman compulsion.

OVER-THE-TOP

While Sarno had reached a new level of luxury with Caesars Palace, he realized he had alienated some customers at the lower end of the market. His second property on the Strip was meant specifically for them. The philosophy was simple: "to attract the mass, not the class,"[76] he said. Initially, he wanted to build it next to Caesars, and call it the Roman Circus, blending well with the theme next door. But when he found another site: "I decided to scrap the plans for a Roman circus, and build a circus like we're all familiar with: a *circus* circus."[77] If the ritzy Roman theme was for *Caesars*, Circus signaled *hoi polloi*.

There was no mistake about it: Circus Circus was a *circus*. The building was a ninety-foot-high tent-shaped big top, in plan the size of a football field (oval-shaped), painted white and raspberry red. But what looked like a curved canvas taut-draped circus tent was actually a stiff Plexiglass structure. No sigh of wind could crease it. No desert heat could warm it (real tents are a lot harder to air-condition).

Sarno commissioned sculptor-performer the "great Montyne" to carve twelve statues, including a clown and a mad gorilla, to stand around a 306-foot-long pool containing five color-changing fountains. Instead of a tall roadside sign, Young Electric Sign Company designed a Coney Island-style carousel, the flashier kind of merry-go-round.

Out of spite for expensive entertainers, Sarno brought in cheaper circus performers and animals. Some of the most notable acts included an acrobat capable of doing the world's only triple-and-one-half somersault on a flying trapeze, and an acrobat who dove sixty-five feet into a wet sponge, placed right in the middle of the casino floor. Sarno's most radical move was to float the midway with the circus acts right above the gambling floor. "A true hybrid structure," the two floors were connected by a fire pole and a slide—which card dealers and waitresses took on their way to their shift, by Sarno's mandate. The floors were also visually interconnected. Children could watch the circus acts on the second-floor midway, while their parents gambled below. Meanwhile, gamblers on the casino floor could see the acts as well, which seemed like a good idea to Sarno.

"All manner of strange County-Fair/Polish Carnival madness is going on up in this space," Hunter S. Thompson wrote. "Right above the gambling tables the Forty Flying Carazito Brothers are doing a high-wire trapeze act, along with four Muzzled Wolverines and the Six Nymphet Sisters from San Diego." He continued:

So you're down on the main floor playing blackjack, and the stakes are getting high, when suddenly you chance to look up, and there, right smack above your head, is a half-naked fourteen-year-old girl being chased through the air by a snarling wolverine, which is suddenly locked in a death battle with two silver-painted Polacks … they are grabbed out of the air by three Korean kittens. … This madness goes on and on, but nobody seems to notice.[78]

Monkeys and elephants wandered through the casino, or ran stores. Sarno said: "You can play a slot machine with our Money Monkey, who jumps for joy if you win or holds his head in sorrow if you lose. There's another monkey who runs a store. If you want something, give him the money and he'll bring you the product. … Here's a fellow leading two little pink elephants, you can ride them or pet them."[79]

One Siamese elephant, Tanya, was capable of operating a slot machine and picking out Keno numbers. Sarno originally planned to have Tanya trapeze through the casino. He had ordered her a custom-made diaper to prevent her excrement from flying around and crashing on the craps tables. After a test drive, however, the idea had to be abandoned. It turned out that elephants, too, could get vertigo—and Sarno could not tolerate Tanya's vomit geyser throughout his casino.

Sarno did not rely solely on architectural clues and circus acts as class signifiers. He also intended to lure people in with the universal appeal of subsidized fast food, like

3.18 Trapeze artists perform right above gamblers at Circus Circus, 1968.

25-cent hot dogs in the "Wiener Wagon," and $1 all-you-can-eat ice cream in "Diet Buster." And he was going to intoxicate them with alcohol, with $1 all-you-can-drink at the "Bavarian Beer Fest." He then added an erotic nuance to the circus theme that was not entirely unisex. "There are certain areas restricted to adult fun," read the brochure. A "Sleeping Beauty" fell out of bed as the target was hit at a baseball toss game. A bar with numbered tables had phones used to flirt with people at other tables. There was also a "very provocatively-dressed shoe-shine girl," in Sarno's words,[80] and the "Lions' Cage Bar," with waitresses dressed up as lion-tamers. "Ooh-La-La theater" featured topless showgirls, while the "Ding-a-Ling-a-Ring Bar" served cocktails with unorthodox views from right underneath the performers and dancers.

Within the plastic tent, it was a free-for-all shakedown. "The customers are being hustled by every conceivable kind of bizarre shuck," Thompson noted. "All kinds of funhouse type booths. Shoot the pasties off the nipple of a ten-foot bull-dyke and win a cotton-candy goat."[81]

The juxtaposition of gambling and the circus did not turn out to be conducive to casino business, however. Sarno said: "We have been careful to train our gaming dealers to keep from looking up at the circus and carnival entertainment."[82] Customers, on the other hand, without such training, were easily distracted from the games. A gaming consultant said: "We'd have a crap game going and all of a sudden Norbo the Ape Man would come down a rope with the trainer chasing him, shooting caps off."[83] Then there was also the case of an acrobat, dressed up as an Indian chief, crashing on the gambling tables.

All of this circus drama unfolded in a tent deliberately painted black on the inside, to make people feel that it was always night, and to provide "a good foil for the brilliant colors of the upholstery and accessories," noted one designer, including "Turn-of-the-century loganberry, cyclamen, red."[84] As a final touch, it had many mirrors, in order to multiply the madness. "The Circus-Circus is what the whole hep world would be doing on Saturday night if the Nazis had won the war," Thompson wrote. "This is the Sixth Reich." Sarno was an easy target for Thompson. "In this town they love a drunk. Fresh meat. So they put us through the turnstiles and turned us loose inside."[85]

Sarno's vision bordered on the militant, with in-your-face acts and surprises, including a Highland Marching Band. Sarno himself, dressed up as a Big Top ringmaster, liked to jump in front of gamblers and ask them trivia questions. Moreover, he made the mistake of charging entrance at the door during circus acts—almost as offensive to gamblers as the odor of the elephant and orangutan.

An even more pressing challenge was that the project opened as a casino without a hotel, since Sarno had difficulty getting loans now that Hoffa had been imprisoned. Without a hotel to force-feed the casino with guests, the economic equation failed. Although he did end up getting a Teamster loan to build a hotel in 1972, it was too late for Sarno. Having suffered millions in personal gambling losses, he eventually sold out in 1974. He planned to build the 6,000-room Grandissimo, but with Hoffa mysteriously disappearing in 1975, four years after his release from prison, Sarno's source of money had dried up. In 1984 he died in his Caesars Palace suite of a heart attack (supposedly after a Jacuzzi date). It was a fate similar to that of his two brothers, who both dropped dead at Caesars's craps tables.

The most lasting lesson of Circus Circus was that Las Vegas had finally seen what "too much" looked like. It revealed the limits of the pop city approach: overstimulation could backfire. (When corporate managers later took over the casino, they built a ceiling between the casino and the midway. The casino, now insulated from the circus, became very successful.)

"I hate to say this," said Dr. Gonzo, Thompson's beefy attorney, as they overlooked the casino, "but this place is getting *to* me. I think I'm getting the Fear."

Circus Circus was a trip too far. "*Nobody* can handle that," wrote Thompson, who— of anyone—would be tolerant of chaos.

"No, this is not a good town for psychedelic drugs. Reality itself is too twisted."[86]

THE LAS VEGAS DESIGN THEORISTS

An unusual group of people attended the gala opening of the Circus Circus: a Yale class of graduate architecture students, led by professors Denise Scott Brown and Robert Venturi. They had come to Las Vegas not to gamble, but to learn. "Yale Professor Will Praise Strip for $8,925," a local paper announced the day of their arrival, after it had found out about their request for a study grant at City Hall.[87]

Why would anyone think they had come to praise the Strip? They could have just as easily come to bury it. "Serious architects still tend to regard exterior decoration as dishonest," Tom Wolfe wrote. "Electric tubing is still *gauche*."[88] Las Vegas was very different from what was taught in architecture departments such as at Yale, where students learned modernism, buildings as boxes, bare, without any decoration.

Las Vegas's architect Homer Rissman, for instance, designed for the city not a concrete casino box but a plastic circus tent. He joked to a journalist that his tent was still an example of the modernist design philosophy "form follows function" (which usually meant a bare-bones structure determined by its purpose, not by preconceived aesthetic considerations). "In this case the function is to attract and entertain."[89]

The Yale academics, however, did not plan to trash the Strip. Venturi already had a name as one of modernism's most vocal critics, having published *Complexity and Contradiction in Architecture* (1966), an attack on the purism and simplicity of modernist architecture, in which he irreverently adapted a maxim of Mies van der Rohe, one of modernism's founding fathers, "Less is more," to "Less is a bore." Denise Scott Brown followed her interest in pop culture, influenced by Richard Hamilton, who challenged fine-art traditions with his art collage assembled from advertisements, including a bodybuilder holding a Tootsie Pop. "We can learn … from Las Vegas as have other artists from their own profane and stylistic sources," Venturi and Scott Brown wrote. The architect pair would draw from Las Vegas casinos like pop artist Andy Warhol painted Campbell's soup cans. Their research expedition, and the subsequent book, had the bold title *Learning from Las Vegas*.

What did they learn? A city like Las Vegas, they argued, managed to communicate messages faster and further than, for instance, Rome. Signs were the new arches, and neon the new mosaics, for the age of the car: "The mechanical movement of neon lights is quicker than mosaic glitter, which depends on the passage of the sun and the pace of the observer; and the intensity of light on the Strip as well as the tempo of its movement is greater to accommodate the greater spaces, greater speeds and greater impacts that our technology permits and our sensibilities respond to."[90]

The Las Vegas roadside sign, such as the Stardust sign, communicated at multiple speeds and distances. The lower part, the "information" whiteboard, has specific information that can be changed at will, visible from up close. The upper part, the stardust cloud with the large logo, has the permanent "heraldry" visible from afar. The academics dissected the roadside sign with the same rigor an art historian would apply to analyzing a Roman temple front.

Even buildings in Las Vegas, such as the Golden Nugget, had evolved to become pure communication: "Like the agglomeration of chapels in a Roman church and the stylistic sequence of piers in a Gothic cathedral, the Golden Nugget casino has evolved over 30 years from a building with a sign on it to a totally sign-covered building."[91]

Scott Brown and Venturi classified buildings into two opposing semiotic types: the "duck" and the "decorated shed." Ducks—coined after a Long Island duck-egg store shaped like a duck—communicated meaning through their form. Venturi mocked modern architecture by classifying it as a duck, since it appropriated industrial aesthetics, mimicking airplanes, cruise liners, and grain silos. But modernist architects never explicitly claimed their use of this reference: they built ducks in denial.

Whereas only the elite, who had a learned appreciation for it, would understand the abstract meaning of modernist buildings, everyone could understand Las Vegas's references to "our great commonplaces or old clichés." These uncomplicated references made the Strip an immersive environment for everybody. Scott Brown and Venturi lauded Las Vegas's "inclusion and allusion" aspects: "the ability to engulf the visitor in a new role: for three days one may imagine oneself a centurion at Caesar's palace, a ranger at the Frontier, or a jetsetter at the Riviera rather than a salesperson from Des Moines, Iowa." The architecture of Las Vegas, Scott Brown and Venturi concluded, was "socially less coercive and aesthetically more vital."[92]

In contrast to the duck, the "decorated shed" was a plain, shed-like building whose signage was applied independently. The Stardust, for instance, where they stayed, was a decorated shed. The advantage of this type was that it conveyed meaning more efficiently than architectural form at higher speeds. Las Vegas showed "the victory of symbols-in-space over forms-in-space in the brutal automobile landscape of great distances and high speed where the subtleties of pure architectural space can no longer be savored."[93]

At the same time, this type could "shed" its identity quickly when necessary: "the most unique, most monumental parts of the Strip, the signs and casino façades, are also the most changeable; it is the neutral, systems-motel structures behind that survive a succession of facelifts and a series of themes up front. The Aladdin Hotel and Casino is

Moorish in front and Tudor behind." And this adaptability is useful, because anything in pop culture is subject to high turnover within the marketplace: "The rate of obsolescence of a sign seems to be nearer to that of an automobile than that of a building. The reason is not physical degeneration but what competitors are doing around you."[94]

However, like their fellow pop artists, Scott Brown and Venturi, for their association with commercialism, also came under fire. *The Daily Princetonian* wrote in 1972 about their alumnus: "Many critics claim that Venturi, by implication, advocates the sentiments that produce vernacular architecture—cheap (perhaps hazardous) construction, pollution, waste of material and land, lack of architectural heritage, and disregard for human needs."[95] According to architectural critic Vincent Scully, Venturi had become "the most controversial architect in America."[96]

Scott Brown and Venturi had never bothered with judging the morals of the Strip. They wanted to analyze it as a "phenomenon of architectural communication" only. They were after the medium, not the message. Yet some critiqued the way Scott Brown and Venturi had misunderstood the Strip as architecture by and for "the people," whereas it was really built in the interests of gambling moguls. A few focused on how *Learning from Las Vegas* was "aesthetic populism,"[97] which helped to move architecture (like other industries) away from standardization (modernism), in order to accelerate the turnover of architectural commodities—incorporating popular imagery would make buildings, just like other products, more quickly passé.

Even though he was there when Venturi and Scott Brown visited his office, Kermit Wayne confessed to never having read *Learning from Las Vegas*.[98] He never needed to: he used his own more profane references. He and other Strip designers had no interest in an architectural discussion about whether buildings should be duck or shed. The Strip was never guided by architectural theory, but by profit: it was Scrooge McDuck, not the Long Island Duck, who ruled the Strip. By and large, however, those few thousand dollars paid out for the Yale academics' visit had major implications. Scott Brown and Venturi's book crowned Las Vegas the undisputed city of postmodernism. Postmodern architects around the world happily learned from Las Vegas resorts' playful and lavish quotations from other times and other places.

"America has become Las Vegasized," heralded *Time* two decades after the book's publication. "Today almost every big-city downtown has new skyscrapers that endeavor to look like old skyscrapers. Almost every suburb has a shopping center decorated with phony arches, phony pediments, phony columns … it is the Vegas aesthetic, architecture as grandiose cartoon, that has become the American Establishment style."[99]

Wolfe located the turning point as early as 1978, years before Venturi won the Pritzker Prize, the most prestigious award for an architect. This was when Philip Johnson, a devout follower of Mies van der Rohe, released a rendering of the new AT&T Headquarters in New York. Where previously modernists had equated "ornament" with "crime,"[100] Johnson built a 647-foot-tall skyscraper, not with a flat modern roof but with the open pediment of an eighteenth-century British cabinet. The ornament alone was blown up seven stories tall.

"The most devoted Miesling of them all had designed a building with a top that seemed to have been lifted straight off a Chippendale highboy," Wolfe wrote.[101]

Like Kermit Wayne in designing the Caesars Palace sign—a decade after the fact—elite architects would not flinch at a faux column or architrave.

POP SKYSCRAPERS

In 1959, Kansas City builder Frank Carroll envisioned his casino as more than a simple high-rise: "I, as builder, saw Las Vegas as the Promised Land, but in designing a hotel for this city, I had to have something different. I don't like to build 'boxes' for hotels."[102] Carroll was going to liberate the high-rise from the oppression of the square.

Departing from the first generation of unimaginative high-rise "boxes," such as the fourteen-story Sahara, architect John W. Jamieson designed a three-story flying saucer on a stem. Where the 1962 Seattle Space Needle had an elevator in the shaft, Jamieson placed hotel rooms with an exterior glass elevator, and where the Needle had an observation deck, he added a casino.

Carroll's tower followed from a natural succession of the sign. Some signs, such as the Dunes pillar, rivaled the buildings they faced. Others, for example the T-bird sign, functioned as a façade unifying different buildings. Carroll's skyscraper would have co-opted the sign's overall form: the casino "saucer" on a hotel "pole" was, as a whole, a supersize sign.

It marked the beginning of an exciting possibility for a pop skyscraper. He called it the Landmark.

Carroll broke ground in 1961. His fifteen-story Landmark was going to be the state's tallest tower—until The Mint announced a downtown tower, twenty-six stories tall. Carroll had to respond. He doubled the height of his tower to thirty-one stories.

But as both towers rose up, the Landmark suddenly came to a standstill. Carroll's loan was stopped. His partially completed tower, a shaft with a hollow shell, became the laughing stock of Las Vegans, who nicknamed it the "Leaning Tower of Vegas." Luckily for Carroll, the Teamsters came to the rescue with a $5.5 million loan, and again his tower rose. But then this financial source dried up as well. He had to put his unfinished property up for sale.

At least by now the tower was built to a full silhouette, a stage that the Viva Hotel, another potential pop skyscraper, had never achieved. This skyscraper would have been the culmination of the pop city age. The designer, Bruce Goff, fit the bill perfectly. He was largely self-taught and known to take his inspiration from catholic sources including Antoni Gaudí, Balinese music, and seashells—whereas his elite contemporaries looked at stern industrial silos. Where the norm was austere shapes, Goff designed spiral and crystalline structures.

The Viva Hotel, the most complex building he had ever designed, was a triangular sixteen-story hotel with concave sides gradually tapering upward. Slanting spire stairs

3.19 A rendering of the Viva Hotel shows an outward-tapering form decked with staircase spires, and a conical rooftop nightclub. Bruce Alonzo Goff, "Viva Casino and Hotel: Perspective Rendering," 1961, graphite on tracing paper, 77.6 × 78 cm. (31 × 31 in.), Gift of Shin'enKan, Inc., 1990.807.1, The Art Institute of Chicago.

3.20 An Ad-Art rendering of the Sands reveals how the hotel tower, the entrance, and the sign share a sculptural language of arcs.

and neon-lined, scalloped balconies accentuated the inverted shape. Three ovals at the bottom housed the casino. A nightclub on top, the shape of a wizard hat, capped it all.

The free-flow tower was never built, though. Tragically, only a few days before construction in 1961, one of the financiers died in a plane crash. Had it been built, it could have changed the future of the Las Vegas high-rise from minimalist box to sculptural form. Moreover, the Viva's soaring outward-slanting atrium could have anticipated John Portman's lauded atrium hotels, changing the future of hotels worldwide.

With the future looking dark for the pop skyscraper, the first Las Vegas pop high-rise was completed in 1967: a seventeen-story cylindrical tower for the Sands, designed by Martin Stern. He crowned it with a coronet of arched windows, and added a smaller version of the tower for the lobby entrance. With their diadems touching the sky, his pair of cylinders animated the skyline, unlike any box-with-a-sign.

Then, billionaire Howard Hughes came in. He bought and finished the Landmark. It ultimately stood 346 feet tall, much taller than The Mint's 290-foot box. Was there hope for the sign-shaped tower?

3.21 The Landmark's casino "saucer" on a hotel "pole," a large sign equivalent of a building, was imploded in 1995. The next year, it was shot down by Martians in the movie *Mars Attacks*.

Rather than setting a new paradigm for the high-rise casino complex, the Landmark would become best known for its implosion, which made it into the movies: a Martian UFO shot down the tower in *Mars Attacks* (1996). And where it once stood, there was now a brand-new parking lot.

Stern's tower had a similar tragic fate, but it was imploded anonymously, by someone avoiding attention, at 2:06 a.m. one Tuesday.

It was ironic that while the pop city critics celebrated the Strip's Electrographic Architecture and Decorated Sheds, influencing architecture worldwide, the Strip was already headed in a different direction. When the Landmark was finally built in 1969, two years after Hoffa was jailed, the Strip tapped into a new source of finance—corporations publicly traded on Wall Street. It came with strings attached. A new generation of casino operators and financiers, no longer of the people, demanded a less extravagant aesthetic. And one by one, they erased all the eccentricities of the pop city age.

Rather than the theories of the design critics, political economy determined the Strip's aesthetics. As the hippies sold out to climb the corporate ladder, so did Las Vegas. Yet just in time, right before its demise, Venturi and Scott Brown captured a snapshot in time of the enigmatic pop era, a long-gone historical period for the ever-evolving Strip. Mass wealth, technological optimism, and Teamster money built extraordinary architectural innovations, with implications worldwide. From cosmetic architecture to three-dimensional neon, from sensual stages to immersive restaurants, from big screen to neon spectaculars, the pop Strip no longer followed other styles, whether Western or Sunbelt modernism, but created its own unique architecture.

As eccentric as it was, it followed a simple logic. The Strip during the pop city age was a perfect example of what happens to a place that follows unfettered populism, unconstrained by elite notions of taste.

4

Corporate Modern (1969—1985)

There isn't as much neon—it's used more for highlighting now. And there's a lot more plastic. I really can't stand plastic.[1]
—Kermit Wayne, YESCO sign designer

Las Vegas Strip and downtown by Garish and Greed, architects.
—Guide to U.S. Architecture 1940–1980

Little did Robert Venturi and Denise Scott Brown know that at the moment their odes to the 1960s pop city Strip were being published, the Strip was already heading toward their worst nightmare. They had celebrated neon signage and symbolism as an antidote to the "less is a bore" of modernist architecture. But just as their book *Learning from Las Vegas* heralded the Strip as a pinnacle of lightness and eccentric signage, developers in the 1970s built massive concrete boxes, devoid of exterior ornament. They had turned to corporate modernism.

Developers put their money in large, efficient hotel buildings that looked little different from corporate hotel chains or office buildings elsewhere in the world. Where the sign had dominated the architecture, now large glass-clad towers loomed over the signs. Architecture had struck back with a vengeance, putting the sign back in its place as an inferior reference to a building.

The corporate modern phase of the Strip was a testament to how finance can give shape to places. Behind it lurked Howard Hughes's arrival in Las Vegas and Nevada's new corporate gaming law, which brought in unprecedented amounts of capital that funded massive hotel towers. Along with the cash, corporations brought international modernist aesthetics, at a time when this style dominated Western corporate architecture.

As the concrete and glass curtain towers rose, they were planted into a faceless base, another characteristic of corporate modernism. Together, the tower and its frame became a single megastructure, eliminating the need for anyone to go outside to get from one place in the resort to the other. These new casino hotels, stripped to their bare essentials, had little or no architectural merit, all the more obvious given they were the world's largest hotels. The Strip had shifted identity once again: it had gone from extrovert to passive aggressive.

But Las Vegas resorts were never clean-cut corporate modernist. Developers encrusted modern *porte-cochères* with bronze acrylics, dotting them with light bulbs. What started as bare concrete and glass escalated into a rococo-corporate splendor of sparkling sheen.

As Nixon planned to save America from the liberalism of the 1960s, so were corporations intent on making Las Vegas architecturally conservative. And by the late 1970s, no other place but Las Vegas better symbolized the Me Decade of Garish and Greed.

GERM-FREE ZONE

The corporatization of the Strip started at Thanksgiving 1966. That night, Mormons sneaked Howard Hughes out of a private train from Los Angeles, onto a stretcher and up the service escalator of the Desert Inn. There they took over the entire ninth-floor penthouse. Without leaving his hotel room for four whole years, Hughes—skin and bones, often naked, with long gray hair and long fingernails—would change the public perception of the gambling industry so much that it paved the way for corporations to own casinos—ironically, since he strongly opposed it.

Hughes's move to Las Vegas happened toward the end of his life. He was still close to a national hero, being an accomplished aviator, defense contractor, and one of the world's most affluent individuals. But after one too many airplane crashes, he lived a life dependent on Valium and codeine. His face scarred, he communicated only through memos and over the phone.

Hughes had big plans for Las Vegas. He knew the city well, since he had made a movie there, *The Las Vegas Story*. Las Vegas was a place where he could avoid California taxes, and a place where he could make a splash. "I'm sick and tired of being a small fish in the big pond of Southern California," Hughes complained. "I'll be a big fish in a small pond."[2]

As soon as he entered the Desert Inn penthouse, he sealed his door with tape so that he could live in isolation from people, daylight and germs. Hughes was adamant about living in a perfectly "germ-free zone," as he suffered from obsessive-compulsive disorder. He used paper tissues to turn doorknobs, put his feet in tissue boxes, and sealed his windows. Yet, in his quest to rid his life of germs, he never once allowed cleaners to enter the room he lived in for years.

A few weeks after Hughes's arrival, owner Moe Dalitz asked him to leave, since the casino was making money neither on the recluse nor on his Mormon crew, who were not allowed to gamble—which was precisely why the Mafia liked to hire Mormon casino managers. Instead of packing up, Hughes put in a bid for the entire resort: $13.25 million. Dalitz and his partners, having grown tired of the constant federal surveillance and close to retirement age, sold. But like anyone wanting to own a casino, Hughes was required to appear before the Nevada Gaming Control Board to get a license. The billionaire refused to leave his room. To everyone's surprise, the Nevada governor exempted Hughes from appearing in front of the Board, knowing what his good reputation could do for Las Vegas's bad image, until then bound up with the Syndicate. It kick-started a more lenient approach to licensing corporations.

Hughes himself was aware of his effect, and took it as a personal mission to change the perception of Vegas: "I want to acquire even more hotels and … make Las Vegas as trustworthy and respectable as the New York Stock Exchange."[3]

"How many more of these toys are available?" he asked his aide. "Let's buy 'em all."[4]

Within months he bought the Castaways for $3.3 million, and the Sands and the Frontier for $23 million each. The Hughes Tool Company, known for building moon vehicles, missiles, satellites, and secret weapons, now added busboys, card dealers, and waitresses to the payroll.

In 1968, Hughes completed his quest to become the "the largest single property owner in the gambling capital,"[5] accumulating one third of the revenue generated on the Strip. He further diversified his portfolio by buying North Las Vegas Air Terminal, the old McCarran airport, as well as a television station, so he could watch Westerns and war movies all night. "Welcome to Las Vegas, Howard Hughes's Monopoly set," Johnny Carson opened to his audience.[6]

Hughes also wanted to sanitize the Las Vegas Strip. "I don't think we should permit this place to degrade into a freak or amusement park category, like Coney Island,"[7] he wrote to his aide. Above all, Circus Circus appalled him:

The aspect of the Circus that has me disturbed is the popcorn, peanuts, and kids side of it. … And also the Carnival Freaks and Animal side of it. … The dirt floor, sawdust and elephants. The part of a circus that is associated with the poor boys in town, the hobo clowns, and, I repeat, the animals. … After all, The Strip is supposed to be synonymous with a good looking female all dressed up in a very expensive diamond studded evening gown and driving up to a multi-million dollar hotel in a Rolls-Royce.[8]

The first casualty of Hughes's civilizing mission was the Silver Slipper. Its revolving sign, a silver slipper the size of a small car, irritated him. Allegedly, after each rotation, the nose of the slipper pointed to Hughes's room, so that he thought it contained a camera spying on him. He ended up buying the place, and filled the slipper with concrete.

When the revolving slipper halted, so did Hughes's buying spree. He tried to buy the Stardust, but state gambling officials blocked him on antitrust grounds, fearing another purchase would give him too much of the Strip. Hughes was severely frustrated, terrified of "excessive competition."[9] Out of spite, he bought acres of vacant land along the Las Vegas Strip, preventing others from building new projects.

Then, his worst fear came true. Conrad and Barron Hilton convinced the Nevada Gaming Commission to allow corporations to own casinos, for the first time since 1955, with the new 1967 Corporate Gaming Act. It opened the floodgates to public companies entering Las Vegas. This was precisely why Hughes tried to stop the law. "I am informed that … everybody and his little dog is filing for a gaming license."[10]

Ironically, while on the surface Hughes had changed Las Vegas's image, his "cleanup" had secretly left the old guard in charge. "'Cleanup' of Las Vegas fails to Oust the Hoodlums" headed the *Wall Street Journal* in May 1969.[11] Even though Dalitz had sold out, he continued to skim the Desert Inn casino as an external "advisor."

But while Hughes failed in his cleanup of the Strip, corporate capital would lend him an unsolicited hand, gradually sanitizing the casinos, stinking animals included, and removing one by one the peculiarities of the Pop City age. Hughes had provided the vision of a sterile environment with cosmopolitan gamblers. Corporations executed it, building corporate modernist casinos and making a more proper, James Bond type of Las Vegas.

THE BAUHAUS CASINO

In 1967, Kirk Kerkorian exploited the new corporate gaming law to sell $26.5 million worth of stock to build a 1,500-room hotel, the International, with the world's largest and most expensive casino, at $60 million.

Howard Hughes was terrified. To scare Kerkorian, he announced a $100 million "Super Sands" with 4,000 rooms. But Kerkorian did not budge. Hughes then came up with another scheme: he was going to scare his competitor with nuclear detonations. He told his assistant: "Please tell Kerkorian the reason I postponed the new Sands is because I learned of the possibility that the testing would be resumed in this area on a heavier than ever basis, and that my architectural and geological experts advised me it will be utterly impossible to get a foothold in this sandy soil, solid and predictable enough to build a really tall building."[12] When this ploy also failed, Hughes put in a bid for the unfinished Landmark hotel, located opposite Kerkorian's resort. Since Nevada politicians realized no one else would ever want to buy this hollow shell, they allowed Hughes to buy one more casino, and continue construction.

While the Apollo 11 crew beat out the Russians on its way to the moon, Hughes and Kerkorian went head to head in a race to build the tallest building in the state. Hughes bought the Landmark because it was thirty-one floors tall, while the International was only thirty. But Kerkorian countered by claiming his thirty floors were actually a little higher, the equivalent of a thirty-seven-story building.

But the battle between the two accomplished aviators was also a clash between two opposing architectural ideas for the casino complex. Hughes had bought into the Landmark tower, a pop high-rise straight from *The Jetsons*: a large saucer on top of a stem. Kerkorian's tower, on the other hand, radiated corporate efficiency like a Hilton Hotel: a tri-form glass building on a concrete base.

4.1 A Martin Stern rendering of the 1969 International reveals a Y-shaped building modeled on the UNESCO headquarters. Stern pioneered integrating all of the casino resort functions into a single megastructure.

By adopting the International Style, the architectural movement that had been equated with corporate modernist architecture, Kerkorian strategically associated the casino with corporations. Even the resort's name, the International, resonated with the International Style. Characterized by its rectilinear forms and bare surfaces, stripped of ornamentation, this elite form of architecture stood miles away from the Mafia-tainted neon of existing casinos.

United States corporations had ceaselessly identified themselves with modernist aesthetics. The first such building was the 1955 Skidmore, Owings, & Merrill-designed Lever House. This thin shimmering green slab, with its Mies van der Rohe glass-and-steel minimalism, made such a visual impact amid the masonry apartment buildings of New York's Park Avenue that it instantly became an emblem of corporate architecture. Pepsi-Cola, General Motors, and IBM then all housed their research branches and headquarters in glass-wall office buildings, which came to symbolize modern management, technology, and economic supremacy.[13]

Kerkorian commissioned architect Martin Stern, who had had left his private practice for the Marriott Corporation, where he became fluent in corporate modernism. For Stern, it was a new exercise in the design of corporate austerity, a throwback to his military roots, when he developed master plans for military camps in California. For the International, he designed a tower in a Y-shape plan, in which three room wings radiated from a central elevator core. This allowed more rooms on a square plot while providing each room with a reasonable view. He borrowed this tripartite structure from the International Style, reminiscent of Le Corbusier's early modernist cities, solitary towers set back from a highway, a scheme that continues to influence cities today.

Stern designed the International as a tower on a concrete base—another classic ingredient of corporate modernism stemming from the Lever House. Unlike original International Style towers, the Lever House stood on a base that contained an exhibition area, since this would not fit on smaller tower floors. Stern used a base to house all of the casino's functions, which previously were placed in separate buildings, into a single megastructure. The hotel's base, as long as five city blocks, contained massive convention and retail areas, and the world's largest casino. The roof accommodated 8.5 acres of recreational space, including tennis courts, a swimming pool, and a lagoon.

This new building typology made the gambling experience more seamless. No longer would visitors have to leave this single structure. They could eat, drink, meet, sleep, swim, and gamble inside a megastructure. Gaming historian David G. Schwartz noted: "Stern-derivative casinos, more structurally integrated than earlier resorts, brought the idea of self-contained pleasure palaces into a new era."[14] The International would influence casinos worldwide.

The opening of the Landmark and the International, scheduled for the same weekend, came to a dramatic climax, driving Hughes to despair, as well as his aides, as he obsessed about the guest list for the opening party until the very end, refusing to pick the food, or set a date. When the invitations were finally sent out, only one day before opening, few people came. But the late invitations were not the only reason guests failed to show. With its relatively small, pie-shaped hotel rooms in the stem, and getting up to the casino saucer through escalators a hassle, people had a hard time appreciating the Landmark as more than a mad architectural addition to the skyline. The paradigm of the new casino complex was set. The down-to-earth efficiency of the International had beaten the Landmark's flying saucer.

In the big picture, however, the International represented more than just a new avenue for casino design. Hardcore architectural critics had already lamented the way corporations worldwide had exploited the International Style's socialist principles of housing the masses efficiently, as once taught by the idealistic design school of Bauhaus. Where the Bauhaus's architects used standardization and a lack of ornament for architecture's sake, to achieve pure and impressive forms, corporations were after building cheaper and faster: "less is more"—that is to say, more profit. Corporate glass boxes, devoid of idealism, were bare-boned versions of the real deal. Tom Wolfe captioned a picture of faceless office towers on New York's Avenue of the Americas: "Row after Mies van der row of glass boxes." He labeled it "Rue de Regret."[15]

Had these critics visited Las Vegas, they would have seen an even bigger mockery of the International Style.

"The International Brings the World to Las Vegas," the advertising stated.

"When you drive up to the new International Hotel, you begin a tour of the world. The flags of the free world are blowing in the breeze. The doorman who opens your car isn't a doorman. He's a French gendarme."[16] Guests were given a passport upon check-in, and each of the hotel's floors was themed in the "International Style" of different countries.

International modernism, in the context of the Strip, had been adapted. It was taken as a theme. True modernist architects would cringe at diluting the purity of the style with such distractions and blasphemy. This was International Style modernism *à la* Las Vegas.

If any moment represented the dead end of modernism, it was the 1969 International casino, when Bauhaus inspired a gambling house.

BOXES AND BOARDROOMS

"There are almost ten new hotels announced," Howard Hughes wrote to his aide in 1970. "The one that troubles me the most is the new Holiday Inn right smack in front of the Sands. To make it much worse, they are planning to make it a showboat sitting in a huge lake of water. A showboat with a pond of stagnant infested water. If they are considering using water from Lake Mead, the effluent in the water would smell to high heaven. Jesus!"[17]

Hughes was filled with disgust when he got wind of "the ship of the Strip," which, although actually planned next to his Sands casino, in his mind was right in front of it. He was somewhat right about the water, however. While initially the Colorado River Water Pact had capped Nevadan imports from Lake Mead, Las Vegas managed to find a surprising loophole. To Hughes's horror and unheeded objections, a 1964 Supreme Court Decree allowed for a "return-flow-credit": for every gallon of wastewater the city put into the lake, it could take out a gallon of drinking water 6.5 miles downstream.

The real question is whether a sophisticated, thoroughly pampered tourist … is going to feel comfortable in the confidence that the water which he is drinking, and in which he is bathing, is the pure mountain spring water pictured in the Coor's Beer advertisements, or whether, instead, he is going to have the uneasy, revolting feeling that the water he is forced to drink, the water used to make his drinks at the bar, and the water in which his food is cooked … that this water is, in truth, nothing more or less than SEWAGE, with the turds removed by a strainer so it can be pumped through a pipe.[18]

Hughes also fretted about the corporate giant behind the boat, Holiday Inn, the first major hotel chain to build a Strip branch. But large corporations were still slightly uneasy about Las Vegas. While Holiday Inn operated the hotel building, they let two local operators run the casino boat in front of the hotel. Holiday Inn benefited from more experienced operators, while at the same time they avoided tarnishing their hotel brand with gambling, which still carried a stigma. The casino was named Holiday Casino, avoiding the banner of Holiday Inn outright.

The architecture of Holiday Inn/Holiday Casino reflected the divided operation. Homer Rissman, Holiday Inn's in-house architect, built a modern white box for the main hotel building. He followed the standard company blueprint, with the exception of adding a cloverleaf-shaped pool. He could have matched the casino boat by designing it as a modern white ocean liner, but instead he designed a replica of a Mississippi River steamboat, complete with fiberglass figures of Tom Sawyer and Huckleberry Finn. Holiday Inn's squeaky-clean box was in total denial of the nineteenth-century gambling boat.

Despite their uneasiness about gambling, corporations flocked to Las Vegas. One reporter wrote: "Firms listed on the New York and American stock exchanges, along with a new breed of gamblers in gray flannel suits, invested in Las Vegas casinos as if they were giant conglomerates."[19] She spoke of a "corporate takeover."

4.2 An eclectic architectural drawing depicts the Holiday Casino, a replica of a nineteenth-century Mississippi gambling steamboat, in contrast to the minimalist Holiday Inn, 1971.

In 1970, Barron Hilton bought the International and Flamingo from Kerkorian, and the Hilton Hotel chain, the world's largest hotel operator, became the first major hotel corporation to both own and operate a casino. By 1976, 43 percent of the revenue of the 163-hotel chain multinational corporation came from Las Vegas.[20] That year, Hilton expanded the Flamingo, now named the Flamingo Hilton. Homer Rissman designed a pink-glass-covered box, the first of a six-phase expansion program of identical high-rise towers, aimed at maximizing profit, not at architectural sophistication. The boxes would gradually imprison the Flamingo's pool, noted a historian: "corporate thinking built the tower that put Bugsy Siegel's pool, the pinnacle of his vision of leisure, in the shade all day long."[21]

Corporations like the Hilton subjected Las Vegas casinos to fiscal and aesthetic austerity. Unlike the previous owners on the Strip, most corporations owned hotels across the United States. Controlled from boardrooms in places like New York and Los Angeles, disembodied from Las Vegas, corporations built stodgy and conservative boxes that matched their properties elsewhere. Architect Rissman said: "Casinos and hotels are now more like department stores."[22]

But with all these similar boxes along the Strip competing with one another, corporations realized that their buildings needed something special. Enter the variations of the box: in 1975, the Marina hotel, a box with long fins; in 1979, the Barbary Coast, a box with a drum-shaped illuminated awning, and the Imperial Palace, a box with a Japanese pagoda roof.

4.3 A postcard depicts the 1979 Imperial Palace, a box-shaped building decorated with Japanese blue-tiled roofs, "wooden" details, and a pagoda-canopy.

Back in 1970, before the boxes had even been built, Howard Hughes had seen it all coming. With corporations aiming for Las Vegas, he had said:

It was this philosophy, that there is no bottom to the barrel ... that led to the 1929 stock market crash and seven of the worst years this country ever faced. It was this same philosophy that led to the construction of a miniature golf course on every corner in Los Angeles, and the horrible, tragic crash of this industry—taking with it all the little people involved.[23]

Cornered between Circus Circus's filthy animals and the showboat's infested water, with the Mafia robbing him of his chips all the while, Hughes had had enough. He decided to move to the Bahamas, another place with gambling, but with a lot less competition. On Thanksgiving Day 1970, exactly four years after his arrival, Hughes quietly left Las Vegas, carried on a stretcher by his Mormon aides down the Desert Inn fire escapes, never to return.

BIGNESS BEGAN IN LAS VEGAS

In 1971, a year after he sold the International, Kerkorian secretly acquired a controlling interest in Metro-Goldwyn-Mayer studios, the renowned Hollywood company, which was rich in nostalgia but low in profits. Knowing there was easy money in Vegas, the corporate raider announced that MGM would "embark on a significant and far-reaching diversification into the leisure field by building ... the world's largest resort hotel in Las Vegas." Having sold off $62 million worth of the company's Los Angeles real estate and historical movie props, including Dorothy's ruby slippers, Kerkorian's "movie" company bought 43 acres of Strip land and planned a $107 million casino. *Forbes* magazine wrote: "From now on the company that brought you *Ben-Hur* and *The Wizard of Oz* will bring you crap—and roulette, slot machines, and all the other pleasure of a Las Vegas casino hotel."[24]

Kerkorian would fully exploit the MGM's logo, one of the world's most recognized corporate logos, by putting it on rugs, walls, and ashtrays. One employee muttered: "I'm surprised they didn't stamp it on the toilet paper."[25]

He then gave his architect, Martin Stern, the following mandate:

"I want to build a hotel," Kerkorian said.

"What kind of hotel?" Stern wondered.

"A big one."[26]

As simple as this was, it summed it all up. The MGM Grand would be above all grand, as in big. Its building volume was as large as the Empire State Building, its base as large as three city blocks, and its hotel tower contained 2,084 rooms, at that time the most in the world. One of the resort's two theaters had a catwalk so long it could drop down as many as a hundred showgirls from the ceiling. It featured a "living curtain," a wall with steps from which dancers descended perilously without railings, and a rotating MGM logo that opened for Leo the Lion, the studio mascot, to roar into the crowd.

But despite its huge size, the MGM was nowhere near as exciting as resorts built a decade before. "By Vegas standards, the MGM Grand is almost sedate," a reporter noted "There are no acrobats and elephants traipsing through its lounges, as there are at the Circus Hotel Casino."[27] Instead, to keep guests animated, architect Stern covered his casino with brocaded walls that were predominantly red, an exciting color. He enlivened the floor by putting high-energy places, such as casino bars, at strategic locations. To prevent people from feeling confined in this large box, which did not have any windows, he made the ceiling higher than usual. He still managed to make the casino the focal point by raising it a few steps, accentuating it with coffered ceilings and crystal chandeliers, and forcing theatergoers, conference visitors, shoppers, and hotel guests to walk past the green felt tables.

On the exterior, Stern's main challenge was to break down the scale of the large complex and add visual interest. In contrast to other casinos, he did not rely on neon but went the corporate architecture route. Stern designed a glass curtain, which hemmed off the street like a massive wall, and thickened the top to allow for bigger penthouse suites. On the bottom he added a chopped-off pyramid, which contained the theater.

4.4 An artist's impression of the 1973 MGM Grand focuses attention on the *porte-cochère*, the resort's new "sign."

Nonetheless, the tower's façade had all the charm of a penal institution, while the base, a band of windowless concrete, made the casino look like a bunker.

Overall, Stern had designed a building with a stylistic contradiction. While the MGM Grand's concrete and glass exterior was modernist, the interior was classic kitsch, including a restaurant with false stone balustrades, an elevator with fake marble, and long corridors with fiberglass "marble" columns and wallpapered "classical" beams—hardly tokens of material "honesty." He decorated the bars with friezes, molds, and cornices, and wallpapered a corridor with photos of MGM stars of yore—all because he knew that gamblers were not yet ready for a true Bauhaus casino interior with concrete crap tables.

"There is a vast Moorish-Bauhaus-Italian Renaissance *porte-cochère* in the front, with fountains and bad statuary all about,"[28] wrote the *New York Times* architecture critic in "Las Vegas: Vulgar and Extraordinary." "The goal here is … to provide the illusion that one has left his or her normal life and become a character in a movie." To help set a luxurious 1920s movie palace context, Stern had indeed built a gigantic *porte-cochère*, as long as a football field, wide enough to accommodate eight lanes and an army of valet boys. He decorated the sides with incandescent lights placed in mirrored vacuum-formed plastic, a new material used by the sign industry, to amplify the glitz. He added two ceiling chambers bathing in light bulbs. Underneath it all, he placed a fountain lined with floral-decorated railings that were deliberately overscaled to match the massive canopy, and plunked an 800-pound marble replica of Bologna's Neptune and sirens in the middle, adding mermaids shooting water from their breasts.

This new entrance had also solved a difficult problem. With thousands of guests, and 4,500 employees, the MGM relied on computers to modernize hotel reservations and credit. Previously, a patron's line of credit had been based on the casino manager's estimation of his assets, which required a personal relationship between the two. The corporatization of the Strip had led to a less personal atmosphere, but the *porte-cochère* would help guests feel important, as if they were attending a red-carpet movie premiere. It rapidly became a staple of casino design in the budding computer age.

The one place MGM did not do "bigger is better" was with its sign. Ad-Art proposed a 207-foot arch-shaped sign, the tallest in the world, with a revolving chandelier the size of an eight-story building. But MGM executives deemed the $700,000 price tag too high, and architect Stern objected to the phallus competing with his building. They argued that since the MGM Grand was so gigantic, it could be seen from a long way away, and no longer needed to rely on signage.

Instead of the pylon, Ad-Art ended up building a 125-foot-tall plastic whiteboard. Like the hotel it referred to, it was nothing special, other than being bulky. Moreover, it was dwarfed beside the mass of the tower. MGM Grand's corporate executives had dealt the death blow to the sign race. Only a few years earlier Venturi had observed the reversal between sign and building, optimizing symbols in space over forms in space. MGM executives negated this principle, undoing his contribution to architectural theory: it was the revenge of architectural mass over symbolism.

4.5 Neptune, sirens, and mermaids shooting water from their breasts stand beneath the MGM Grand's porte-cochère, the size of a football field.

But while Stern had managed to guide the International into an overall iconic shape, the MGM Grand was a sprawling megastructure without an overall iconic form. In its defense, it was constructed in only eighteen months, thanks to a "fast-track" building process in which materials were arriving on site while Martin Stern and his team were still busting out drawings and designing details. But speed led to construction waste and mistakes, including not installing a sprinkler system, and very little architectural quality.

"Beyond a certain critical mass, a building becomes a BIG Building," architect Rem Koolhaas wrote two decades later, in "Bigness and the Problem of Large."[29] "Such a mass can no longer be controlled by a singular architectural gesture, or even by any combination of architectural gestures. ... Bigness is no longer part of any urban tissue. Its subtext is fuck context." In the years that followed, similarly massive and insular developments would flock to American cities. In 1992, one critic wrote of "megalomaniacal complexes tethered to fragmented and desolate downtowns." He criticized them for "their abuse of scale and composition, their denigration of street life, and their confiscation of the vital energy of the center, now sequestered within their subterranean concourses or privatized plazas."[30] These were also buildings with conference centers and malls inside a bunker-like base, hotel towers and offices standing on top, with the only difference that they lacked a casino.

While it eventually sucked the life out of American cities, Bigness began in Las Vegas, for one simple reason: to make a bigger mousetrap.

THE WHITE SQUARES AND PLASTIC PLANES

On November 16, 1973, at the height of the energy crisis, exactly one month after the Arab Oil Embargo, Las Vegas's lights went dark and stayed that way for five whole months. Casinos had decided to comply with Nixon's request for voluntary energy cutbacks. "We were visible," a Nevada Power manager explained. "People complained about the lack of oil and how we were burning lights all day and night."[31] Only the Hilton's sign was lit, powered by an aging method that ran circles around a generator. A spokesperson recalled, "All it cost us was a little bit of hay."[32]

When the oil embargo ended, developers went as far as demolishing entire neon signs, replacing them with supposedly more energy-efficient "whiteboards"—white acrylic reader boards illuminated from within. The 1950s development of acrylic plastics made sign faces translucent so they could be backlit, rendering obsolescent the neon letters or incandescent light bulbs on sheet metal that had until then illuminated the painted messages. Whiteboards substituted neon signs throughout American cities, as they would in Las Vegas. Developers even dared to take down the Aladdin's neon sign, so celebrated in art journals, and replace the shapely figure with a white plastic box. Kermit Wayne, designer of the original Aladdin neon sign, said: "I really can't stand plastic."[33]

Neon fell out of favor because of the way it was perceived. Once dubbed "liquid fire," neon was now seen as "clutter" in the landscape, a sign of declining morals and "XXX" theaters, or of urban decay, sputtering in abandoned downtowns. In 1971, the city of Denver had banned neon altogether. Back in Las Vegas, neon signage was also a symptom of lower class, financed by the blue-collar Teamsters in the 1960s, before the arrival of corporate board members, who preferred a better class of signifier. One by one the Strip's eccentric neon signs were replaced, until a sea of whiteboards prevailed. The new signs had little "personality": They had standard, not custom, typefaces. They didn't glow anywhere near as brightly. And in contrast to neon's sensual silhouettes, the acrylic signs were literally "square."

Nevertheless, within the Strip's whiteboard logo-land of the 1970s and 1980s, three exceptional plastic whiteboards popped up. In 1976, the $1 million, 123-foot-tall Lucky the Clown rose at Circus Circus. Designer Dan Edwards managed to give Lucky a silhouette, and highlighted it with neon. He gave the whiteboard feet, and placed them on toadstools. He then added one hand pointing to the entrance, the other holding a spinning pinwheel. Lucky's head extended from the top, his waving hair carrying a cone hat, a bulbous nose protruding from his face. Edwards, a former confectionery carton designer, dressed his clown in exciting colors such as red. "Although money is green, it's not a good color for signs," he explained. "It's too cold."[34] Hot colors are more visible in the sun, whereas blues and greens can be soporific, or worse: as one owner noted, blue light can make older women appear "devastating."[35]

The 1980 $1 million Sahara sign featured a large metal wedge on top of a whiteboard reaching a total of 222 feet, the world's tallest. But one of the designers of the 1983 Westward Ho sign, the final extraordinary whiteboard, balked at "bigger is better." "Spectacular doesn't necessarily mean immense," he said of his 80-foot sign, which consisted of five truncated spheres, built of polished aluminum ribbons dotted with light bulbs. "You can't equate spectacular with size … it's very important to us that we don't overkill."[36] Had he dared to make that statement a decade ago, he would have been committed to the Strip's mental institution.

While sign designers had little reason to be excited about the new roadside signs, they would nevertheless find another outlet. They evolved from designing roadside signage alone to entire interior ceilings, for instance the 1979 "leaded glass" ceiling, a copy of an existing San Francisco 1880s Art Nouveau ceiling, but made out of plastic. They also increasingly designed façades and *porte-cochères*, such as the 1975 Aladdin, which, in envious emulation of MGM Grand's giant brass canopy, was practically a freestanding building over the access road: twelve Doric columns carried the gold polished ceiling as large as an Olympic swimming pool, with three chandelier fixtures, each the size of a truck. One art critic reported: "The new Las Vegas look brings … 'the inside outside.'"[37]

A full war between casinos for the most pompous and illuminated *porte-cochère* followed. While canopies are typically made out of marble, stone, stucco, or wood, and designed by architects, Las Vegas's sign designers dotted them with light bulbs and, to amplify the glitz, plastered them with mirror glass, brass plating and fiberglass, simulating expensive finishes.

The plastic *porte-cochère* came out on top. According to one architecture critic, it replaced "the roadside sign in projecting the primary imagery of a Strip hotel."[38] With large buildings crowding the Las Vegas skyline, vertical signs had less impact. While the *porte-cochère* was not visible from a distance, from up close, underneath all the mirrors and light bulbs, it transported guests into an elevated state. And so, by the late 1970s, Las Vegas developers shifted their focus from neon vertical pylons to plastic horizontal planes, with maximum levels of sheen.

Even a hybrid between a vertical pillar and a *porte-cochère* appeared: the 1977 Silverbird sign. Costing $1.8 million, it was the most expensive sign to date, and also the most reflective, featuring wings covered in mirror glass and sparkling light bulbs. If one structure came close to Liberace, this was it, although the Stardust's new mirrored façade, as long as five football fields, also came close. The mirrors helped reflect the light bulbs, consuming only a third of the energy. Reflective film even appeared on hotel towers to throw back solar heat, and reduce air-conditioning. Finally, as an added

4.6 An Ad-Art rendering by Jack Dubois of the Aladdin's gold-polished *porte-cochère*, effectively a freestanding building with massive "chandelier" fixtures, 1975.

bonus of all this Plexiglas, polished aluminum, and reflective film, Las Vegas glittered by night as well as by day.

But despite all these reflectors, a decade after the oil embargo Las Vegas still consumed a ton of energy. Seven of Southern Nevada's ten largest power consumers were Las Vegas casinos. Moreover, the city still had millions of energy-wasting light bulbs. There were so many that the Las Vegas Convention Authority, the agency that counts everything from the total number of Keno balls to the sequins on the outfits of showgirls, even stopped estimating.

Even the shift from neon to whiteboard led to minimal or no energy reductions, since the plastic signs were illuminated from within by fluorescent lights, containing the same argon gas as exposed neon. And while developers might have hidden neon in a waterproof box, instead of it being "exposed," the whiteboard signs still required a lot of maintenance. YESCO's maintenance team was as busy as ever. In 1985, the servicemen twisted more than a quarter-million light bulbs and 300 miles of neon in Las

4.7 A sign-canopy hybrid with mirrored wings and outward-radiating lights defines the Silverbird, formerly known as the Thunderbird, 1979.

Vegas's signs.[39] On one occasion, more than 1,300 bulbs had to be replaced in Lucky the Clown alone. Imagine climbing inside a ten-story clown to replace a light bulb. "When it's 100 degrees outside, the temperature inside the signs is enough to melt the socks right off you,"[40] said Daniel Kempf, one of YESCO's bulb changers. With transformers going up to tens of thousands of volts, there were some additional challenges. "I get shocked all the time," he said. "It's better than a morning cup of coffee."[41]

Kempf, a former auto mechanic, began his light-bulb-changing career filing plastic letters in YESCO's warehouse, where letters were permanently kept for superstars like Frank Sinatra, but run-of-the-mill stars had to share with others. Kempf then moved on to changing the whiteboard's sign panels. "A real hard day is when you have to take Wayne Newton down and put Dean Martin up," he said. "You go home physically and mentally exhausted."[42] With the Newton letters weighing between 50 and 75 pounds each, they were not easy to carry up an 80-foot ladder. "I once got a hernia lifting Wayne Newton," he said. And as for any bulb changer in the business, one fall was inevitable; Kempf's was a 55-foot tumble from the Tropicana sign, tearing his ligaments and shattering his teeth.[43]

Kempf, dubbed by his colleagues the "most astute dead-bulb tracker,"[44] went on a two-hour patrol every night. He would be on the lookout for slightly darker patches in whiteboards, an indication of a dead light behind. Speaking into his voice recorder, he then marked the dead lamp's location by describing its position within the sign:

"Indirect light, Stardust, behind 'soup,' south side."

"Circus Circus clown, indirect, tip of toe, flat foot."[45]

With his eyes on the lights, talking into his voice recorder, all the while driving his car, Kempf was a bit of a road hazard. "I've gotten into some wrecks," he acknowledged. Sometimes the police pulled him over for weaving in his car. They usually let him go, except for one time when, while looking up at Lucky the Clown, he ran into a lady.

"I got a ticket for that one."[46]

A GLITCH IN THE CORPORATE GLITZ

By 1980, a decade after the corporate gaming law, the five biggest gaming companies in the state of Nevada were no longer Mafia factions but publicly traded companies: Hilton, MGM, Del Webb, Harrah's, and Caesars World. The law appeared to work, and it should have improved Las Vegas's reputation.

Yet Las Vegas reached rock bottom in the popular estimation. "I suspect Las Vegas has a highly secret Bad Taste Committee," wrote a *New York Times* reporter. "Builders are not given construction site permits unless their plans show a requisite degree of egregious gracelessness."[47] Las Vegas was also a place of "super-galactic people watching," she added. "Genuine Pa Kettles, wearing overalls and straw farmer's hats," and "blue-rinse perm grandmas in print dresses wearing cat-eye glasses with sequins on top."

The city was considered a retirement home for fading stars, where an overweight and drug-addicted Elvis performed until his death. Then there was the even more extravagantly dressed Liberace, who flew into audiences like a glitter-ball Peter Pan on wire. Reporters characterized the Las Vegas of the 1970s as an "uncool polyester dump,"[48] and "a blight to spirit and soul."[49]

During the early years of the corporate age, Las Vegas suffered from a lack of innovation. The city was now led by conservative boardrooms watching the bottom line, or someone like Howard Hughes, who had failed to build new casinos and prevented others from doing so too, buying up most of the land along the Strip. In 1974, the Department of Health even closed ninety of the Desert Inn's rotting hotel rooms. Two years later, Hughes, now a slum hotel owner, boarded a plane to Houston and died en route, an autopsy weighing him at only 90 pounds. In 1978, the administrators of his company finally remodeled the Desert Inn, building a 14-story box covered in one-way mirror glass. It could have been mistaken for a corporate headquarters, had they not stopped short at filling the casino with office cubicles.

4.8 In 1978, the Desert Inn, Howard Hughes's former headquarters, discarded its neon cactus for a new 14-story addition to the existing building (left), both clad in one-way-mirrored glass ribbons.

Nevertheless, the Xanadu, an exciting proposal from architect Martin Stern planned for real estate tycoon Donald Trump in 1975, had the potential to blow the life back into Las Vegas. Stern envisaged a 1,730-room pyramid-sloped property decked with a soaring atrium and "firefalls" across the site. He had taken his cues from John Portman's spectacular atrium hotels, which proved more profitable than maximizing floor area in boxes with long corridors. But Stern's Xanadu was never built; the developers quibbled with the authorities over who should build the resort's new sewer line.

Gaming corporations were less interested in building in Las Vegas than they were in Atlantic City. In 1978, in response to the recession, Jersey voters legalized gambling in Atlantic City, breaking Nevada's forty-five-year monopoly on legal gambling. When the city announced a Las Vegas-style Strip along the Boardwalk, Las Vegans shivered. Atlantic City had a better location, with the entire North Eastern Seaboard population in proximity. By 1982, Atlantic City had twenty-three million visitors, about double the number of Las Vegas, where visitor numbers rose only marginally.

4.9 An artist's impression of the Donald Trump-proposed Xanadu, 1975, inspired by the pyramid-sloped Acapulco Princess, final residence of Howard Hughes.

Still, the Atlantic City strip lacked Vegas's pizzazz. City planners, worried about inheriting Vegas's "crass" design, allowed only modern towers on concrete casino bases, refusing Sin City's glitz. "We're trying to create an effect that's reasonably tasteful,"[50] a local city planner said. But without the light bulbs and reflective mirrors, all that was left were bunker-like casinos ruining the boardwalk, a city of faceless concrete walls.

Back in Las Vegas, an additional problem behind the lack of new developments was finance. Both legitimate and illegitimate investors were turned off by some highly publicized series of FBI raids and wiretaps, and brutal Syndicate murders. A new Syndicate generation from Chicago, led by the brutal Tony "The Ant" Spilotro, had taken over Las Vegas, violating the "purity code" by tainting the city with blood—the death of Culinary Union leader Al Bramlet, found buried naked under a pile of rocks in the desert, shot in both ears. A 1976 FBI raid of the Stardust revealed a supremely masterful skim involving a rigged counting device and a secret coin vault that would have made Houdini envious.

Murders and raids showed that corporations controlled only part of the Strip. Lurking behind the glitz were Syndicate factions. But with growing internal disputes, and FBI heat intensifying, their ranks quickly thinned out—if they were not behind bars, their fate lay in a steel drum or a hole in the desert. To add to the misery, in 1980 two columns of black smoke spiraled up from the MGM Grand. A refrigerated pastry display case had caught fire, which spread rapidly for lack of sprinklers. It grew into a massive fireball at the entrance, feeding off the *porte-cochère*'s shimmering plastics. In what was Nevada's worst tragedy ever, eighty-seven people died, many killed by toxic fumes. Inspections showed that the MGM Grand, in its rush to finish construction, violated fire codes, and this was overlooked by lenient county inspectors. To make matters worse, only ninety days after this disaster, the Hilton also suffered a fire, which killed eight people. The speed with which the modern mega-resorts were built had literally backfired.

All these issues, along with the early-1980s recession and high interest rates, put the damper on new projects in Las Vegas. But little by little, the Mafia influence waned and the corporate revolution grew in strength. Corporations modernized many aspects of the gaming industry, replacing one-way mirrors with computerized camera surveillance systems, mechanical slot machines with electromechanical and later electronic slot machines. They continued to transform signage, introducing "computerized electronic message centers" that could constantly change their message, rendering whiteboard signs obsolete. They constantly held Las Vegas casinos to new standards of taste. In 1984, the Golden Nugget's sign, one of the world's most photographed, was taken down. A few years later, the Stardust's sign changed its electro-jag font for a corporate Helvetica. "We were heartbroken," the designer said. "We basically screwed up our own sign."[51]

It would be only a matter of time before the city recovered. The increasing legalization of gambling in other parts of the United States over the years would not damage but benefit Las Vegas, as it enlarged the market of gamblers. The new pupils of chance would eventually make a trip to the undisputed gaming Mecca: Vegas. In addition, the casino basics were solid. In 1978, a gaming consultant noted that a casino earned on average $1,000 per square foot, compared to $150 to $250 for a typical retail store. "It seems certain," he said, "that once the economics of the industry are evaluated objectively, conventional long-term financing will become available."[52] When investors took notice, a new Las Vegas would come to dominate the world.

The corporatization of Las Vegas highlighted the role of finance and management in the shaping of cities. It helped the Las Vegas Strip to expand, as well as change its nature. It explains why corporations built lean corporate modernist casinos first. But over time, as competition escalated and the Mafia still lurked behind the scenes, the square boxes were enhanced with glittery *porte-cochères* and disco ball chandeliers. It was as if developers built shrines to Liberace, the one-man diamond mine, his Rolls-Royce covered in tiny mirrors, his sequined suit cape embroidered with jewels, one of them weighing more than 200 pounds alone.

Preceding Madonna's *Material Girl* (1984) and Gordon Gekko in *Wall Street* (1987), the 1970s Strip, from the Stardust reflector to the Aladdin's gilded canopy, glittered unfettered materialism night and day—thanks to the Mafia glitch in the corporate glitz.

5

Disneyland (1985—1995)

I'm more of a Disney person than a casino guy. … This is what's gonna protect Las Vegas in its next generation … we're building fantasy resorts.[1]

—Steve Wynn, casino mogul

The town will never be the same. … Today it looks like Disneyland. And while the kids play cardboard pirates, Mommy and Daddy drop the house payments and Junior's college money on the poker slots.

—Ace Rothstein, Casino

At the north end of the Strip, a fire-spitting volcano erupted every fifteen minutes, spewing piña colada scents. Next door, skirmishing pirates set a battleship on fire, then sank it, every hour. Two seven-story felines outstared each other on the Strip's south end: an Egyptian sphinx backed by a laser-shooting pyramid, pitted against King Looey, paws stretched out, with Dorothy, Scarecrow, and Tin Man walking the yellow brick road from underneath his chin. If those clues were not enough to guess the new identity of the Strip, a bright white castle with oversized turrets made the new paradigm crystal-clear. You could fool yourself into thinking it was Sleeping Beauty Castle, were it not for a casino lurking behind the moat.

Welcome to Disneyland, Las Vegas! In the 1980s, Disney became the largest entertainment conglomerate in the world, making films, owning television channels and theme parks. Casino developers hoped to draw their own share of the traveling family and baby-boomer market. From 1985 to 1995, departing from the lifeless office blocks and square whiteboard signs, they injected "entertainment value" into their casinos, adding layers of fantasy architecture and theme park fun. By the end of this new phase of the Strip, Disney's Animal Kingdom had been imported too. With all the bottlenose dolphins, white tigers, and toucans flown into the Mojave Desert, just a rodent was missing to complete the picture—if only his copyright had expired, the Strip could have added a mouse-ear-shaped casino to its skyline.

Developers could not exactly copy Disney. The highly conservative Disney would never have endorsed gambling. His company had long fought against casinos coming to Florida to tarnish the state's family reputation. Imagine his reaction had he found Winnie the Pooh in Las Vegas, holding a honey pot filled with casino chips. Nonetheless, the Strip managed to find its way around copyright issues, bringing in its own supply of G-rated fantasy tales. It quickly succumbed to pharaohs, pirates, knights, and the Wicked Witch of the East.

Behind the new wall of Disney-associated aesthetics also lurked Walt's corporate structures and strategies. Developers emulated Disney's design principles, immersing visitors in a story. They also copied Disney's merchandising divisions and corporate culture of employees as "cast members," acting out a fantasy storyline. By unsolicited association, Disney helped Las Vegas shed its negative stigma, and become a respectable family destination. Just as McDonald's had borrowed a clown to put a smiling face on junk food, cartoon caricatures warmed up children for gambling—a word that had been sanitized to "gaming." And while the yellow brick road paved the way to Main Street, it did the same for Wall Street. Encouraged by the conversion from Sin City to the Emerald City, high-yield bonds gushed in, ushered by Michael Milken, junk bond king.

Cultural critics, however, were less enthusiastic about the Strip's new phase, which they saw as the nexus of a worldwide trend of "Disneyfication." They criticized city managers for emulating Disney. Just as Mickey was a hairless and commodified cartoon caricature of a mouse, so were cities sanitized, reconstructed in purely visual terms, and placed under private ownership and control.

A closer look, however, revealed that the Las Vegas Strip could never become a Disneyland. Unlike the serenity of Disney's monopoly of Main Street U.S.A., multiple companies competed for the Strip. In this distortion of Disneyland, pharaohs, pirates, and hawkers all vied for attention. For a good ten years, Las Vegas led the world not in classic Disney, but in a Disney collage, juxtaposing a bronze pyramid, an erupting volcano, and a sinking eighteenth-century ship, smack on the Strip.

And best of all, unlike Disneyland, it was free.

FAMILY HOOKS

Casino signs used to attract customers with topless showgirls. The Tropicana, on the other hand, had a five-acre waterpark with a jungle and zoo, featuring flamingoes and penguins.

"We're probably the only casino hotel in the world with a fish and wildlife department,"[2] said the president of Ramada Gaming, who during strategic business meetings had to decide where to put the talking macaws and parrots, and what they would say.

The Tropicana's approach would come to define the new phase of the Strip, providing an answer to Las Vegas's economic and image crisis. By the beginning of the 1980s, as we saw in chapter 4, Las Vegas had reached rock bottom in the popular estimation. The city became known as a retiring home for worn-out superstars, like Frank Sinatra, or celebrities at the peak of their career woes, like "Las Vegas Elvis," obese and dulled by prescription drugs. The phenomenon even led to the expression "going Vegas," describing the malady of entertainers past their prime, who were on the Strip because they had no other place to go.

Las Vegas suffered from the deep national "Reagan" recession of the early 1980s, which brought high interest rates and did not encourage investors to develop. With nationwide state lotteries, riverboat casinos, and gambling in Native American reservations, the city had lost its monopoly on legalized gambling. In the midst of this slump, there was a big surprise. In what was the first institutional stock in the gaming industry, and one of the most successful initial public offerings on Wall Street that decade, financier Michael Milken had floated Circus Circus Enterprises as a public company in 1983. With Circus's books revealed, it turned out that its business model of running a family-oriented "grind"—a casino that does not go after a few high-rolling "whales," but after the masses—was highly profitable.

The middle class, it turned out, put plenty of quarters in Circus's slot machines. They had more capital available thanks to credit cards, a result of the 1970s deregulation of consumer interest rates. Companies provided high-interest credit to high-risk, lower-income customers, who happily spent, in spite of surging personal bankruptcies. The 1978 Airline Deregulation Act made air travel cheaper for families and helped double the number of airlines serving Las Vegas's airport. Moreover, baby boomers, the largest demographic, were getting older and had more leisure time and disposable income than before.

Circus Circus had been mining this demographic since Jay Sarno opened it in 1968, and surrounded slot machines with acrobats and animals, all in a circus tent. But no developer since had dared to mimic Sarno's mad visions, especially after Circus Circus initially failed financially when gamblers did not appreciate corridors smelling of orangutan.

The Tropicana had taken Circus's approach, but instead of attractions above the casino, it built a theme park in its "backyard." It rode a trend of water parks placed in unorthodox locations. The 1985 West Edmonton Mall, the largest mall in North America, for instance, had the world's largest indoor water park, in hope of attracting shoppers with their children.

The Tropicana's theme park succeeded in bringing in the middle-class crowds. With a centerfold feature in *Casino Gaming Magazine*, it was seen as a way to entertain customers and to "differentiate" the casino, the antidote to "uniformity." Interior designer Charles Silverman explained: "A certain owner is looking for the extra hook, that extra gimmick as an attraction. 'Go to Casino A because Casino A is exciting to look at as opposed to Casinos B and C, which are ordinary and plain vanilla.'" He was not overly concerned with design theory. "We're basically in the marketing business."[3]

The theme park quickly became an icon of a new casino design paradigm, "theming."

Central to theming was the notion of a single identity that dominated all aspects of the resort, from interior design to employee outfits. Designers even themed the slot machines—which by 1986 surpassed green felt table games in bringing in revenue—and decorated them with cartoon characters, sports themes, or patriotic red, white and blue, which was popular during the Gulf War.[4] Some design companies used marketing research techniques, such as focus groups and interviews, to make their designs more appealing. One firm even added an environmental psychologist to the team. The company learned how to use focal points in the casino to prevent people from getting lost, or how to help alleviate the boredom of waiting around elevators: "It's amazing how much longer you'll wait if you look at yourself in the mirror."[5]

In contrast, at the inception of the Strip's corporatization during the 1970s, companies paid little attention to design, building dull modernist boxes fronted by square whiteboard signs. Only the Strip's Caesars Palace and Circus Circus had proper themes.

In 1987, two years after the Tropicana's water park, Caesars built a little gimmick that would multiply tenfold the daily entrance into the West casino: a domed pavilion with holographic video projections of Cleopatra, backed by sounds of feasting Romans. As families stepped into the pavilion, a one-way conveyor belt dragged them across the parking lot.

The Las Vegas theme park war had begun.

THE VOLCANO SHUTDOWN

A stroll down the Strip used to take pedestrians past buzzing neon and swaths of asphalt. In 1989, enter Steve Wynn's lagoon and eight-story volcano, spewing columns of smoke and burning flames.

Steve Wynn successfully ran his family's bingo parlor in Maryland, moved to Las Vegas, bought a stake in downtown's Golden Nugget, and managed to stage a takeover. In 1973, at the age of thirty-one, he became chairman and president of the Golden Nugget. He then wanted to build a Golden Nugget in Atlantic City, but lacked the necessary capital. Wynn's cousin's college roommate, Michael Milken, entered the picture. Milken happened to be the legendary king of junk bonds—below investment-grade loans at high interest rates. In 1979, he raised $160 million from Mormon bankers, the highest amount ever loaned to a casino. When his casino became the most profitable in Atlantic City, Milken then backed Wynn with $535 million worth of bonds for a new $630 million Las Vegas Strip hotel, the Mirage, which would open in 1989, the world's most expensive casino-resort. But Wynn needed a million a day in revenue to service the debt alone. It was the skeptics' heyday.

With this budget, Wynn could spend $30 million just on a volcano to "hook" people away from Caesars Palace. Lighting designer David Hersey, who had had initially been charged only to light the exterior of the hotel tower, came up with the idea. A 12-foot-tall prototype was made so that it could be tested. Hersey explained: "Steve's first reaction to the volcano was concern that it would look like a cigarette lighter going off."[6] The source of the flame was a pipeline delivering 400 million BTUs of natural gas, guaranteeing a 40-foot blaze. Edward Lewis, director of Rock and Waterscapes Inc., said: "The volcano is just a pipe with gas in it."[7]

Lewis's firm was charged with decorating the pipe with rocks. Wynn wanted the rugged formations from the Santa Rosa Mountains near Palm Springs. They made a mold of the rocks and built the mountain out of fiberglass, adding a few layers of paint to achieve a "natural" rocky look. Lewis explained: "You get a very artificial appearance with real rock."[8] A landscape architect, charged with constructing a river to flow over the rocks, quoted Wynn: "Steve told us, 'I need the cascading water to be white so I can light it. Niagara Falls has white water, and I want white water.'"[9] They poured water over the fake rocks to see when it would go perfectly white. 128,000 gallons of water a minute did the trick.

All of this was enhanced with sounds of chirping birds, giving way to roaring thunder at punctual fifteen-minute volcano eruptions. To simulate the lava, water spewing up from the lagoon appeared to be on fire, thanks to underwater gas jets. But the gas also gave off a smell of sulfur, which could frighten guests. An artificial scent was added, to make the volcano smell like piña colada.

"It's what God would've done," Wynn joked, "if He'd had the money."[10]

That summed it all up. The volcano, as well as the resort's other "natural" features, were built on the theme park contradiction of making nature "more realistic" with "fake" elements. At the entrance, Wynn built an interior jungle with real palm trees and orchids, but over 20,000 square feet of fake plants. "Mummified" trees, implanted with a steel rod and injected with formaldehyde, could be twisted into more exotic shapes than had been possible when they were alive.

"You can really pretend you are in a rain forest jungle setting without the mosquitoes and the dengue fever and the so forth you get when you're in the real ones," an interior designer said. "The fantasy is kind of a jungle effect that you don't find in nature and it's really better as a consequence."[11] Plus, with fake plants, "people are trying to figure out which are real." This philosophy was in line with the resort's name, the Mirage, evoking an imagined, exotic oasis. Wynn bought the name from a Las Vegas motel, which renamed itself the Glass Pool Inn (it had a glass pool).

Wynn also built an interior jungle, underneath a 90-foot-high glass dome. He was breaking the taboos against bringing natural light and calm into a casino, typically dark except for the nervously artificial glare of the slot machines. These were the interiors inherited from the dark, smoky, illicit gambling joints of decades past, *à la* film noir. Only a few plants survive in dim lighting, such as the Philodendron, which is overused as a result. But the brighter, natural lighting broadened Wynn's plant choices and his demographic. He explained: "I was trying to appeal to women."[12]

5.1 Strip passersby halt for the Mirage's fire-spewing, roaring volcano reeking of piña colada, 1989.

Instead of such casino classics as scantily dressed women, the Mirage's attractions were flora and fauna. Included were sharks and rays, placed in a 20,000-gallon aquarium behind the registration desk to keep guests entertained as they waited in line. Wynn also added a white tiger habitat for the tigers that performed in the Mirage's main show with Siegfried and Roy, a duo of German illusionists. The Roman-column-lined habitat was painted white, the apparent assumption being that white tigers like white.

But Wynn also catered to high rollers, building villas at the back with swimming pools and putting greens—Michael Jackson's suite had outdoor air-conditioning. The hotel tower's top five floors contained suites. Wynn did not like the fact that the Golden Nugget's colored glass sometimes had a greenish tint. So Hersey bathed the hotel tower in a special 24-carat gold film. No matter what the weather, or the time of day, it would always be gold.

Now only the volcano had to be tested, full-scale, in the live situation of the Strip. With each explosion, some startled drivers even got out of their cars to see what was going on. It caused a major traffic jam. In any town but Las Vegas, less lenient officials might have objected to having a volcano erupt in public.

All these attractions brought so many people, 200,000 on opening day alone, that the sidewalk had to be widened. But some analysts wondered if Wynn should have placed the volcano at the rear of the hotel, so viewers were forced to walk through the casino. Many now just walked away to Caesars Palace.

To everyone's surprise, Wynn made $661 million in revenues the first year, and managed to pay back the bonds after only eighteen months. For him it was just the beginning. He later built an artificial coral reef in the casino, and flew in bottlenose dolphins. "This place will always be changing, and we'll always be adding things," he commented. "This is a Disneyland."[13]

Wynn's success kick-started what has been coined the "Mirage phase." According to one researcher, "a new psychology of pride and growth took over the town."[14]

The Mirage's universal appeal attracted an entirely new demographic of average Americans to Las Vegas. "This place is filled with people like me and you—none of whom think of themselves as gamblers," Wynn said. "They think of themselves as folks who are on vacation, and while they're here—hey, let's put some money in the slot machine."[15] This demographic contrasted heavily with the Sin City crowds, Marc Cooper noted in the *Village Voice*:

Anxiously gathered at the foot of the Mirage volcano was this herd of beefy middle Americans, almost all dressed in short pants, T-shirts and baseball caps, and enough of them wearing those pastel-colored fanny packs around their waists that the city looked as though it was immersed in a continuing convention of colostomy patients. … If so much as one old-time Vegas showgirl had shimmered by in boas and pasties, this assembled decency league would have stoned her to death.[16]

But the Mirage represented much more than that. The volcano was the first full-size theme park attraction right on the Strip, ending the reign of surface parking lots. Moreover, the Mirage turned Las Vegas into the national test bed for company loans and consumer spending, up to their ears in junk-bond and credit-card debt.

Of Drexel Burham Lambert, Milken's firm, Wynn told a *Forbes* reporter: "They made me."[17] Drexel funded companies like CNN and gaming corporations including Circus Circus, Bally's, and Harrah's. But the same year the volcano spewed, Milken was indicted for racketeering and securities fraud, and sentenced to ten years in prison.

Even the sweet-smelling volcano had unforeseen dangers. It burnt so hot that it scorched the Mirage's palm trees. A sprinkler system had to be set up, timed to match the volcano's flames. Wynn also failed to equip his volcano with a security fence, so he was taken by surprise when he saw a teenager wade into the water. With the volcano scheduled to erupt, Wynn exclaimed: "He's about to get third-degree burns in his crotch."[18]

"It was a nightmare. It was a category three mistake." Luckily, his security staff came to the rescue. "One of my plainclothes jumped in and grabbed this guy by the neck and pulled the dipshit out."[19] He then gave the volcano another vital feature: a beam-and-eye security system, so if someone stepped through, the whole volcano would shut down.

THE ARTHURIAN MEGAMALL

Like a huge Jeff Koons balloon dog sculpture, Las Vegas's next addition to the skyline had the features of a toy castle, but blown up twenty-eight stories tall. Mounted security guards were dwarfed in the face of the cartoonish white crenelated walls. A drawbridge the length of two football fields crossed a vast swath of asphalt and a moat where every day, at 6.00 p.m. sharp, above three-quarter million gallons of water, Merlin exchanged fireballs with a three-story dragon.

This was Excalibur, completed in 1990, Circus Circus Enterprises' new casino hotel. "We found the theme of a *castle*," it wrote in its annual report. "Tournaments, heraldry, chivalric orders, knighthood, high ceremony and singing," the report stated, would provide the modern person with "a temporary release from the chores of daily life."[20] Like other casino companies, Circus Circus had established a professional marketing department, plowing through demographic data, psychological profiles, and market research. They estimated that seven million Americans participated in Renaissance fairs in 1989. It then crowd-sourced the name Excalibur from a public "Name the Castle" competition, drawing more than 183,000 entries.

Veldon Simpson, the architect, toured European castles, theme parks and Renaissance fairs. But Excalibur, with its 4,032 rooms, was to be a lot bigger than any castle built before: "The challenge is to create the authenticity of a castle at a scale that no actual castle ever approached."[21] Moreover, the bulky hotel towers were difficult to mold into spire shapes. As a solution, he implemented a "castle-within-a-castle" scheme. He placed four hotel boxes around a square courtyard and decorated them with small turrets, to make them look like castle walls. Within the courtyard he built a smaller castle, but with overscaled towers, battlements, and spires, which were colored bright red, blue, and yellow, to make this smaller castle recognizable from afar. But as a result the large central spires looked out of proportion compared to the small turrets on the hotel buildings, which made the whole thing look like a bizarre caricature of a castle.

A few local architects did not see the humor of Excalibur's absurd castle situation. "There is no real relationship to contemporary society in that building," noted one architect. "It's obviously out of scale," another said. "Each element is oversized. It's a caricature, that's what it is."[22]

However, they failed to grasp the castle's relationship to contemporary entertainment. While nobody at Circus had dared to mention the "D" word, the referent of the Excalibur was crystal-clear: it was a clunky version of Disneyland's Sleeping Beauty and Cinderella Castles, which were also castles-within-castles. If Wynn had targeted the Disneyland crowds by using architectural detail and universally likable attractions, Circus Circus had dared to co-opt Disney's most recognized symbol, second only to Mickey's trademarked ears. It approximated the cartoon castle logo of the Disney Corporation and incorporated it into the Las Vegas skyline. Where Mirage's volcano only spewed fire at night, the Excalibur advertised fantasy for miles around, in all directions and at all times of the day.

5.2 A drawbridge crosses a moat and a driveway into the Excalibur's central "castle-within-a-castle," with deliberately overscaled turrets to make the castle more recognizable from a distance.

This castle was built at record speed in only twenty months. When William Bennett, Circus Circus's majority shareholder, drew a sword from a stone at the groundbreaking ceremony, the interior design was still not finished. It was never fully refined, leaving lots of walls with not much more than a scant banner, an iron chandelier, or a crenelated ceiling border. But the price tag was only $290 million, hundreds of millions of dollars cheaper than the Mirage. Excalibur's room rates were less than half of Mirage's cheapest rate. "Be King Arthur's guest for less than a King's ransom," the brochure promised, appealing to Circus Circus's low-rolling crowd. "It's the time-honored K-mart concept,"[23] Wynn said of what he named a "Chuck E. Cheese on steroids."[24]

Circus Circus Enterprises preferred to explain the concept as an "entertainment megastore." The company's 1989 annual report described this business idea as a new stage in the evolution of the supermarket. The one-stop shopping innovation, which had revolutionized grocery-buying when it was invented in the 1930s, had continued to grow. By the 1950s it had evolved into a downtown shopping center, by the 1970s into a suburban mall, and by the 1980s into a megamall that even offered entertainment.

Glenn Schaeffer, Circus Circus's chief financial officer, clarified the analogy: "What works in the shopping mall is you draw the broadest range of customers for longer periods of time."[25] A casino, like the megamall, could draw its success from having an abundance of choices: "We're rather indifferent as to which cash register we pull the dollars out of at the end of the day. What we want is to make sure that we own all the cash registers."[26] Moreover, he made sure that 2,630 of the "registers" in his megamall were slot machines.

To draw people in for longer, Circus's new casino would incorporate all of this: "a blend of casino, theater, festival and shopping mall."[27] Instead of spending money on an expensive shark tank, cheaper performers entertained the "ladies" and "lords" standing in line at the reception desk. While the company cited the exciting street life and performers from then-popular festival marketplaces, such as Boston's Faneuil Hall, the idea was a throwback to the Middle Ages. Just as medieval merchants used buffoons to attract people to their stalls, Excalibur employed sword swallowers, fire eaters, magicians, jugglers, mimes, minstrels, harpists, and contortionists. Even belly dancers made it into the castle, coming all the way from the Sultan's palace. The performers wore medieval garb, but enhanced with sequins and lamé. The creative producer said: "We've made it a little Las Vegas."[28]

The performers were free to stroll around the public areas of the hotel—the lobby fountain underneath a fake blue sky, for instance—but they were strictly banned from the casino. Circus Circus had learned its lesson two decades earlier, when it had allowed performers in the casino, an experiment that ended when acrobats crashed onto the gambling tables.

Excalibur was designed as a four-level "Realm," with the casino sandwiched by entertainment and restaurants. Escalators from the casino led families down to a "dungeon" of Merlin's Magical Motion Rides and the Hansel & Gretel Snack Bar. It also featured the King Arthur's Arena, a circular theater with an earthen floor hosting a jousting tournament where kids, served by "wenches" and "serfs," got to eat chicken with their hands, bang on the table, and scream *Hoorah à la* Shakespeare: "Huzzah!"

The escalator going up from the casino pulled guests into a royal medieval "village," a "street" lined with faux medieval façades, decorated with battlements, Robin Hood murals, and stained glass. Restaurants and shops themed in a medley of medieval styles, from Arthurian to Bavarian, included Lance-A-Lotta Pasta and Octoberfest Beer Garden, with a German oompah band performing sing-alongs. The final level up was Camelot, where at the Canterbury Wedding Chapel fiancées could walk the aisle wearing a crown and a velvet robe, and holding a sword—in case someone objected to the marriage.

Designers had trouble finding proper room furnishings. Unlike Victorian, for instance, "nobody specializes in medieval," a designer noted. They had to design their own carpets and wallpaper. But rather than studying castle interiors, they looked at movie sets. He pointed out that if you made rooms "as they literally looked during the traditional period, they would be dark, dingy and dirty."[29]

Imagine staying in one of the rooms covered in imitation stone wallpaper. You call one of the costumed damsels at reception to summon a carpet vacuumer wearing doublet and tights. She salutes: "Have a royal day!" Your eye glimpses a brochure. "Hear ye! Hear ye! His Majesty the King would like to welcome each of you to the land of Excalibur. He hopes you have a royal stay and would like to remind you that all Spectradyne in-room movies are $7.95 each."[30]

Like Excalibur, Cinderella Castle had elevators, air-conditioning, and television. All of which was OK, Disney's design chief said, since the castle was only "to say something about the idea of being a castle."[31] He had made each story of the castle slightly smaller than the one below, so that it appeared higher, following the optical illusion of forced perspective. This made for a more recognizable and fantastic visual experience. Cartoons are made on the principle that we recognize caricatures more easily than the real object they represent, since the brain works by exaggerating difference. Walt Disney himself said: "All cartoon characters and fables must be exaggeration, caricatures. It is the very nature of fantasy and fable."

Despite the obvious resemblance, Disney's copyright lawyers could not sue Excalibur. While Excalibur was derived from Disneyland, Disney's castles were themselves derived from Neuschwanstein, a castle built by Ludwig II of Bavaria. Deemed insane in 1886, he wandered between fantasy and reality. "I want to remain an eternal mystery to myself and others," he once said. His powers limited as a constitutional monarch, he ignored statehood for extravagant artistic and architectural projects like Neuschwanstein, built at a time when castles had lost their practicality, since cannons had long made fortified walls obsolete. His theater designer drew up a dramatic mishmash of Romanesque walls and Gothic turrets. It gave a nostalgic sense of release to a mad king, who, like a nineteenth-century Liberace, liked taking nighttime rides in ornate coaches and sleighs, dressed in historic costume. He would have done well in Vegas.

Architects then derided Neuschwanstein's thin blue spires, failing to appreciate their lightness and iconography, which draws so many tourists today. Similarly, architects mocked the Excalibur and Disney's castles, whose fiberglass was an inadequate token of material honesty and whose fortified walls did not fit the "form follows function" mantra of a proper building, but were a symbol of useless ornamentation. They did not appreciate that the fake castles were much bigger, erected much faster, and built to conform to fire code. Neither did they appreciate the construction complexities, like trying to hoist the cones up 265 feet, where a gush of wind could crash them into the hotel buildings.

King Ludwig, Walt Disney, and Circus Circus Corporation, while divided by half a century each, all had a fantasy castle in common. It was a telling symbol of changing leisure patterns. What was a palace in the late nineteenth century and a theme park attraction in the mid-twentieth century had now become a casino.

WIENIE AND FENDI

Imagine taking a stroll along the Strip. Out of the blue comes a Cleopatra impersonator, like an ancient showgirl, wearing a golden bra and a crown with plumed feathers. She lures you past a Trevi Fountain, into the Palazzo Poli. You meander through vias and piazzas, past palazzi of Fendi and Versace. Music fills the air. The sky turns from bright blue to rosy dusk. A Bacchus statue gives a toast, rising his fiber-optic cup.

"Your typical Roman via," architecture critic Aaron Betsky wrote on the occasion of the opening of the Forum Shops, the new mall at Caesars Palace, "where the sun sets and rises on an electronically controlled cycle."[32]

The designer of the mall, Terry Dougall, had designed the 1992 Forum Shops not as a typical mall, but as a story. "You need a story,"[33] he said, designing the mall as "a play in three acts."

"The opening number" was the "festival fountain" that featured Bacchus. After the wine god's toast, his eyes rolling, Dougall had visitors hooked. He could gradually build to a climax: "Then the next street becomes more and more opulent, and just when you think it can't get any better, you step into the large domed area with the large fountain. That seems bigger than life."

Dougall was referring to the replica of Bernini's Fountain of the Four Rivers. But despite his interest in historical accuracy—"we draw, we don't reinvent"[34]—he had dared to adjust this classic masterpiece. For instance, he replaced the original Egyptian pillar with a lower colonnade, since he could not have the obelisk pierce through the painted moon in the blue-sky ceiling. He also replicated Venus and Neptune instead of the more anonymous river gods at the original, added a few winged horses, and changed the water squirts for waterfalls. This "rococo version of the Fountain of the Four Rivers" was so loud, Betsky noted, it "drowns out the sound of nearby slots."[35]

After the four river gods' act, the "finale" was near: "Then you step to the last area, which is more money per square foot, about $1,000 a square foot, because of the height of the ceiling, and every square inch of that is either real or faux marble."[36]

As Dougall built to a thousand per square foot spending climax, about four times as high as a typical retail store, he left pedestrians exhilarated, right at the entrance of the casino. But ideally, before unleashing themselves onto the slot machines, they had already entered at least a few shops, the Caesars store for instance, selling Caesars branded T-shirts, hats, and fragrances. Now you could bring your favorite casino back home, or even smell like one—in the Mirage that meant like coconut, which it pumped

5.3 Below a changing sky, Neptune holds his spear on a shop-lined "piazza" at the Forum Shops, 2008. Photograph courtesy of Vladislav Bezrukov, Flickr.

through the casino not only to mask the smell of cigarette smoke, but to increase brand remembrance through the nose, the most sensitive organ, and until then untapped, other than by the piña-colada-scented volcano.

Disguised in Roman aesthetics, crowd control devices commonly used in theme parks took people away from the volcano, through Caesars's new mall, into its casino. The Forum Shops represented the closest approximation to Disney yet. The mall's press release boasted: "The newest landmark in town could have come from the imagination of someone like Walt Disney." The Forum Shops were a symptom of Disney's growing influence. The same year as the mall opened, Disney opened Euro Disney, 4,800 acres near Paris, two and a half times more land area than the Gardens of Versailles. It built Disney stores selling Mickey ears, key chains and mugs around the world. Rather than suing Caesars, they opened a Disney store in the Las Vegas Forum Shops, headed by Mickey Mouse himself, wearing a laureate and riding a chariot.

Dougall had followed to the letter all of Disney's design principles, starting with storytelling, one of the disciplinary crossovers from Disney's movies to theme parks. Many of the designers hired in 1952 to oversee the design and construction of Disneyland Park were art directors working on Disney animations who brought animation techniques to theme park building. They subjected an attraction to a single defining narrative, the central theme. This led to a very different design approach. Rather than guessing the architect's artistic intentions, the design followed a simple narrative that could be easily understood by the masses—at the cost of dumbing down the complexities of the original literary work.

Dougall also relied on "wienies," visual attractions, to pull people through the story, such as the Trevi Fountain replica right near the entrance. Walt Disney coined this term, remembering how he had once lured a dog home with a wiener on a string. Disney's chief designer, John Hench, who started as a story artist, designed large attractions, mostly with high-contrast colors to suggest action, to draw people through Disneyland. They included the Matterhorn and Sleeping Beauty Castle. He said: "Main Street is like Scene One, and then the castle is designed to pull you down Main Street toward what is next, just like a motion picture unfolding."[37]

Back at the Forum Shops, Dougall was careful to reveal the successive wienies gradually, designing meandering streets with end points that were out of view, to create a sense of mystery and discovery. But it was not just Disney aesthetics the Forum Shops were after. Retailers around the world learned how Disney had profitably blurred the boundaries between entertainment and shopping in their theme parks, coaxing people into buying merchandise. When researchers found that spending is directly related to the amount of time people spend at shopping centers,[38] they used entertainment to keep customers inside longer. Malls became sites of "immersion shopping," or "experiential retail."

The Forum Shops manager said: "We like to compare ourselves with Disneyland, where you feel good about where you are. And when people feel good they tend to want to stay longer … and they might think 'Gosh, you know what, I might love to get a new blouse for this evening.'"[39]

The Forum Shops became the most profitable retail space per square foot in the United States for most of the 1990s and 2000s. As soon as other resorts took note, large indoor malls appeared in more Strip casinos, faux blue skies included. Along with the Disney aesthetics and theme park attractions, the Disney phase of the Strip led to a diversification from just gaming to entertainment and shopping.

Now that Disney's design and shopping principles had arrived in Las Vegas, the hunting season for Disney alumni was open. Dougall made a final pitch: "Unless you work for Disney or a movie theater, the next best place to let your imagination get carried away is the casino business, and they have the money and freedom to let your imagination go crazy."[40]

Disgruntled Disney employees around the world flocked to Vegas.

THE BLOCKBUSTER PYRAMID

In 1993, a mysterious bronze pyramid took the Las Vegas skyline by surprise. This smooth object looked like one of Donald Judd's minimalist sculptures, blown up to astronomical proportions. Like a glitch in the glitz, its simple shape and dark façade stood out from the bright, ornate buildings around it. The architectural lesson here was that in an area with buildings screaming for attention, rather than succumbing to the Las Vegas maximalist aesthetic, it took a stark pyramid for people to really take notice. However, this pyramid, the Luxor, to enhance its pulling power, also had a ten-story Sphinx perched in front of it, its laser eyes projecting Tutankhamun. And then there was the 38-billion-candle-fueled laser shooting from the pyramid, the world's brightest beam, and supposedly the only human object astronauts could distinguish from outer space, besides the Great Wall of China.

"You don't need neon," Veldon Simpson, the pyramid's architect, said. "When you have something as powerful and dynamic as that. … It would be an insult to the

5.4 A driveway cuts through the Sphinx, sandwiched between a misted obelisk and a glass pyramid with the world's brightest beam, 1993.

architecture to sign it. It would be like holding up your thumb and putting a sticker on it that says 'thumb.'"[41]

Three years earlier, Circus Circus Enterprises had had the audacity to copy Disney's logo with the Excalibur. Now it had dared to do something even more audacious. Luxor's name did not accurately represent its iconoclastic form, as it stole from Egypt's revered Sphinx of Giza, cut a driveway underneath its belly, and turned it into the entrance to a glass pyramid casino.

But while the Excalibur was mainly a derivative, a lesser version of Disney, the Luxor, on the other hand, was a blockbuster of a pyramid. The Las Vegas Sphinx was one and a half times bigger than the original, to match the scale of the hotel pyramid behind it. Moreover, in contrast to the real one, whose nose was missing, this one was given a nose job, plus cosmetic coloration. And where the original Sphinx lay in the desert alone, in Las Vegas it backed into the pyramid, and was fronted by an obelisk.[42]

"Only the desert is real," architecture critic Ada Louise Huxtable wrote,[43] placing the Luxor on the cover of her book *The Unreal America*. "All fakes are clearly not equal; there are good fakes and bad fakes. … What makes the good ones better is their improvement on reality."[44]

What allowed the Luxor to outdo the Excalibur was its truly interdisciplinary team. Circus Circus's CEO William Bennett said: "This is a collaborative production of imaginative architects, cutting-edge movie producers, science-fiction writers, special-effects designers, and experienced casino operators."[45] This team conceived the Luxor not as a building but as "sets" that invite "interactive" and "participatory adventures."

Simpson's pyramid had upward-slanting rooms on four sides, forming the skin of the structure. Initially, it would have been higher than the Great Pyramid of Giza, were it not located opposite the airport, and the Federal Aviation authorities were worried about airplanes ramming into it. Inside the hollow pyramid, 2,526 rooms looked out over the world's largest atrium, rising up thirty stories, big enough to stack nine jumbo jets. It was a major deviation from the standard double-load corridor of Las Vegas hotels. This new setup called for unusual features, for instance sixteen "inclinators," inclined elevators that traveled at a ski-lift 39-degree angle up the slope of the pyramid. In case of fire, eight giant vortex fans at the bottom would redirect smoke away from the rooms in a spiraling column up to an exhaust at the apex. It would have been one hell of a show if they had tested the fire system nightly.

The apex also housed a room crammed with forty-five searchlights shooting up the pyramid's phallic beam. The aviation authorities were lenient in classifying this potentially blinding light to pilots as a "navigational aid," even though the "aid" had an unusual animation sequence with airport strobe lights running up and down the pyramid's ribs, followed by the beam's ignition. Then, all the lights would switch off. The beam's creator said: "It's a really slow fade, and about the time it gets to the point where you can't see it, BOOM!"[46]

Imagine meandering along the Strip, running into the Ramesses obelisk and its four sacred baboons. You pass a line of criosphinxes, duck underneath the Sphinx, and walk

5.5 A cutaway model shows a "city" within the Luxor pyramid, including a Manhattan skyline, a ziggurat-style temple, and a black monolith featuring a vertical movie screen, 1993.

inside the Great Temple of Ramesses II, the entrance to the casino. After checking in at the registration desk, you step inside a vessel floating on a chlorinated Nile. A guide at the helm sails you past a temple and truckloads of Egyptian ornaments, telamons, and hieroglyphics, leaving you at the inclinator lobby in the corner of the pyramid.

The Luxor team designed the bottom of the pyramid as an "archeological dig," where the mysteries of ancient Egypt are revealed as though in a state of "excavation." It displayed one of the reasons behind the Luxor's name, other than its evocation of luxury and luck. Luxor was the site of Tutankhamun's tomb, and a full-scale replica would make a fine addition to the basement of the casino.

"All the pieces were built in Egypt, and we had an Egyptologist from Cairo make sure we did things right,"[47] said Cliff Hay, director of rides and attractions, an unusual position added to the casino's croupiers, slot managers, and security guards. His credentials included starting his film career as a vampire movie stuntman, specializing in drowning in quicksand. Hay spoke of the "realism" the Egyptologist contributed to reproducing the hundreds of treasures in King Tut's tomb: "We needed to bind stuff together with leather, and he said, 'No! This is cow leather,' so we wound up getting deer leather because we couldn't find antelope leather in the large quantities we needed."[48] While these fake artifacts were displayed in the "museum," real ancient coins were sold in the next-door gift shop.

"This hotel is a special effect!" Hay exclaimed. "We created crypto-Egyptian," he said of the casino's hieroglyphs. "We fed the signs into a computer and told it to generate random sequences … about 40 actually said something, and we had to take them out."[49] Luxor could not have a Keno player fluent in ancient Egyptian deciphering an accidentally obscene obelisk inscription.

Luxor's upper lobby level had motion machine rides housed in an incongruous bunch of theaters, including a Mayan stepped pyramid, a New York skyline, and a black monolith. The theaters blew air streams into viewers' faces and shook them up and down with electromagnetic actuators, the same technology that controls motion in space shuttles. So many top-of-the-line computers were used, it even bedazzled *Wired* magazine. As one writer said: "Technologies evolve in the strangest ways. Computers were created to calculate ballistics equations, and now we use them to create amusing illusions."[50]

But as fantastic as the pyramid was, it had some spooky features. Its dark angled glass made rooms and views obscure. The atrium was also poorly lit, since the laser room sealed the top, preventing daylight from coming through. Only a web of green lasers shooting from an obelisk periodically lit the cavernous space. This, combined with the replicas of funeral receptacles, made for a macabre atmosphere. It was perhaps prophetic of what would become an infamous suicide spot on the Strip, where the counterfeit sarcophagi indirectly commemorated the real fate of desperate gamblers, leaping into the atrium to their deaths. Meanwhile, outside, the laser beam turned out to be the world's largest bug attractor *and* killer, with a whole ecosystem of moths, bats, and owls feasting on one another.

Construction errors added to the misery, including dozens of incorrectly installed water pipes bursting from hotel rooms, causing twenty-story waterfalls inside the atrium. All of this became known as the "Luxor Curse," which, some suggested, could be averted only by placing a giant glass eye on the pyramid's capstone. Nevertheless, the interdisciplinary team built one of the most recognized symbols in the world, at the rapid rate of only eighteen months. Circus Circus Enterprises, Nevada's largest employer with 18,000 workers, had professionalized the production of spectacle, and Wall Street seemed to notice. After Luxor opened, the company was rewarded with $750 million in unsecured bank credit, then the largest line of bank credit ever extended to a gaming company.

With its roller coasters of different times and spaces, mixing of different media, and integration of cutting-edge technology, Luxor belonged to the avant-garde of contemporary building. The beam's builder even imagined that the Luxor would change cities forever, with "a new kind of skyline created by lasers."[51] Moreover, the Luxor was an instantly recognizable icon. One image of the black pyramid and the yellow-blue Sphinx, and people thought of Las Vegas.

In fact, a few months after opening, the Luxor was featured on the cover of *Time* magazine. It stood as a symbol of Las Vegas, "The New All-American City." Where typically media featured the customary Las Vegas showgirl, now there was the "improved"

5.6 Room corridors overlook the attractions level of the Luxor, Las Vegas's first atrium hotel, 2015. The former Manhattan skyline (left) was remodeled in 1997 to look Egyptian.

Sphinx. Of the "splendidly pyramidal new Luxor," the magazine wrote: "The bells and whistles are more prominent and accessible than the casino itself, and are not merely a cute, quick way to divert people as they proceed into the fleecing pen."[52] At the Luxor, American showmanship had upstaged the casino.

As a finishing touch, the pyramid featured two audio-animatronic dromedary camels, Elias and Jody. Within this first new pyramid in the desert for six thousand years, the two camels' chatter quickly turned sentimental.

"This place reminds me of home," Jody said to Elias.

"It's made me a little bit homesick," Elias added.

"I miss my mummy."[53]

As kitschy as they were, interior designer Zoli Kovacs understood their charm. "There will always be people in T-shirts, with their bellies hanging out, who you won't see in tuxedos at the Hilton," he said. "But who will be very comfortable standing in front of the talking camels."[54]

"Captain of the *Britannia*, prepare broadside, Ready, Aim, Fire!"

Further down the Strip, a pyrotechnics company ignited a salvo of firebombs and fireworks from the Dunes hotel, until 1,600 liters of aviation fuel powered an all-consuming fireball. Then the demolition company kicked in, exploding pounds of dynamite. The tower imploded while the red Dunes sign tumbled on its side, spelling "No Vacancy" for the occasion. More than 200,000 spectators witnessed the event, yelling deliriously and in awe. Architectural preservationists, however, lamented the demise of the tower, a fine example of midcentury modernism, and the Dunes sign, celebrated by Tom Wolfe as the work of "designer-sculptor geniuses." But the *Las Vegas Sun* headlined with the general consensus: "Fall of Dunes much greater than its rise."[55]

While the paper coined the event "D-Day," the event stood less for the Dunes than it did for Disney. On October 27, 1993, the day on which Steve Wynn dramatically combined the opening of his newest resort, the pirate-themed Treasure Island, with the implosion of the Dunes, the Disney era reached its climax. Wynn orchestrated the most spectacular implosion in the history of Las Vegas, featured live on television. He personally triggered the cannons of an eighteenth-century warship, and even made a cameo as "head pirate" in his hour-long infomercial, "Treasure Island: The Adventure Begins," written by the screenwriter of the Disney film *Hook*.

"My hero was Disney," Wynn said to a reporter on the day of the event. "I would be just as happy building theme parks as casinos, but it's been done already."[56] Although most Las Vegas gaming executives would pursue the Disney paradigm, no one embraced it more than Wynn.

Wynn's new resort, Treasure Island, was effectively a lower-end overflow hotel to the adjacent Mirage. But Wynn could not copy the Mirage outright. By having different themes, he could grow his consumer base in a lower market segment without devaluing the brand of the higher-end Mirage. He learned this from Jay Sarno, who diversified from his palatial Caesars Palace with a cheaper, unruly alternative: Circus Circus, a raspberry tent filled with hobo clowns and elephants.

Pirates also conformed to the old-school Disney book, going back to their *Peter Pan* (1953) animated movie. *Pirates of the Caribbean* (1967) was the last ride Walt Disney designed before his death. But the animator, noted for his wholesome family values, would have surely turned in his grave, had he known that Wynn would front his casino with not one, but two galleons of Peter Pan.

"There are going to be things for the family and for young adults that people haven't seen before—not even at Disney," Wynn promised at the press conference, dressed in a pirate captain's jacket and hat. He even immersed his designers in the pirate story, forcing them to watch pirate movies and wear pirate costumes. All workers were called "cast members" who assented to each other by saying "Aye." Roger Thomas, chief interior designer, said: "Every time we had a decision, it's 'what would the pirate have done?' … We lived and breathed Pirate. … We all talked about 'Yo ho ho' and said 'Arrr' a lot."[57]

Wynn's designers now overtly experimented with Disney's method of theme park design. They even commissioned Disney alumni to make the architectural drawings. In contrast to the monotone blueprints of architects, they drew in full color, the better to communicate expectations to the craftsmen. "They are very expensive, these guys, but they are worth it," Thomas said.[58]

Illustrator Charles White was commissioned to design the ships and the pirate village. The difficulty of designing a resort supposedly built by pirates lay in the fact that pirates, rather than erecting new buildings, were known to take over buildings designed by others. "The pirates wouldn't build anything themselves," White figured. "They would just take over what was there and build out from it." He conceived of Treasure Island as a Portuguese outpost in the Caribbean taken over by the Spanish before it fell to the pirates. "That way we could rationalize a lot of Middle-Eastern attitude and Moroccan influence,"[59] he said. "We wanted it to be eclectic."

Designers developed a pirate-parasitical form of architecture. They used ship parts, and objects pirates would have plundered. The pirates were quite the decorators with their spoils inside the casino, decking the ceiling with booty baskets and bone chandeliers. They dressed up a restaurant named The Plank as a pirates' library, "raising fascinating questions about buccaneer literacy, and whether Blackbeard preferred lyric poetry or philosophical works or maybe the *Iliad*," a tongue-in-cheek *Smithsonian* wrote.[60]

At Buccaneer Bay, the pirate village at the entrance, the pirates carefully placed Blackbeard heads on floral engraved architraves. They fashioned balconies from the sterns of ships. They made door grips out of a skull, which, at opening, split lengthwise. But it could not be too spooky. The team had initially designed a grotto casino entrance. White said: "That was too scary for Steve."[61]

The casino's façade was made to look like a hillside pirate village, with sun-faded buildings, an outdoor hearth, palm trees, and a wharf with kegs, pilings, drying sails—even the skeleton of a perished pirate. "We wanted to have a real village, as real as you could make it,"[62] White said, by which he meant as "real" as a theme park could get. Rock and Water Scapes Inc. made the wharf with "wooden" pilings by plastering steel pipes and pounding them with wood-grain mold. The company built "rocks" by manufacturing natural rock formations, but they broke new ground with Skull Mountain, a giant skull peeking behind shrubs, watered by horticulturalists trained to scale up and down the rock pile.

The village hosted The Battle of Buccaneer Bay, a simulated sea battle between two 90-foot ships: the *Hispaniola* versus the *Royal Britannia*, a 75,000-pound ship running through a million-gallon lagoon. "These are not toys in Disneyland—these are complete, $10 million ships," Wynn said. "People's appetites get bigger. It takes more for people to go 'Wow.'"[63]

White thoroughly researched eighteenth-century ships, and worked with three English sculptors to carve out sterns and figureheads. "I wanted them to be over the top, but to have an authentic look,"[64] he said of the steel and fiberglass ships. The galleons

5.7 A pirate leaps from his ship into the whitecaps of Buccaneer Bay, Treasure Island, 1993.

would shoot 45-foot fireballs at each other, bombs even exploding in the village. At the end of the show, the *Britannia* would sink completely, water covering the entire deck. The press release stated: "After all, this is Las Vegas—the pirates always win."

But Wynn did not want just your average sinking ship. "He also wanted it to keel as it sunk so that it didn't look plastic, just going straight under,"[65] explained Bill Mensching, who was in charge of building the boats. Wynn demanded two-inch swells in the lagoon, and whitecaps on the waves. Sixty wave machines did the trick, with the added bonus that the waves would also prevent the stagnant pool from fostering bacteria—they could not have the pirates suffering from dengue fever.

However, Wynn had difficulty getting the boats through the county fire, building, and highway departments. Requesting permission for propane storage, the blasting of flames, and a moving ship raised a deep existential problem: administrators did not know how to classify the ships. They considered "unoccupied buildings," but finally settled on two completely different categories. The *Hispaniola* was classified as a sign. The moving *Britannia*, on the other hand, was named an "amusement transportation vehicle"—an unusual special designation inserted in the Clark County planning code.

To create more space for his spectacle, Wynn had arranged for a 24-foot setback from the Strip instead of the 50-foot county setback rule, arguing that his company would maintain the sidewalks. Quite literally, the pirates had invaded the Strip by covering the public sidewalk with a 500-foot-long stretch of wooden boardwalk. It reduced the remaining sidewalk to a sorry strip of concrete, so that everyone naturally walked on Treasure Island's privately operated grounds. Indeed, pirates do always win in Las Vegas. Wynn even moved the car entrance traditionally located on the front, the Strip side, to the South side in order to accommodate the show: another proof that casinos no longer fought for car traffic, but for pedestrians. He could not have a limo cut through the skirmishing pirates.

To get pedestrians into the pirate story, the village was designed in the form of a cove, with hillsides going up toward the Strip, so that the further people went over the boardwalk, the less of the Strip they would see. But it was more difficult to make Treasure Island's 2,900-room hotel tower, looming above the village, disappear. Architect Jon Jerde had to play a tricky scale game to humanize the size of it. He perfectly executed an optical illusion named the "window eye trick": he combined four sets of windows into a single visual element appearing as one window, fashioned out of shutters and a balcony décor. Whereas there were four rooms in the façade, there now appeared to be only one. This made the building appear four times smaller, but it also made the whole thing seem like a grotesque cartoon—like "a perfunctory version of a New Orleans townhouse stretched to 36 floors,"[66] noted Aaron Betsky.

If three decades before sign designers outclassed architects by building signs bigger than hotel towers, now theme designers dominated the image of resorts, all the way from the tower elevation to the false-front buildings and artificial sea cliffs. Wynn relegated his in-house team of architects to developing only the layout and construction details. They suffered under this tyranny of the theme. One architect said: "So many of

5.8 Guests cross a long wooden bridge into "a living fantasy—the pirate capital of the world," 1993. To humanize the Treasure Island's gigantic hotel tower with the smaller village, four rooms were clustered into only one window opening, each with fake shutters and a balcony.

the designs from so many of the casinos in Las Vegas did not come from architects, but set designers, who say, 'Hey, make this real.'"[67]

But the outsourcing of the resort's image to specialist image-makers signaled a new moment in the professionalization of Las Vegas's spectacle. Disney perfected his theme parks with teams drawing expertise from animators to engineers, so Las Vegas did too. Two architecture critics noted: "Only at Buccaneer Bay does it so far meet the standards of Disney."[68]

"Just tea and crumpets for the likes of them!" the pirate captain yells as the *Britannia* sails into the bay, calling his British counterpart a "son of a footman's goat." A tennis match of fireballs follows: "That's one for you, British scum!" The pirates appear to lose, their mast snaps, but they fire one final shot. The galleon is hit! Scorching flames engulf the deck. The galleon plunges into the sea, the British sailors jump, but the commander goes down with the ship. "Ahoy, you landlubbers," the pirate captain shouts to the spectators. "It's time to enter our village and share in our victory celebration."[69]

The crowds go along the wooden walkway into the casino. A guard watching the pier estimated between 4,000 to 8,000 people attending each show. "Three thousand of them walk away," the guard said, "but the rest—it's a steady flow; they go right in."[70]

"The name of the game is the walk-in business," Wynn said of the show that, at seven battles a night, drew seven million people in 1994.[71] The problem was that the exploding galleons also "hooked" passing car traffic, causing major jams. But Wynn had learned his lessons from building the volcano. Unlike the Mirage's more isolated "hook," he fully exploited the scorching frigates by building a restaurant overlooking them. Moreover, he had built a perimeter alarm system from the outset, so as soon as someone entered the water, it shut the whole crossfire down.

On the night of the Dunes implosion, financier Michael Milken said: "I met Steve in 1978 and felt that Steve embodied Walt Disney."[72] He had helped finance Treasure Island with $300 million worth of junk bonds—just before he had been indicted on 98 counts of racketeering and securities fraud, and spent two years behind bars. And so "D-Day" represented the peak of the new paradigm, with professional designers following Disney to the letter in building an "Adventure Resort." A Mirage Resorts spokesperson said: "It will take a lot to stay in competition if all you have is casino, rooms and food—and don't have a theme park."[73]

The opening of Treasure Island also signaled the end of the naked breast: whereas in 1957 the Dunes's trucker-owners had brought in the Strip's first bare-breasted showgirls, in 1993 Wynn built a $26 million theater for Cirque du Soleil, the French Canadian circus with *clothed* acrobats.

As the modernist tower and the red spade turned to ashes, with fireworks topping Disneyland's, the Strip's Disney phase rose to its peak. But it also invited a crucial question: Had Las Vegas taken the Disney mold too far?

The infomercial scripted the Dunes implosion as a treasure hunt beneath the building.

"Hey, mate, it appears you like pirates," Wynn said to little Robbie, vacationing at his casino with Mama and Papa.

"To me it's more than a hotel," he explained of Treasure Island to his new twelve-year-old pal.

"It's a gateway between fantasy and reality."

THE MICKEY MOUSE TRAP

Imagine walking up to a ten-story cubist lion, his paws stretched out, his eyes staring across the Luxor's Sphinx. You duck through the hole beneath his chin. Stars twinkle in a blue dome above a shimmering forest of green glass spires. Thunder roars, lighting bolts flash, but the storm subsides and a rainbow appears. You walk through a corn-stalk field where a tree scolds Dorothy, Scarecrow, Tin Man, and the Cowardly Lion for stealing apples. The yellow brick road kicks in. It takes you through the Emerald City gift shop, past rows and rows of beeping slot machines and a wizard flying a hot-air balloon, and drops you at the haunted mine. And this is just one of twelve rides at a massive theme park, at the end of the rainbow ceiling.

"Although other parks [casinos] have themed attractions, this is a full budget theme park compared to something like Disneyland,"[74] bragged a spokesperson for the new MGM Grand Hotel and Theme Park. This was not exactly true, since that same year Circus Circus added a $90 million amusement park which included robot dinosaurs munching plastic leaves. But MGM's $100 million theme park covered a whopping thirty-three acres, as large as Disneyland when it opened.

With "one in two people in the world visiting a theme park last year," the press release stated, a theme park would turn the casino into a "must-see." Moreover, it would bring in a new susceptible demographic. MGM Grand President Bob Maxey was optimistic: "Last year, only 5 percent of visitors to Las Vegas were children. That can go much, much higher."[75] The assumption was that as the children came, so would their

5.9 Dorothy, the Scarecrow, the Tin Man, and the Cowardly Lion walk the yellow brick road from the green-glass Emerald City, below twinkling stars, 1993.

parents—a demographic labeled by MGM Grand's chief executive as: "the ADDICTS—Adrenalin Driven Dual Income Couples That feel guilty about keeping their kids at home."[76]

By building a full-fledged theme park, Kirk Kerkorian, MGM's majority shareholder, had taken Disney literally. He never was a person to take on projects subtly anyway. At 5,005 rooms, it was the third time Kerkorian built the world's largest resort. He cunningly managed to circumvent lawsuits by making "sufficiently transformative" ripoffs of Disney's rides. The Lighting Bolt, his indoor space-themed roller coaster, resembled Disneyland's Space Mountain, but was just different enough to be a legal "original." But Kerkorian walked a fine line against a venerable opponent. In 1998, Disney would almost singlehandedly extend United States copyright regulations by twenty years, with legislation known as the Mickey Mouse Protection Act.

MGM also invented cartoon characters, including Wack E. Wolf and King Looey the Lion, an emasculated version of the studio's mascot, Leo the Lion. Looey was blown up ten stories tall to become the entrance to the casino, and, since there was no entrance to the theme park except through the casino, the figurehead also became the theme park entrance. The giant cartoon camouflaged the true goal of the theme park: to get parents to stray from the yellow brick road on their way to the rides, lured by the blackjack tables.

However, industry insiders questioned the theme park. Although some gaming analysts saw it as "a clever baby-sitting device,"[77] others worried that time spent at the rides could take away from time at the slot machines. Steve Wynn pondered: "I wonder if kids' rides, gambling and a hotel are really compatible. Gamblers don't like to trip over children."[78]

Designers were concerned with MGM's architecture. Other than the lion and the emerald-green façade, nothing of the cubist composition on the exterior revealed the Emerald City theme. One architect noted: "Aside from the fact that it's green, what else do you notice about it?"[79] The MGM Grand was precisely that: grand—as in huge, not architecturally sophisticated.

But MGM predicted that the theme park alone would lure 20,000 extra people a day into a giant Mickey Mousetrap, fresh meat for a ravenously hungry gambling machine. They even added a 15,200-seat event arena, bigger than Madison Square Garden.

Hoteliers doubted whether the company could get high-quality labor, particularly since Kerkorian had shunned union workers. But MGM had fully taken on Disney's attitude toward both organized labor and management: Disney "cast" employees, schooled them at the "Disney University to work "on stage," dealing with visitors as upper-case "G" Guests, not lower-case "c" customers. Meanwhile, at the MGM Grand, rainbow-colored-outfitted "cast members" were to go to the "University of Oz," so they could greet Guests more perfectly with: "Have a *grand* day."

In dedicating thirty-four acres solely to children, had the MGM Grand taken the Disney model too far? At Treasure Island and at the Mirage, the theme attractions were built as a lure to enhance the gaming experience. But at MGM the rides were almost

5.10 A 10-story cubist Looey the Lion is the entrance to the emerald-green MGM Grand Casino and Theme Park, 1994. Photograph courtesy of Alan McFaden, Panoramio.

as important as the casino. "It's one thing for the place to be user-friendly to the whole family because the family travels together," Wynn said. "It's quite a different thing to sit down and dedicate creative design energy to build for children. I'm not, ain't gonna, not interested. I'm after Mom and Dad."[80]

But the MGM Grand managed to draw between 50,000 and 60,000 visitors a day. And with gambling deemphasized, it was the first resort that could structurally rely on corporate sponsorships, with Coca-Cola logos and products—another idea from theme parks such as Disney's.

MGM Grand's King Looey, as well as its competing Sphinx, the pirates, and the erupting volcano, had broadened Las Vegas's appeal. It led the Las Vegas Visitors and Convention Authority to adopt a new marketing slogan in 1994, "A World of Excitement: In One Amazing Place," without making a single reference to gaming—it would have taken "the Happiest Place on Earth," if Disney had not copyrighted it.

Las Vegas was still very different from other parts of the United States; it had legalized gambling, and was in close proximity to legalized prostitution. Architecture had blurred the difference between image and reality. "The place is no longer considered racy or naughty by most people,"[81] *Time* magazine wrote. The Disney strategy helped give Las Vegas a G rating. But hardcore gamblers saw their Sin City defiled by wholesome family fun. *The Village Voice* wrote: "The traditional sleaze and cheese that had always made this place a great weekend refuge from the monotony of an ordered and decorous life are being swept away by a lava flow of respectability and Family Values."[82]

Encapsulating gambling in fantasy and fairytales helped to remove gaming's stigma, but it also achieved something more cynical. It led families astray.

"You go up to a woman sitting in a casino," Wynn said, "and she's playing a slot machine with both hands and you ask her, 'Are you a gambler?' and she says, 'Me? Oh, no, I'm just here on vacation with my husband and kids.' And you know, she's right. She's not a gambler."[83]

Moreover, a major ethical dilemma arose. Much as the Ronald McDonald clown had given unsavory fast food a smiling face, Looey the Lion familiarized minors with gambling. Not that this was a dilemma the gaming industry liked to entertain, especially since the Disney strategy appeared to work. In 1994 visitor count was at 29 million, up a staggering 20 percent over the year before, whereas Atlantic City's grew only 3 percent. In 1995, 30 percent of all Americans had visited Vegas, twice as many as in 1989. Las Vegas now had nine of the world's ten largest hotels, and the world's most hotel rooms at 87,000. But the key question was: as the families came, would they blow their savings?

The *New York Times* described a San Diego couple who, in a departure from previous trip behavior, brought their newborn and a nanny. "[Her] eyes were like saucers when we walked into the Emerald City at MGM," the mother said. "She even sang the words to 'We're off to see the wizard' as we walked down the Yellow Brick Road. That's why we came."[84] But the reporter also noted that the couple, in another departure from their typical trip behavior, had "left their bankroll at home." Perhaps the Mickey Mouse trap was a double-edged sword: on one hand more families, on the other miserly gamblers.

Until the numbers rolled in, it was up in the air whether the MGM Grand's Emerald-City-colored façade, and with it the closest Disney approximation of a casino to date, was going to be a reference to the color of money.

THE DISNEYFICATION OF LAS VEGAS

The 1992 opening of Euro Disney in Paris ignited a cultural interest in "Disneyfication," as European intellectuals were forced to theorize how American consumer "culture" had arrived in the epicenter of "real" European culture. The term initially referred to Disney's "shameless process" of making cartoons by "reducing" original works, one researcher wrote. "Magic, mystery, [and] individuality, were consistently destroyed when a literary work passed through his machines that had been taught there was only one correct way to draw."[85] But the term quickly came to represent much more, as the process by which the principles behind Disney's theme parks came to dominate the world. It referred to the rapid increase of themed environments that defy the historical and geographical context and rely on privatization, control, merchandising, corporate sponsorship, and company culture[86]—Disneyland's business model.

While Disney lay at the roots of this global trend, the new center was Las Vegas. Where some malls had theme parks, Las Vegas went above and beyond, with a robotic Bacchus toasting from his cup. Where themed restaurant chains such as Planet Hollywood had elaborate décors, Las Vegas's restaurants still outdid them: for instance at Caesars's "Magical Empire," with a five-story stage and fireballs shooting from a dragon-toothed cave. Where other places had fantasy accommodation, such as West Edmonton's Fantasyland Hotel, with beds inside an igloo dome, Vegas still topped it, with rooms overlooking a spewing volcano and scorching frigates. "These hotels naturally proliferate in Las Vegas," wrote the *New York Times*, "the Galapagos Islands for fantasy hotels in terms of sheer diversity of the species."[87] The sociologist Mark Gottdiener, in *The Theming of America*, considered Las Vegas the "theme park capital of the United States."[88]

Critics saw pure evil at play, going back to Walt's "lifelong rage to order, control and keep clean any environment that he inhabited."[89] In his cartoons, he had turned a real mouse into a wholesome, hairless, sterile and, as a consequence, more universally likable mouse. Even cows were drawn udderless, and forced to wear clothes. He manipulated theme park visitors just as easily, through people-movers, lines, and security checkpoints. Philosopher Umberto Eco wrote: "Disneyland is a place of total passivity. Its visitors must agree to behave like robots."[90] The most sinister side of Disneyland was the way Walt had hidden his corporate agenda. Not a single police officer could be seen on the street, yet it was under high surveillance by a single, omnipresent private corporation. Eco objected to the false fronts: "The Main Street façades are presented to us as toy houses and invite us to enter them, but their interior is always a disguised supermarket, where you buy obsessively, believing that you are still playing."[91]

Las Vegas was not much different. Casino developers had hidden their ulterior motive by wrapping gambling in fantasy and fun. They had deliberately placed restrooms, check-in desks, people-movers, and escalators inside casino mazes so complex that visitors were bound to lose themselves to a craps game. They placed unknowing guests under surveillance with undercover private security and CCTV. They had even gone beyond Disney's level of control, creating human drones so glued to slot machines that they are too oblivious to move when ambulance personnel try to rescue neighboring gamblers dying of a heart attack.

City governments nationwide had deliberately adopted Disney strategies too. As conservative governments reduced urban-renewal funds, they implemented laissez-faire urban planning to attract private-sector investments, typically privatizing streets, squares and parks, placing them under private-sector management. They looked at Disney's iconic image culture of public space, along with its seamless private management of urban areas: spotless, tourist-friendly, and without "blight."

Critics saw this as by far the most threatening strand of Disneyfication, which grew to become a metaphor for the sanitization of urban life. For instance, in the early 1990s, the New York City government partnered with the private sector to rid Times Square

5.11 An LCD canopy projects video over five entire city blocks in Fremont Street, among casinos' flashing neon and flickering light bulbs, 1998.

of sex shops, X-rated movie theaters, and live nude shows. In came the squeaky-clean company flagships of Ernst and Young, Reuters, and a Disney store. The quintessential urban square had been turned into what the *New Yorker* described as "a cold-blooded corporate simulacrum of an amusement park."[92]

Still, Las Vegas would top that. In an effort to avert an economic slum in downtown's Glitter Gulch, Las Vegas's epicenter of "grind joint" casinos, the city government decided to build a pedestrian zone. Jon Jerde, Treasure Island's architect, came aboard. He covered Fremont Street with a large vaulted canopy, seven stories tall, covered in LCDs, the world's largest electric screen.

If Disneyland, according to Michael Sorkin, was a "television city,"[93] television-financed and *like* television, broadcasting a universal image for mass consumption, downtown Las Vegas had taken it further. It had actually become a television, the size of five city blocks, sponsored by Coca-Cola.

By 1995, Las Vegas had become the undisputed overlord of Disneyfication—but with serious chinks in its armor.

"Consider Las Vegas, the experience capital of America," wrote Pine and Gilmore in *The Experience Economy*. "Virtually everything about Vegas is a designed experience, from the slot machines at the airport to the gambling casinos that line the Strip; from the themed hotels and restaurants to the singing, circus, and magic shows."[94]

Was there something to learn from the new Disneyesque Las Vegas? Just like Disney, Las Vegas had professionalized the design of customer experience. The city had become a pioneer in the "experience economy," in which companies compete by orchestrating memorable events for their customers. Architects could perhaps learn from Disney that design is not only about practically accommodating bodies in concrete boxes, but also about delighting the mind with narrative. For instance, in contrast to Disneyland, one critic wrote, "most of the vast concrete plazas filling our downtowns today are helpful only to those whose fantasies lean toward Kafka."[95]

However, critics objected to the Strip's "Disneyfication." But were their objections nothing more than an elitist critique of middle-class aesthetics, just like movie critics trashing Disney's universally likable movies, enjoyable for millions of people?

Even on city planning grounds there was something to learn from Disney, as there was from Las Vegas. Disneyland, with its advanced technology and management, had clean streets, no blackouts, with fireworks and parades running like clockwork. Special tractors in underground tunnels made deliveries, without disrupting the peace and quiet on Main Street, U.S.A. Disneyland also had no need of garbage trucks, since trash was pumped down through vacuum tubes to underground garbage stations. Moreover, since all the utility lines went through the tunnel, there would never be a sewage truck stinking up Magic Land. Back in Las Vegas, individual casinos had underground tunnels with hidden superior infrastructure—even including miles of liquor lines, automating alcohol supply.

Moreover, the Disney strategy seemed to be faring well in Las Vegas. By 1994, the six Disney-themed mega-resorts were generating 50 percent of the city's revenue. In addition, Las Vegas's Disney style had already started to spread. The city led the world in creating themed environments. The entire theme design industry's slogan had even become "You don't look up 'volcano' in the Yellow Pages."[96]

But despite all the developers' efforts, from the scorching frigates to the pirates growling 'Arrr,' there was something odd about Las Vegas's version of Disney. "Theming is still in its infancy in Las Vegas and the quality is uneven," noted architecture critics Frances Anderton and John Chase. "Hotel/casinos frequently jumble multiple conflicting themes, or stop and start themed areas without thinking about the edges or juxtapositions."[97]

While Las Vegas's designers appeared to follow Disney to the letter, the requirements of gaming in Las Vegas always superseded Disney's rules of Imagineering. A casino space is a difficult animal to theme, because most gamblers prefer not to be distracted. In the Egyptian-themed Luxor, for instance, designers had to abandon the theme at some points—at a sarcophagus craps table, for example.

Moreover, in contrast to Disney's in-house production of its theme parks, casino companies outsourced theming and construction. The gaming corporations typically only designed the layout of the casino and hotel, hiring specialized companies to develop the overall concept. This "extreme segregation of the roles of designer, architect, builder, and engineer," noted one researcher, created "considerable difficulty of managing."[98] And unlike the perfectionist Walt Disney, Las Vegas's developers built fast to get a quick return on their investment, even if this meant a less refined execution of the theme.

Furthermore, Disney had managed to avoid the "Danger of Contradictions" between different thematic lands. Disney's chief designer said: "Walt was the inventor of the three-dimensional cross-dissolve. He didn't want people to turn abruptly from Main Street, U.S.A.—*bang!*—into Adventureland."[99] Subtle clues gradually indicated change: concrete walking surfaces changed to cut stone, or musical sounds gave way to animal growls.

But in Las Vegas, pharaohs, pirates, and "wienies" competed, rather than complemented one another. Disneyland could make Cinderella Castle appear larger, thanks to the lower surrounding context of Main Street, U.S.A., with its forced perspective directed toward the castle. Back in Las Vegas, the Luxor's ten-story Sphinx did not anticipate another large feline, Looey the Lion, staring back from across the road.

Unlike the monopolistic Disneyland, there are multiple competing "Disneylands" on the Las Vegas Strip. And whereas the people-movers in Disney were employed to manage traffic for the park as a whole, on the Strip developers use people-movers against each other as weapons of mass traffic.

The paradox is that the competition on the Strip that led to the culmination of the Disney paradigm would also lead to its exhaustion. In contrast to Disneyland, where there is no internal competition, competing resorts were more eager to use the latest technology, special effects, and fashionable colors—all of which get obsolete quickly, as technology and color palettes date as fast as seasons change. Even worse, it turned out that the new family image sat uneasily with a town previously known as Sin City—with gamblers just as uncomfortable dodging baby-strollers as parents were exposing their kids to smut peddlers handing out leaflets advertising "dancers." The final fall came when it turned out that Disneyfication did not prove to be the massive profit engine it was in other places. A 1997 survey showed adults spending $500 per day at luxury casinos, but only $100 when their kids were with them.[100]

By then the backlash had already begun. The planning of Disney monuments was stalled—for instance, the Desert Kingdom, an Indiana Jones-style casino. Or Countryland U.S.A., a family-friendly casino with two hotel towers the shape of cowboy boots—a classic case of form follows footwear. The River Nile was filled in, the camels were discarded, the skull and crossbones axed, the buccaneers fired to make way for "sexy sirens." MGM Grand's theme park was demolished in favor of an adults-only pool, Dorothy and her crew got sent down the gray asphalt road, and the ten-story lion was cut down with chainsaw swipes—although this change was as much a function of

5.12 The Las Vegas skyline is a battle between the Strip's clashing and competing "Disneylands."

the fallout with Disney as it was with *feng shui*: Chinese gamblers found it inauspicious to enter a casino underneath a lion's chin.

Today, only the Excalibur's castle and the MGM Grand's emerald-green façade continue as larger-than-life monuments to Disney, since they were too expensive to change.

Ironically, while the Strip never achieved full Disneyfication, this was precisely why Las Vegas was more interesting than Disneyland. Where Disneyland's private Main Street, U.S.A. would always be free of picket lines or homeless people, in Las Vegas, on the public space of the Strip, protesters, street vendors, and a few remaining neon casinos advertising nude showgirls clashed with the fairytale castle and Peter Pan galleons. All these elements of a "real" city led to dangerous but exciting contradictions within the Disneyesque myth corporations tried to re-create.

However, during the Disney phase, Las Vegas's gaming industry had consolidated. Only three companies owned the majority of the Strip. If this oligopoly intensified further, architects Steven Izenour and David A. Dashiel III observed, Las Vegas's designers would be hindered, just like Disney's, by the demands of a single client, resulting in "sameness." Las Vegas could become like the "blandly homogenized good taste of Disney World … boring as only paradise can be?"[101]

Whether this moment would come or not, in the meantime, the Strip's partial Disneyfication created a unique collage of Las Vegas-style Disney, where pharaohs clashed with hawkers, a pyramid with a castle, and a ten-story Lion with a Sphinx.

6

Sim City (1995—2001)

Our buildings command a special kind of attention. An architecture of spectacle, where in the tradition of the grand palace or the gilded opera house or the soaring civic monument, or even that notable American instance, the skyscraper, we provide a show to the public that starts on the sidewalk.[1]

—Glenn Schaeffer, president of Circus Circus Enterprises

Built to be exactly what it is, [Las Vegas] is the real, real fake at the highest, loudest and most authentically inauthentic level of illusion and invention.[2]

—Ada Louise Huxtable, New York Times

By the late 1990s, developers like Mirage had evolved from mimicking Disney fairy tales to simulating authentic architectural heritage. Blossoming with historical monuments, the Las Vegas Strip offered visitors a condensed version of a Grand Tour, now endowed with American commercialism and convenience. Renaissance connoisseurs could scrutinize the replica Campanile and the Bridge of Sighs. Beaux-Arts fans would recognize a full-scale knockoff of the Paris Opera House. Modernist architecture buffs, too, could witness icons such as the Seagram building. Even Steve Wynn, who once saw himself as Walt Disney, now presented himself as the "Count" of Bellagio.

Although Las Vegas developers had exploited the past before, building replicas of nineteenth-century Western structures in the 1940s, developers now went to great lengths to reproduce well-known monuments from cultural tourist destinations, including Paris and Venice. They did not simply cite historic buildings, with an occasional column or architrave. Taking postmodernism to the next level, they aimed to replicate cities, complete with cobblestone streets and gondola-filled canals.

Las Vegas fit into a worldwide trend of "manufacturing" heritage.[3] World expositions had been organized in Europe as early as the nineteenth century, featuring entire copied streets. But by the 1990s, whole neighborhoods were built in traditional architectural styles, most notably by the urban design movement "New Urbanists," whose residential communities, such as Celebration in Florida, harked back to an idealized early-twentieth-century version of small-town America.

As the Strip lined up with icons of historic and modern architecture, architectural theorists lined up to object. The Strip, they claimed, displayed extreme symptoms of society's preference for the superficial "fake"—a simulated and commercial bastard of reality.

But while theorists saw Las Vegas's architecture as the epitome of simulation, they failed to notice how the Strip's investors had feigned the "real" too. Developers financed the Sim City monuments with large collateral loans, secured against a tiny percentage of equity, which failed to reflect the actual risks of the investment. When bankers finally took notice, there was nothing fake about the way Las Vegas's economy tanked.

And these billion-dollar structures were not, of course, true replicas. The Strip could not accommodate entire cities, nor did casino developers desire them. Designers reconfigured a city into an instantly recognizable and easily consumable image by focusing on its most iconic period: Manhattan of the early twentieth century, Paris of the nineteenth century, and Venice of the sixteenth century. They incorporated only the best-known monuments, and took plenty of artistic license—leading to symbolic tensions with the original. At times, the "hyperreal" copy may have been perceived as more "convincing." Philosopher Umberto Eco, having seen too many wax versions of the Last Supper, when he finally saw the real painting at the Getty, was disappointed: "I cast absent glances on these drearily authentic pictures."[4]

And so the Las Vegas Eiffel Tower stood on top of a Paris Opera House, Venetian canals hovered above a casino, and the Manhattan skyline was amalgamated into a single structure, circled by a yellow-cab-style roller coaster. Migrating heritage to Las Vegas led to juxtapositions so incredible that the Strip became the world's center of the *original* fake.

THE ENCHANTED AXE

In 1996, only three years after its opening, MGM Grand, the resort that had so slavishly co-opted Disney, spent a quarter of a billion dollars to remove all associations with the *Wizard of Oz*. Management closed the theme park and razed Emerald City.

The eviction of Dorothy marked the beginning of a process of de-Disneyfication for the entire Strip. Until then, developers had catered to middle-class families, giving them more theme park rides and fantasy fun. But gaming analysts came to the conclusion that families were spending more time at the Disney attractions than at the gambling tables. As of 1996, Las Vegas surpassed Orlando as the leading hotel room capital in the United States, with more than 99,000 rooms, yet gaming revenues remained nearly the same.[5]

The backlash was swift and brutal. The Luxor pyramid filled in its "Nile" river ride. The company's vice-president said: "The first thing guests should see when they enter the Luxor is its casino. Period. Not hieroglyphics, not boats, not fancy rides."[6]

MGM Grand's "Emerald City" morphed into the "City of Entertainment." Its "Yellow Brick Road" became a "Studio Walk." The Tin Man and 700 cast members were axed.

Rather than presenting the elimination of the *Wizard of Oz* family theme as the correction of an error, it was presented as something Walt Disney would have done. MGM Grand's chairman said: "It's like when you go to Disneyland, you want to see something new."[7]

But the truth was that Disney's Las Vegas fairy tale had come to a brutal end.

ICONIC FAILURE

By the time Disney was written out of Las Vegas, developers were desperately searching for a new casino design paradigm. The first alternative came from Las Vegas developer Bob Stupak, whose extravagant approach earned him the nickname "Vegas Guy"— a throwback to the 1960s, before corporate boardrooms ruled the Strip. "With his 1,000-decibel sports coats and dress shirts opened to the Vegas minimum two buttons deep," his biographer wrote, "Stupak was a ringing stereotype of the old-style operator as one part craps dealer, one part con man."[8]

Stupak came to Las Vegas in 1971, and built a casino on an unpromising piece of real estate just north of the Sahara. To draw attention to the casino, he christened it with the name, along with a massive sign to bear it: *BOB STUPAK'S WORLD FAMOUS MILLION DOLLAR HISTORIC GAMBLING MUSEUM.* Stupak said: "The name was about 10 feet longer than the casino."[9]

But an air-conditioner caught fire and burned his gambling "museum" down. Stupak then built Vegas World, lined his casino with silver wallpaper, and hung astronauts and satellites from the ceiling. When others had long abandoned "tacky" neon, Stupak commissioned the world's largest sign, shaped like a rocket, for his casino. After a windstorm blew the sign down, Stupak wanted to build a bigger one. He hired Ned Baldwin, the architect of Toronto's CN Tower, to design the world's tallest freestanding tower, at 1,815 feet.

The design called for a three-legged structure, "The Shaft," carrying an observation deck, "The Pod," outfitted with laser lighting. The Federal Aviation authorities, however, objected to the light-shooting phallus obstructing airplanes descending into the nearby airport. Stupak compromised on a tower of 1,148 feet—even so, he could still boast that it was the United States's tallest freestanding tower, complete with the world's highest wedding chapel.

But the construction made it only so far. Stupak's contractor built the tower's north leg at an incorrect angle, then his money ran out. The structure stood incomplete at

6.1 The Stratosphere, America's tallest observation tower, features a "Big Shot" thrill ride that catapults guests up the tower's mast, 2011. Photograph courtesy of Antoine Taveneaux, Wikimedia Commons.

510 feet, with one crooked leg, when Lyle Berman of Grand Casinos joined the venture, allowing Stupak to complete an initial public offering. Stupak and Berman finished the project and expanded it into a half-billion-dollar mega-complex with a 1,500-room hotel. The partnership made it clear that individuals like Stupak could no longer compete against corporations.

Stupak then paid special attention to the twelve-story circular pod, including its revolving restaurant and the "Big Shot" and "High Roller" rides around the tower's mast. The designs called for a giant, six-million-dollar mechanical gorilla, "King Kong," climbing up on one of the structure's legs. A few dozen tourists at a time would be "In the Grip of the Gorilla," strapped around the primate's belly. "In New York, it was just a movie," Stupak said of his simulacrum. "In Las Vegas, it's real."[10] As he anticipated, the tower opened to hordes of visitors—445,000 in only five weeks. But something happened that he did not expect. Of the $26.8 million revenue, only a $7.1 million profit was generated from the casino.[11] After visiting the pod, people did not stay in the casino. While the Stratosphere succeeded as an icon, it failed as a mousetrap.

Stupak resigned as the board's chairman. King Kong was axed. Five months after the opening, Stratosphere filed for bankruptcy. The largest tower in the United States had become the largest bankruptcy in Nevada.

The Stratosphere's failure left a lasting impression on developers. Although Stupak's tower offered an exciting architectural possibility for the casino complex, they ultimately had to look elsewhere for a model that made business sense.

THE *BELLE ÉPOQUE* OF THE MEGA-SHED

On the other side of the Strip, two months after the Stratosphere premiere in 1996, the Monte Carlo opened with a completely contrary architectural approach. If the Stratosphere was a tower of the future, then the Monte Carlo was a bastion of tradition, complete with replicas of the Paris Opera House, Beaux-Arts statues, and gaslit cobblestone promenades.

Glenn Schaeffer, the key person behind the Monte Carlo, came to Las Vegas from Wall Street, and with the polished lingo of a writer quickly rose to become chief financial officer of Circus Circus Corporation. Schaeffer started with demographic research. He said: "As baby boomers are aging they are becoming more affluent and we are coming into the biggest market we have ever had."[12] Since their nests were empty, with more discretionary income and time to play, Schaeffer chose baby boomers rather than families.

But how to get them to the casino? "Travel entertainment is a big part of what these people want,"[13] assumed Schaeffer, noting the growth of mass tourism. He decided on an architectural strategy not too dissimilar from Stupak's. "Our job in this business is to create a crowd. So you build monuments that must be seen," he said. By monuments, however, he did not mean a tower like the Stratosphere. He was going to build *literal* monuments, by replicating historical ones.

In contrast to Circus's fantasy approach a few years earlier, Schaeffer mandated Dougall Design to produce "a classical theme."[14] Roving the globe for tourist city monuments, they chose Monte Carlo as a reference, less for its gambling history than for its association with wealth. But designer Terry Dougall was not going to be confined by Monte Carlo alone. He wanted to evoke that particular Monte Carlo *feeling*. He developed a script around the period, rather than the place, of Monaco's casino by settling on the French *Belle Époque* architectural style. He furnished the casino with marble floors, crystal chandeliers, Victorian paintings, and cherry wood armoires. For the exterior façade, he obviously picked Monaco's Place du Casino, but then added the Paris Opera House and San Francisco's Palace of Fine Arts.

But even before they decided what it was going to be, architects and a gaming consultant had already designed the casino floor plan. Instead of radically reinventing the casino complex, like Stupak, Schaeffer relied on a tried and tested casino complex typology: a standard three-winged hotel tower containing thousands of rooms, standing on a one-story base housing the casino. Not only was it fast to build, it was highly tactical: the design would force thousands of guests staying at the 3,002-room hotel above into the casino below.

Only after these plans had been made did Dougall, who thought of his firm as "package designers," decide on the Monte Carlo bells and whistles.[15] The endeavor was similar to what the Stardust had done forty years earlier: only after the company had built the industrial barracks did it plaster a sign as long as a football field on the façade, which would later come to be known as a prototypical "decorated shed."[16] The Monte Carlo, a standard international-style skyscraper with a Styrofoam Paris Opera House in front, was effectively a high-rise version of this prototype: a decorated mega-shed.

In fact, not all the details of the *Belle Époque* imagery had been drawn out. Even during construction, the design was still being developed. One day during the building process, Construction Department head Bill Richardson laid down an important rule to avoid offending guests: the semi-clothed, two-story male and female Beaux-Arts statues could expose only "tits, but not dicks."[17]

In this high-speed building process, construction quality was sacrificed. Yet it was enough to make an impression to the undiscriminating customer, for a relatively low price. Although the Monte Carlo evoked wealth and class, it was built on a dime. It was a profitable paradox. As a result of the resort's private contracting company and adherence to the standard mega-shed, construction was completed under the $350 million budget, within its sixteen-month schedule. Never had this amount of square footage been built faster in the United States. Moreover, relative to the Stratosphere, it was built three times faster, almost three times cheaper, and contained double the rooms. But Stupak's tower won on originality. "This isn't a substitute for the real thing," the Stratosphere spokesperson said. "This is the real thing."[18]

Nonetheless, the standoff between the Monte Carlo and the Stratosphere, between Old European and contemporary architecture, had left a clear winner.

6.2 A rendering of the Monte Carlo shows a copy of Paris's Fontaines de la Concorde and other Belle Époque-inspired monuments below the generic hotel building.

While the replica Monte Carlo was still a skeleton, Las Vegas developers soon fixated on fleshing out the copy.

The hunting season for heritage had opened.

A CITY SO NICE, THEY BUILT IT TWICE

Imagine King Kong randomly rearranging the Manhattan skyline, grabbing only the most cinematic of all icons: Lady Liberty, the Chrysler Building, and the Empire State Building. Throw in a green felt Central Park, and you have New York New York, the Strip's latest casino complex. Far from Hollywood fiction, this was sound business strategy by two seasoned companies, Primadonna and MGM Grand. They expected to eclipse the Monte Carlo by choosing the Greatest City. It was not that Monte Carlo's monuments were camera-shy, but to Americans, the Big Apple was better understood.

New York's skyline was distilled to a mishmash of ten skyscrapers, congealed into a single mass like a souvenir slow globe. The Lever House and Seagram Building were scaled down to about one third of their original size. The lesser-known CBS Building, the "Black Rock" of the New York skyline, was added for contrast. Together they formed one single 2,100-room hotel building with a nice skyline arrangement—unlike the Monte Carlo, whose monotonous mass and thousands of identical windows meant it was known as a "maximum security resort."

The interior of the hotel building, however, did not match the exterior tower slices. This led to an odd situation in which one could go up the Empire State elevator to end up in the Seagram Building, simply by passing through a corridor. But down in the casino, areas were themed after New York public spaces and neighborhoods, for instance the Central Park-themed casino, complete with benches, street lamps and a green-carpeted floor. Greenwich Village-themed eateries brought New York street scenes to Las Vegas, including mock graffiti.

The exterior of the casino building was a recombination of New York's most recognizable and respectable icons, including the New York City Public Library, the United Nations Building Assembly Hall, and the Ellis Island Immigrant Receiving Station. As icing on the cake, a roller coaster with yellow checker cabs circled around and through the fake New York skyline, bringing the nostalgia of early-1900s Coney Island into Manhattan. The coaster even hosted wedding ceremonies (just don't puke on the bride).

"If you just went down and photographed New York," one designer said, "you wouldn't get that picture."[19] The resort represented the epitome, not the photocopy, of the Greatest City. More New York than New York, it was the quintessential simulacrum: *New York New York*.

But while New York New York appeared tongue in cheek, it had achieved something devious. By cannibalizing New York City's monuments of political and corporate culture, the casino successfully rode on their reputation. For instance, a 150-foot-tall replica of Lady Liberty, two water-spraying fireboats at her side, stood as the resort's new roadside sign. She even graced the casino's logo. In creating this juxtaposition, New York New York associated gambling with the quintessential symbol of America.

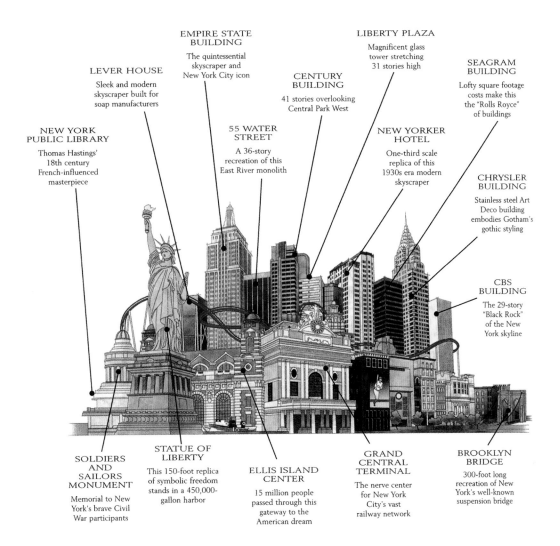

LEVER HOUSE

Sleek and modern skyscraper built for soap manufacturers

EMPIRE STATE BUILDING

The quintessential skyscraper and New York City icon

LIBERTY PLAZA

Magnificent glass tower stretching 31 stories high

SEAGRAM BUILDING

Lofty square footage costs make this the "Rolls Royce" of buildings

CENTURY BUILDING

41 stories overlooking Central Park West

NEW YORK PUBLIC LIBRARY

Thomas Hastings' 18th century French-influenced masterpiece

55 WATER STREET

A 36-story recreation of this East River monolith

NEW YORKER HOTEL

One-third scale replica of this 1930s era modern skyscraper

CHRYSLER BUILDING

Stainless steel Art Deco building embodies Gotham's gothic styling

CBS BUILDING

The 29-story "Black Rock" of the New York skyline

SOLDIERS AND SAILORS MONUMENT

Memorial to New York's brave Civil War participants

STATUE OF LIBERTY

This 150-foot replica of symbolic freedom stands in a 450,000-gallon harbor

ELLIS ISLAND CENTER

15 million people passed through this gateway to the American dream

GRAND CENTRAL TERMINAL

The nerve center for New York City's vast railway network

BROOKLYN BRIDGE

300-foot long recreation of New York's well-known suspension bridge

6.3 A New York New York brochure spells out the architectural references of the resort's "skyline," which is in fact one single hotel tower.

Not all New Yorkers appreciated their replica. The New York Stock Exchange was shocked to find Wall Street-derived signage, such as "New York $lot Exchange," in the casino's "Financial District," where the cashiers were placed. There was even a replica of its Corinthian-columned façade. The Stock Exchange sued the resort, accusing it of tarnishing its reputation.

Architecture critic Ada Louise Huxtable, in her book *The Unreal America*, wrote: "The themed environment that so frequently and profitably trashes its sources is a bowdlerized and impoverished version of the real thing"[20]—even though rumor had it that the New York author had never visited Las Vegas. But critic Paul Goldberger argued that New Yorkers should be "flattered" that the Strip chose the Big Apple: "After all, nobody's making a resort called 'Pittsburgh, Pennsylvania.'"[21]

Meanwhile, just as New York New York was a sanitized version of the original city, the real New York had been sanitized too. Mayor Giuliani had made Times Square "safe" by ridding it of street hawking and peep shows. In contrast, the space in front of New York New York thrived with all the "messiness" associated with a real city, including smut peddlers. Historian Nezar AlSayyad asked: "Has Las Vegas become *the* real [New York] city?"[22]

The tension between New York City and its copy in the Mojave Desert led to another incident in 2011. The United States Post Office had issued a Forever "Statue of Liberty" Stamp, supposed to show the Statue of Liberty. One stamp collector, on closer inspection, realized the stamp did not depict New York's Lady Liberty, but her Las Vegas bastard sister. The stamp designers had accidentally chosen the wrong stock photo. By the time the error was discovered, over 10 billion Forever stamps—the postage that never, ever expires—had already been printed. This led to frustration in New York, and great amusement in Las Vegas. An MGM spokesman responded: "Everyone thought the post office was honoring just one great American institution when in reality they were honoring two—the Statue of Liberty and Las Vegas."[23]

THE COUNT OF LAS VEGAS

A decade before, casinos had announced entertainers like Liberace or topless showgirls. In 1998, the Strip's latest casino, created by Steve Wynn, was different. The man responsible for a roaring volcano now maintained that "people care for quiet moments of reflective beauty."[24] To all his guests, he showed a $47.5 million Van Gogh, *Woman in a Blue Dress*.

What started with an art budget of $10 million ballooned into a $300 million museum collection. Going against the casino design tradition of avoiding impressive decorations at all costs—a gaming consultant claimed that it "draws the attention of visitors away from the gambling equipment"[25]—Wynn commissioned artist Dale Chihuly to create a 50,000-pound glass-blown flowered lobby ceiling. Immediately behind it, Wynn placed an ornate botanic garden with birds and butterflies.

Steve Wynn, who had dressed up as a pirate only a few years before, now presented himself as a cultured patron of the arts. The new image was the luxurious town of Bellagio.

Wynn's new resort used nineteenth-century masterpieces to lure a more upscale demographic. He persuaded high-end designer brands Chanel and Hermès to open boutiques. He seduced celebrity chefs to bring their gourmet restaurants, including Le Cirque. A decade earlier, they would never have dared to branch out to Las Vegas, home of the five-dollar buffet. The Bellagio marked the beginning of a process of gentrification that gradually displaced the middle-class Disneyland crowds.

To give customers a luxury experience, Wynn's architects innovated by placing the entire back-of-house, the countless service hallways and maintenance rooms, underground instead on the periphery. It gave Bellagio's front-of-house views of the surroundings. The restaurants looked out over patio lawns, and the shops along the "Via Bellagio," a glass-domed knockoff of Milan's nineteenth-century Galleria Vittorio Emanuele II, had views of the pool.

Architect Jon Jerde was tasked with making the giant hotel appear boutique-like and small. While Renaissance-style villas broke down the scale of the building's large base, he overscaled moldings and friezes to reduce the scale of the hotel tower. He also perfectly executed the "window eye trick," making four rooms appear to be only one window in the façade. As a result, the thirty-seven-story colossus looked as if it had only sixteen floors. Meanwhile, the gigantesque sign was made to look like a sixteenth-century bell tower.

"Bellagio is one of the few casinos in Las Vegas that actually looks good in daylight,"[26] the *New York Times* noted. "The master builder of Vegas,"[27] *Time* said of Wynn.

To capture that "resort" feeling, Wynn set the hotel a thousand feet off the Strip, so he could dig an eight-acre replica of Lake Como. A 1990 ordinance, however, had barred new artificial lakes, characterizing them as a "wasteful" use of the limited water supply in the Mojave Desert. Wynn persuaded legislators to allow the lake in exchange for the water rights of his property, thanks to a new ordinance so specific that only the Bellagio could exploit it. Inside the lake, Wynn built a $40 million musical fountain as extensive as three football fields. Despite its grand scale, he gave pedestrians intimate views of the fountain by surrounding the lake with idyllic alcoves. Special underwater cannon "hyperscooters" were developed, shooting 75-gallon water bursts up 460 feet into the sky, while robotic nozzled "oarsmen" sprayed water gracefully from side to side. The fountains were then taught to dance to American classics and Italian arias, including recordings by great singers such as Pavarotti, by the Emmy-Award-winning choreographer of *Dirty Dancing*.

The fountain operated every fifty minutes, keeping up to 17,000 gallons of water up in the air at a time. As its water evaporated, it dramatically lowered the temperature—as well as Las Vegas's freshwater supply. Ironically, vanishing water was a theme inside the resort as well, where Cirque du Soleil's new show "O" was being performed in, on, and above a 1.5-million-gallon pool, made to appear and disappear. (It was going to be called *Eau*, French for water, but it was feared that Americans would pronounce it "Eww.")

6.4 Fountains burst 460 feet upward from an artificial lake at the Bellagio, an amalgamation of Tuscan-style villas, domed Galleria arcades, and a stretched-out Italian Renaissance palace, 1997.

Wall Street bankers, however, saw disappearing profits. Wynn had managed to fund his $2 billion resort with collateralized loan obligations, a new financial structure pioneered by Michael Milken's company, which secured an above-average amount of financing at a relatively low percentage of equity. But the Bellagio needed to generate a staggering $2.5 million revenue a day to service the loans.

The Bellagio marked a shift in financing from equity markets to commercial banks and collateral financing. In 1996 alone, banks lent a total of $10 billion to ITT Corporation, Circus Circus, Mirage, and MGM Grand. This unprecedented amount of capital—*Casino Journal* spoke of a new "Gold Rush"[28]—helped corporations expand with billion-dollar casinos. But this type of collateralized debt—the culprit behind the 2008 global financial crisis—also led to towering interest payments.

Wynn, however, had a plan: he was going to charge about 30 percent more than the Mirage rates at the time. "With 90,000 rooms in town, you can have 2,600 that cost more,"[29] he reasoned. But when three other developers followed that philosophy, and opened within a period of twelve months, that new business model was stretched to its limits.

THE MEGA-CASINO CLUSTER

In 1999, pedestrians could zigzag along a path of statues of Oriental griffins, vine-covered cliffs with waterfalls, and a looming stupa. Arriving at British colonial style buildings, they could scuba with sharks in an aquarium, or surf on six-foot waves on a white sandy beach. This new resort, called Mandalay Bay, referred less to Mandalay, the largest city in Burma (which has neither ruins nor a bay), and more broadly to the edge of the British Empire in Asia—enhanced with a whole lot of marble, and minus the dengue fever.

Even Circus Circus Enterprises, a company known for catering to RV crowds, had gone the way of Mirage's Bellagio casino. Mandalay Bay replaced the Hacienda, which had pioneered catering to the middle classes in the 1950s. At exactly midnight Eastern Time, 9 p.m. in Las Vegas, New Year's Eve 1997, it blew the Hacienda to pieces. It used so many fireworks that Fox cut their coverage of the Times Square ball drop for it.

Mandalay Bay was the last piece of the puzzle of the Masterplan Mile, Circus Circus's mile-long contiguous piece of 230 acres of real estate along the south end of the Strip. This, the largest single-owned cluster of mega-resorts in the world, contained 12,000 hotel rooms altogether. By connecting Excalibur, Luxor, and Mandalay with internal moving walkways and a monorail, the mega-casino cluster had strung together the best experiences from empires spanning three millennia: from shark diving in colonial Burma to beer-drinking in medieval Bavaria.

This clustering of mega-resorts enabled casinos to share facilities and services, and, more importantly, helped to keep gamblers on Circus's property longer. The larger master plan included owning properties at all freeway exits to the Strip. No matter where cars turned off the highway, they would always find an off-ramp taking them to a Circus property nearby. Like owning all the consecutive properties in Monopoly, the mega-casino cluster worked better as a game of Mousetrap.

The company also built a series of skywalks to detour existing pedestrian bridges, which spanned Strip intersections to allow people to cross the road safely. "Today, they deposit customers on the sidewalk," Circus Circus President Schaeffer said. "We have a better idea. We are going to deposit customers onto a drawbridge at Excalibur so they can go directly into the casino."[30] In Las Vegas, pedestrian bridges, moving beltways, escalators, and monorails are never built for people's sake. For casino corporations, they are weapons of mass transportation.

The irony was that the casino developers had moved to the Strip's unincorporated land, outside of city limits, to avoid zoning plans and other restrictions. But the companies that had dodged city planners seventy years ago had become so large that they ended up conducting master planning after all, including land use and transport integration, as well as a warped form of community development. For instance, the mega-casino cluster effectively operated as a "Strip within a Strip," serving all key segments of the Las Vegas tourism market. Excalibur grabbed the low end, Luxor targeted the $60,000 to $80,000 crowd, and Mandalay was aimed at the $80,000 plus. This one mile of casinos, a sort of demographic black hole, sucked in all types of customers, then filtered them by price point.

"Somebody turns forty-nine years old every seven and a half seconds," Schaeffer explained of his key Mandalay demographic.[31] This "rock 'n' roll generation," the assumption was, wanted a "Woodstock without the mud": to party like it was 1969 but also enjoy *haute cuisine*, a 30,000-square-foot spa, and a fake beach. The fifty-year-olds would also like to imbibe wine from a four-story wine tower, complete with black-bodysuited waitresses scaling up and down the racks. They would appreciate chilled vodka from an ice block bar at "The Red Square," fronted by a 16-foot statue of a beheaded Lenin, complete with pigeon droppings streaking down his jacket.

Mandalay Bay even included a luxury Four Seasons Hotel on the upper floors of the gold-clad tower, pioneering multiple hotel brands within the same resort. This new business model seemed like a logical trend in the evolution of the ever-larger casino complex. As resorts were getting bigger, and wanted to cater to more types of crowds, they had to bring in specialist operators. The cluster had effectively become a frame for others to fill in, including hoteliers, restaurant and nightclub operators, almost in the way real cities are parceled out.

As the cluster brought in new elements, it also had to correct things that were not working. The Luxor, for instance, had trouble holding onto its demographic. Vice-President Anthony Alamo was in charge of a $350-million renovation to save the casino. He found that Asian customers avoided staying in the Luxor, since the pyramid's angular forms were reminiscent of a tomb and therefore represented bad luck for Chinese gamblers, plus the inclinator elevators crossed diagonally, like "killing breath energy lines"—a "Feng Shui *faux pas*."[32]

6.5 Mandalay Bay's fake beach attracts to the Mojave Desert pool revelers who might have gone to real beaches otherwise, 1999.

Alamo then built 2,000 additional rooms in separate ziggurat-shaped towers—not a pyramid. He also sharpened the Luxor's identity by removing the miniature Manhattan skyline inside the atrium to achieve the "consistency" of a solely Egyptian theme. As a final touch of authenticity, he had a plan to replace the fake Tutankhamun in the basement: "I want to put a real Egyptian mummy on display."[33] He negotiated renting a specimen from the Egyptian government. But when a government official inquired about the mausoleum venue, he was shocked to find that Alamo wanted to stick his forefather *inside* the casino: "You must build a special museum for it *outside* of the casino."

"If your mummy can't go in our casino," Alamo responded, "then we don't want it."[34]

No real mummies ever made it into the casino cluster mousetrap.

THE 22-CARAT STYROFOAM CITY

In 1996, businessman Sheldon Adelson anonymously imploded the famous Sands Hotel, former home of the Rat Pack, at the ungodly hour of 2 a.m. on a weekday. Three years later, he opened the Venetian with trumpets and fluttering white doves, while singing gondoliers, glassblowers, and mask-makers throughout the property added to the "streetmosphere," in the spirit of the annual Carnival celebration in Venice.

Adelson, who had bought the Sands and expanded it with America's largest private conference hall, initially did not want to conform to the Las Vegas dogma of replicating cities. On the road to raise money for his new resort, one analyst asked him about the theme of his new casino. "How about 'making money'?" Adelson replied. "Where does it say in the Bible 'Thou shalt have a theme' when you build a Vegas hotel?"[35] But despite his proclamations, even he realized that a theme was inevitable. "Look at New York New York," noted his marketing executive. "The real success of that project is the attraction of other people's business—all of these people staying elsewhere, but who want to come see it."[36] Adelson then turned from iconoclast to the most zealous theme-builder the Strip had seen.

Venice was the obvious choice. It was the birthplace of the first public casino (for those who could afford the dress code of tricorn hats and masks), and the city whose romantic canals lie so deep in people's imagination. Moreover, its architecture exuded opulence, as Adelson knew: "These are the most ornate, luxurious buildings in the world."[37] Unlike previous attempts at copying cities on the Strip, which were looser in their reference to the original, Adelson wanted an exact replica. "We believe New York New York is a 'faux' New York," he stated. "We are not going to build a 'faux' Venice. We're going to build what is essentially the *real* Venice."[38] Moreover, he realized that the more accurate his copy, the more difficult it would be for others to top. "The whole purpose was to create longevity," he later said. "Something that couldn't be outdone by somebody else."[39]

This Las Vegas Venice had copies of the Campanile Bell Tower, Rialto Bridge, and Doge's Palace, built to the standards of their original glory. Adelson had demanded that the Las Vegas Venice buildings feel old, but not run down. "He wanted aging, but

6.6 "The Rialto Bridge and the Campanile Di San Marco together in one picture, complete with a portico!" the photographer of this Venetian photo wrote. "The Rialto Bridge had escalators, I bet the steps of the real bridge will be a disappointment to many tourists!" Photograph courtesy of mararie, Flickr.

he didn't want weathering," said John Hlusak, who was in charge of all the statues and ornaments. "He said, 'Let's strip a couple hundred years off the face of Venice.'"[40]

"We went over to Venice and we spent about three weeks taking about 3,000 photographs of the things we were going to replicate," said Hlusak, who built 80,000 Venetian cornices, pilasters, capitals, pediments, columns, finials, statues and balusters. "But obviously we couldn't do that in stone and marble because they had about, oh, 600 years to do it, and we had about two."[41] This was a pious Venice, with thousands of statues representing mainly arcane Christian religious figures, including the Winged Lion and the Archangel Gabriel, sword in hand.

"So they're made out of Styrofoam like you drink from a cup," Hlusak said. "That's the archangel Gabriel and he's actually another foam and polyurethane piece although he's gilded with real 22 carat gold."[42]

This was a Venice built with American efficiency. It updated stone and marble with gypsum- and urethane-covered polystyrene foam. Builders glued, bolted and cemented these synthetic parts onto rapidly built steel frame substructures. Computer-assisted multiaxial cutters automated the slicing of foam, with the ease of cutting cheese. "It's so fast, it's wonderful,"[43] said a sculptor as she finished a foam column. Another sculptor insisted that Michelangelo, if he were alive today, would work in foam.

This Las Vegas Queen of the Adriatic bustled with hordes of sculptors and painters, who flocked to Las Vegas to train. "There's a two-week-to-a-month learning curve, but if they have an eye, they become trained in a new medium, and you are training a new genre of artisans," Hlusak said. He recruited primarily clay sculptors. "You can't go to a university and say, 'Give me your three best foam sculptors.'"[44]

"Vegas is the Vatican of the 90's," said Karen Kristen, owner of Sky Art, the company spray-painting the sky ceilings above the Venetian's fake canals and St. Mark's Square. As she held her walkie-talkie and laser pointer, she shouted to her ceiling painters on high-suspended platforms: "I want wispy over there, lumpy over here. Deepen the sunset!"[45]

But the Venetian wasn't all gilded Styrofoam and fake-blue skies. Adelson used real marble in prominent public areas, to make them look more authentic. The entrance colonnade consisted of solid Botticino marble columns. But where each original column in the Doge's Palace has a different capital, for the Venetian only two versions were made, each with four different faces. Yet simply by turning them one-quarter they achieved a similar effect, at a much lower cost. "It seems like every one of these capitals is different," Hlusak said. "You have to walk past eight columns before you see the repetition."[46]

Above all, Adelson's concept of authenticity lay in the reproduction of the visual appearance of individual monuments. He had assembled a team of Venetian architecture consultants to draft detailed drawings, since the original blueprints no longer existed. A Venetian historian was even flown into the desert to supervise the accuracy of construction on site, making sure that the fiberglass-coated Styrofoam looked "authentic." However, despite the commitment to authenticity, the Venetian monuments were still infused with a little bit of Las Vegas. The St. Mark's clock tower, while a perfect copy with an enamel clock and Virgin and Child, was turned into the base of an arched roadside sign, as tall as the tower itself. A glaring video screen now disrupted the idyllic Venetian scene, looming over Baby Jesus and the fake St. Mark's Square.

The clock tower was one of many original monuments that were adapted to fit Las Vegas. The Rialto Bridge spanned a vehicular access road, not the Grand Canal, and had a moving beltway pulling people into the casino. The Bridge of Sighs, on the other hand, was more appropriate: while in Venice it connected the Doge's Palace to the prison, in Las Vegas it led sighing gamblers from high-roller slot rooms to the VIP lounge. And where the original Biblioteca Marciana was a library, the Strip version housed a wax museum: an archive of Vegas classics, including Liberace.

The Venetian's architects also re-created some sense of Venice's urban mystery by designing twisting roads leading to unexpected piazzas, for instance the second indoor St. Mark's Square, with fine dining on "outdoor" terraces, under a painted blue sky. They built a 630-foot meandering replica of Venice's Grand Canal, hovering right above the casino floor. It irrigated a mall, The Shoppes, with an incessant stream of pedestrians. Fake Venetian canals, it turned out, added real value.

6.7 The Venetian's Rialto Bridge spans not the Grand Canal but a vehicular access road, 2015.

6.8 Gondoliers steer guests along the Venetian's Grand Canal, dyed monthly to keep its azure color, past St. Mark's Square, one floor above the casino.

So zealous was Adelson in replicating Venice, he commissioned Italian artists to hand-paint frescoes including Bambini's *Triumph of Venice* and Veronese's *The Apotheosis of Venice*, out of fire-retardant paint. He then featured them in Art and Architecture guides given out to patrons: "Experience a Masterpiece."

Adelson had constructed his Venice with such precision that it caught the attention of Italian scholar Giovanna Franci: "The frescoes and canvases by Tiepolo and Veronese, often hard to see in dark Venice churches or on the high ceilings in Palazzo Ducale, are well lit, visible, and brand new!"[47] The Venetian provided tourists with a "post-modern Grand Tour," she claimed. While Venice during the eighteenth century embodied the epitome of the Grand Tour, whereby ancient monuments cultivated Europe's upper classes, the Venetian offered a strange twentieth-century version. Best of all, the Vegas version was more convenient, and free. And while the canals in Venice were filled with raw sewage, the Venetian's Grand Canal was chlorinated, and frequented by motorized gondolas and trained performers, who could sing "O Sole Mio" more beautifully than

6.9 At Paris Las Vegas, the half-size replica of the Eiffel Tower stands partly outside on the Strip, partly inside the casino, against the backdrop of the stretched-out Parisian city hall.

their Italian counterparts. When the canals were not blue enough, Adelson ordered them to be drained, and their bottom surface repainted. They ended up dyeing the water blue. "We dye the water every couple of weeks to maintain the color," the gondola operation manager said. "It's an ongoing process to keep it up to standards; to make it appear more blue; otherwise it would be clear."[48]

"I've been to Venice," a woman said to Hlusak as he talked to a writer for *Preservation* magazine. "And tacky as Las Vegas is, this is a lot nicer than the real one. It smells a lot better."[49]

"In the treacherous sunlight we see Venice decayed, forlorn, poverty-stricken, and commerceless—forgotten and utterly insignificant," wrote Mark Twain in *Innocents Abroad* (1869), ambivalent about all the fuss over old Europe. Today, the pressure of tourism makes the real Venice more like a theme park, overflowing with tourists, while rising prices force out locals. Franci hinted: "Haven't you ever had the impression that Venice also has unfortunately turned a bit into Las Vegas?"[50] Besides, today many tourists experience an equally shallow encounter, zipping through Italy on four-day package tours, peeking through the window of a tour bus.

Walter Benjamin, in his 1936 essay "The Work of Art in the Age of Mechanical Reproduction," wrote that art reproductions lacked the original's "aura": the fabric of tradition in which the original was made. But he did acknowledge a potential positive effect. Mass reproduction could lead to art's popularization. Would the Venetian copy lead to the democratization of heritage, providing a luxury experience to the masses who otherwise would never have visited Venice? The fake Venice doubled the Venetian experience, in 2006 recording eighteen million visitors annually, about as many as the real Venice.

Whether or not, in the age of mass reproduction, the Venetian democratizes Venice, one thing is clear: should the real Venice sink into the Adriatic Sea, at least one record of its glory remains, frescoes and monuments included, built out of impossible-to-rot Styrofoam, high and dry on the caliche of the Mojave Desert.

But more likely than Las Vegas becoming a zoo for cities that may become extinct, a serious drought in the American Southwest could sap all the Venetian's canals—or worse: a relentless developer like Adelson could blow the whole thing up, at 2 a.m. one weekday.

CECI N'EST PAS PARIS

Paris Las Vegas opened with fireworks from a replica of the Eiffel Tower, with music from *An American in Paris*, and French actress Catherine Deneuve flipping the switch that lit up the Las Vegas version of the City of Light. Simultaneously, in Paris, the great-grandson of Gustav Eiffel extinguished the lights of the real Eiffel Tower. Arthur Goldberg, head of Hilton's gaming division, even visited the mayor of Paris. The mayor, as he looked over the drawings, was "impressed by the gigantism of this project … by its quality and its chic."[51] Paris, so it seemed, had endorsed its copy.

Business strategists had endorsed the new Paris too. It cost only $785 million to build, almost half the cost of the Venetian. One analyst noted: "What this will highlight to management teams is that you can create must-see attractions at under a billion and still generate attractive returns."[52] Paris Las Vegas was a "must-see" on the cheap.

Goldberg made a career out of penny-pinching, rather than casino mogul flamboyance. He wanted to tackle the problem of the "Vegas trap": outrageously expensive hotel complexes with low returns on capital. He packed Paris Las Vegas with casino space, which yields twice as much return per square foot compared to restaurants and retail.

While this strategy did not give him access to the same high-end crowd as the Venetian, it still returned more for its capital. *Fortune* magazine wrote: "He doesn't measure [the space] by how much glitter there is per square inch. He is more apt to talk of the 'beauty of cash flows' than of floor shows."[53]

The theme of Paris was chosen because it was sure to strike a chord with the typical American. "The average person will not get to Paris in their lifetime, so we're giving them a part of Paris," interior designer Charles Silverman said.[54]

Paris Las Vegas was a lesson in theming at low cost. "Are they going to realize the back of a column is finished?" Silverman asked. "I don't think so. It's the overall effect."[55] Casino design, he later said, "is just merchandising. … Nobody is looking for awards."[56]

Designers had to strike the difficult balance of re-creating the Eiffel Tower and other monuments with less expensive materials, while still creating an "authentic" depiction. While the 1889 Eiffel Tower was made of wrought-iron pieces fastened with millions of rivets, architect Joel Bergman built the Vegas version from less laborious welded steel, adding fake rivets for show. Bergman intended the tower to be full-scale, but the Federal Aviation authorities halved the size, to prevent airplanes on their descent into the nearby airstrip from crashing into the iron lady. Yet, despite its diminished size, Bergman fully exploited his Eiffel *Towerette*. On the eleventh floor he placed a restaurant, which featured the best views of the Bellagio fountains—better than that of the Bellagio's ground-level restaurants, to Steve Wynn's great frustration.

Moreover, unlike the Campanile at the Venetian, a tower visible only from outside, three of the Eiffel's legs pierced through the casino, landing in between the gambling tables. This meant that the tower was visible all the time, to guests both outside and inside the casino.

Bergman grabbed Paris's Arc de Triomphe and scaled it down by 60 percent so it could mark the driveway, and guests driving up to the casino could get that *Champs-Élysées* experience. It consisted of 1,146 cast pieces; the designers managed to cut costs by copying only the two most famous of the four sculptures, "La Marseillaise" and "Le Triomphe de 1810," and reproducing them twice—a glitch only the observant cabby going up and down the driveway would notice.

Paris's exterior ornaments required only 10,000 pieces, eight times fewer than the Venetian. Where the Venetian copied dozens of buildings, Paris picked only the most memorable few, including the Louvre Palace and the Opera House, rebuilt at 60 percent. The four-story Hotel de Ville, the Parisian city hall, was stretched out to thirty-four stories and turned into an X-shaped hotel tower, which crammed in more rooms at the expense of views.

But not just any part of Paris was re-created. Paris Las Vegas was narrowed down to the early-twentieth-century time bracket, a period that people associate with romance. "That's the Paris that most people think of,"[57] Silverman said. This was the Paris of the Art Nouveau Métro entrances, which were placed around the blue-sky casino. But the eighteenth-century Montgolfier balloon, with Louis XVI's royal monogram, was an anachronism designers could not resist. It was used as a roadside sign. It was just like

6.10 The Aladdin's video screen honors troops amid onion-shaped domes, minarets, and faux-sandstone cliffs, 2003.

the original, had the balloon not been striped in neon and the basket made of video screens within gold picture frames.

All of it seemed to work. As much as Paris Las Vegas impressed investors, it also impressed tourists. A fake-tree-lined "Rue de la Paix" shopping street had a French wine and cheese shop, a Parisian pastry shop with *croissants*, and a *boulanger* to supply the resort with fresh *baguettes,* delivered by a French cyclist in a striped shirt riding the resort's cobblestone streets—things American tourists would expect to see in Paris, but never do.

In fact, the gap between tourists' towering expectation of Paris and the reality on the ground appears to be a major cause of "Paris Syndrome," a psychological disorder that strikes in particular Japanese tourists visiting Paris, about twenty per year. Symptoms are extreme distress, dizziness and sweating, even hallucinations. While the media worldwide idealize Paris, the Japanese especially glorify the city. It can be a rude awakening for Japanese tourists to realize that the French do not all dress like fashion models and smell of Chanel No. 5.

The cure? Perhaps visit Paris Las Vegas, which, from the vibratos of Edith Piaf in the elevator to the greeting of guests with *Bonjour*, offered a ringing American stereotype of Paris.

"Forget Paris," the *Washington Post* wrote. "Las Vegas is about to offer you a much, much better version: One without French people."[58]

THE MAP AND THE TERRITORY

Despite developers' attention to heritage, and the relatively accurate copies of other places, architectural theorists teamed up to condemn Las Vegas as a center of inauthentic experience.

At the heart of these critiques lay the notion of the simulacrum: a representation of something that is so hyperrealistic, it is preferred to the real. In order to explain this warped sense of the "real," French philosopher Jean Baudrillard referred to a Borges fable in which cartographers had drawn a map so detailed that it covered the territory entirely. But where in Borges's story the map frays, Baudrillard inverts the story as a metaphor for today's world: "if we were to revive the fable today, it would be the territory whose shreds are slowly rotting across the map."[59] The map had superseded the territory.

Book after book discussed the phenomenon, with a special focus on Las Vegas. Another French philosopher, Bruce Bégout, delivered the most sneering critique: "It is a city without shame that swallows up other cities to the point of re-appropriating their urban icons, in its own style, and supplanting them as a tourist destination."[60] But Bégout ignored the fact that his city, too, has had its share of reappropriated icons. At the 1889 Paris World Exposition, a Cairo street had been copied, complete with imported donkeys, buildings made to look shabby, and a mosque filled with belly dancers—even though no such street existed in Cairo. These and other representations of the "uncivilized" Orient justified the French civilizing mission.[61] At least the Las Vegas replicas had no ulterior motive, other than recruiting gamblers.

In addition, many other cities besides Las Vegas exploited heritage, even when it did not exist; for instance colonial Williamsburg in Virginia, which was, in the words of Ada Louise Huxtable, restored to "the way it never was." In Santa Fe, New Mexico, authentic-looking "adobe" structures are actually built of wood frames plastered with cement, which is why some people call the city "Santa Fake."

In Las Vegas, on the other hand, "any claim to the reality of history is clearly secondary to its potential to generate commercial profit,"[62] historian Nezar AlSayyad has argued. Whereas a city like Santa Fe was a "fake authentic," Las Vegas was an "authentic fake." Moreover, Las Vegas had *original* fakes. The monuments were never exact copies. To make them fit the casino they were reassembled into a pastiche, pasted together into new original creations—a photo-collage of a Manhattan skyline, for instance, with a roller coaster snaking in and out of the building.

If theorists had not been so obsessed with dismissing Las Vegas's heritage copies, they might have noticed how the paradigm of replica cities really ran its course. The Aladdin, for instance, would become the last resort of the Sim City Age in 2000. In 1998, the original Aladdin was torn down, only the name surviving the implosion. In line with Las Vegas's replicas, the new Aladdin had copies of buildings from Middle Eastern cities, including Cairo and Marrakesh. It had a mall with a series of "ancient trade routes" leading from North African settings into a mountainside village, through high domed ceilings, arabesques, and Moorish archways. Moroccan street performers completed that bazaar-like feeling.

Then 9/11 happened. People deliberately avoided the Aladdin. Some deemed it a potential terrorist target, seen by extremists as a casino mocking Arabian architecture. Others considered the ersatz caves and Middle Eastern structures to be a retroactive tribute to Al Qaeda, a Bin Laden-themed casino. Barely two weeks after 9/11, the resort filed for bankruptcy. The resort that had survived its own implosion could not survive the collapse of the World Trade Center towers.

With its referent under siege, New York New York, on the other hand, took center stage on the Strip. The replica Statue of Liberty, the quintessential symbol of the American spirit, was spontaneously treated as a shrine. People placed flowers, flags, firefighter helmets, and T-shirts with handwritten notes in front of the statue.

The 9/11-triggered response to the Aladdin and New York New York showed that even simulacra could be imbued with deep social meanings. It disproved the argument that Las Vegas, as Bégout had claimed, "ingests" worldwide urbanity, "without actually digesting it."

But while the Aladdin's bankruptcy signaled the end of the Sim City Age, there were deeper problems with the paradigm. Las Vegas was becoming saturated with a room inventory of 120,000 in 1999, almost double the number of a decade earlier. Nonetheless, commercial banks happily financed the Sim City monuments with large collateral loans, secured against a very small percentage of equity. Even risky projects were now able to get access to credit. The Aladdin's financial advisor spoke of a "national flood of liquidity,"[63] one of hundreds of corporations benefiting nationwide from the 1970s deregulation of the banking industry.

Just as the fake cities cease to refer to the real, so did the Strip's investors feign the "real." Banks financed the ever more expensive casinos and at one point ceased to reference the actual risks of the investment, laying the ground for a big crash. During the Sim City Age, investment structures, as well as the Strip's architecture, became lost in representation.

As the Aladdin failed, the planning of more replica cities was stalled, including the London Hotel and Casino, with its Tower Bridge and Palace of Westminster. A City by the Bay copy of San Francisco, with all the trappings including the Golden Gate Bridge, was permanently delayed. Bob Stupak's new resort did not make it either. He proposed a half-size replica of the sinking *Titanic*, with 1,200 rooms placed in an "iceberg."

And while in Las Vegas the paradigm had ended, its influence lasted, with lesser versions of Vegas replicas appearing elsewhere. For instance, the Southern California company "Moonlight Molds," which made reliefs for the Bellagio, now added these ornaments to private Bel Air homes. These and other designers exported Las Vegas lucre to other places, from fake sky ceilings in private jets to Roman-style ornaments in McMansions. "Casino Chic," *The New York Times* concluded. "It may be coming to a home near you."[64]

"Call it our Belle Epoxy," *Preservation* magazine wrote. "Everything now strives to look like something else, to evoke a distant place or era."[65]

But even scarier was Las Vegas-style finance, "casino capitalism,"[66] dominating the globe. This brand of financial risk-taking and instability, with vast sums of capital secured against small amounts of collateral, would set the world's companies and homeowners on a dangerous path. It also fundamentally restructured the Strip. When Mirage Corporation's stock fell in 2000, MGM bought the company and then owned most of the Strip. Hilton bought Caesars, turning Park Place into the world's largest gaming company. MGM Mirage, Park Place, and Mandalay Resorts combined now owned almost the whole Strip. The fact that each of the casinos looked different concealed the real conditions of ownership. The Strip now actually seemed like a Sim City, an entire "street" owned by only three corporations.

Moreover, a new brand-centric demographic was on the rise. This younger, wealthier demographic did not want fakes. They wanted originals. For them, Las Vegas would build "authentic" contemporary architecture, not copies but originals, designed by celebrated architects.

Nonetheless, from 1995 to 2001, Las Vegas had led the world in its pursuit of the original fake. It became *the* place where old monuments were recast into 22-carat Styrofoam. From New York skyscrapers to the Eiffel Tower, Las Vegas had become a permanent World Exposition of global culture. The Las Vegas copies, rather than the originals, became the main frame of reference for millions of visitors. Best of all, they were convenient, open twenty-four hours a day, and free—at the cost of potentially losing your shirt.

Las Vegas's designers already knew that the show of replica cities had run its course. "We're running out of cities," Silverman said. "Look what we have … Rome, Paris, New York, Egypt, King Arthur's England, Venice, the tropics at Mirage and Mandalay Bay."[67] There were few territories left to map.

Some locals wondered if someone was going to build a Las Vegas-themed casino: a miniature version of all the cities in the world, with a whole lot of retro neon.

It would be called *Las Vegas Las Vegas*.

7

Starchitecture (2001—Present)

CityCenter [casino complex] bridges the vitality of Las Vegas with the experiences travelers see … spectacular architecture, culturally significant art, great public spaces. … It is an evolutionary destination that aims to transform Las Vegas … like the Guggenheim in Bilbao.[1]

—Bobby Baldwin, CEO of CityCenter casino complex

[CityCenter casino] is a fitting coda to the decade of celebrity architecture and overextended real-estate mania … the complex is a palace … for the age of towering debt.[2]

—Christopher Hawthorne, Los Angeles Times

Right next to New York New York's fake skyline, with its fiberglass Chrysler Building, ultramodern towers rose from crystalline titanium structures. Unlike the Styrofoam buildings next door that lacked luster, the new towers' curtain wall façades blinked in the desert sun, emphasizing the fact that they were not another knockoff of an existing building. They were originals, designed by star architects.

In the new millennium, casino moguls moved from building replicas to authentic architecture. They vigorously embraced the "Bilbao Effect": the belief that a building designed by a star architect would attract visitors, as Frank Gehry's Guggenheim museum had brought millions of tourists to the city of Bilbao. They went so far in trying to attract a higher-end customer that, to everyone's surprise, the Strip, once known for its five-dollar steaks and neon-lit grind joints, became a hub of high design and contemporary art.

Las Vegas's new casinos now rivaled New York's finest contemporary buildings. Star architects and interior designers added light-filled atria and entire parks to casinos, traditionally places that shunned natural light at all cost. They fronted them with trees, terraces and multimillion-dollar sculptures, bringing the Strip, once a sea of asphalt and cars, close to major pedestrian boulevards like Broadway. Meanwhile, the Strip's new model of a sophisticated urban casino was considered such a success that cities around the world desired it. Macau reclaimed hundreds of acres in the South China Sea, only to build a Las Vegas Strip. Even Singapore, known as a model city for urban planning, built its new flagship business district around a Las Vegas casino.

But this global age of the Strip also coincided with exotically leveraged collateral bank loans and risky real-estate speculation. When the world's economy adopted Las Vegas-style "casino capitalism," the crisis that followed almost brought the Strip down. Yet ironically, by the time the global financial recession had turned Las Vegas into the poster child of crisis, the city was even more relevant than ever. Las Vegas had become the quintessential model of how to build cosmopolitan urban gambling.

THE BILBAO EFFECT

In 2001, the venerable Guggenheim and Hermitage museums opened a branch inside the Venetian, the casino known for its knockoff Renaissance frescoes and gilded Styrofoam sculptures. "High-brow critics will criticize us,"[3] Russia's minister of culture predicted. "The Hermitage in the capital of gambling?"

World-renowned architect Rem Koolhaas designed one of the galleries, a seven-story steel minimalist box, which contrasted sharply with its ornate Venetian surroundings. Frank Gehry designed the first exhibit space with his trademark wavy metal shapes. While both designers delivered world-class work, the Las Vegas context made Gehry uncomfortable. He worried that the surroundings would taint even the most pristine design: "the fear is that it would all just become another theme."[4]

Although the galleries lasted only a few years, with few visitors willing to pay to see the art, they foreshadowed where the Strip was headed. By importing the cultural prestige of the Guggenheim and the celebrity architects, Las Vegas joined a worldwide trend of cities exploiting the "Bilbao Effect."

This new philosophy replaced the casino design paradigm of replicating cities. In 2003, Mandalay Bay, previously known for its British colonial buildings and Burmese stupas, expanded with a new hotel tower, which was deliberately *not* themed. "We believe that style is going to be the next phase of Las Vegas,"[5] Mandalay's marketing director said. Where Mandalay Bay had a Red Square with a replica Lenin Statue, the new hotel tower had a rooftop nightclub with an ultramodern coral-like ceiling, and a lobby scattered with Andy Warhol's Pop Art.

All of this high design and contemporary art were important signifiers for what would be the Strip's next target demographic. Instead of baby boomers, casino operators were after "Generation X." This generation, born after the baby boomers, had more disposable income and was less averse to travel. The millennials were also targeted. Designers assumed that this brand-centric demographic would not identify with a copy of a place they had either already explored or planned to visit.

The Bellagio, themed after the tranquil Lake Como destination, allowed a minimalist Ibiza-style nightclub to intrude on its elaborate Mediterranean surroundings. Treasure Island renamed itself "TI," rebranding its signature pirate show, "The Battle of Buccaneer Bay," into the sexier "Sirens of TI," where naval officers were replaced with scantily dressed sirens, and masts became stripper poles where "booty" was shaken, not looted. The Mirage, which had tragically lost its family-friendly act Siegfried and Roy when Roy got mauled by his tiger, reinvented itself by opening numerous nightclubs including the "Bare Pool Lounge," where "European-style" sunbathing allowed women to take off their tops. Even Cirque du Soleil, known for its family-friendly shows, opened Zumanity, its first "erotic cabaret"—with replica genitals, since total nudity was illegal in Clark County. (The French couturier explained: "What we'll give them is even bigger.")[6]

Even the city itself was rebranded into a sensual nightlife destination thanks to the tagline "What happens in Vegas, stays in Vegas." But some criticized how the local authority, initially called the Clark County Fair and Recreation Board, had moved from supporting recreational activities for locals to using tax money for implicitly advertising sleaze.

All these combined efforts did not go unnoticed. In 2004, a decade after it appeared as "Las Vegas U.S.A." heralding wholesome family fun, the Strip appeared again on the cover of *Time*. Where in 1994 the cover showed the Sphinx, it now showed young women dancing on a table at MGM Grand's new Tabu lounge: "It's Vegas … hotter than ever." Moreover, the reporter noted, a sensual architectural element had been mushrooming in hotel rooms, nightclubs, and even gaming areas: stripping poles[7]—a symptom of society's growing "striptease culture,"[8] with pole-dancing as legitimate a recreational activity as yoga.

"After Nice, a Return to Vice,"[9] headlined *The New York Times*. Las Vegas was "hip" and "cool" again, having realized there was more money to be made by going back to its sleek and sinful roots. With the new image, and a younger demographic, it was waiting for the first high-design resort built from the ground up.

THE SURREALIST CASINO

Casino mogul Steve Wynn used to build hotels themed after pirates and Italian towns. Now he said: "Why would you set out to build something not as good as the original?"[10]

Wynn's own signature became the logo of his new 2005 casino, featuring prominently on the building. It also decorated a three-story "eraser" going up and down a ten-story video screen, "erasing" it like a blackboard. Inside the building, the Wynn logo was put on roulette tables, bottled water, and bedsheets. "The Wynn" was the first casino to have its own line of home furnishings and accessories, so that people could take the logo home, and even sleep on it.

Departing from the tri-wing tower that sacrificed views for packing in more rooms, Wynn built a single-slab hotel tower that was sleek and curved. To make this 2,700-room building appear more "boutique," his designers used the "window eye trick." They drew a white line on the copper façade every two floors, not every floor, making the forty-five-story tower appear to have twenty-three stories only.

The resort was originally named *Le Rêve* (French for *the dream*), after the famous Picasso that Wynn owned—almost the world's most expensive painting, until he accidentally pierced it with his elbow. The name was dropped when focus groups had trouble pronouncing it, yet surrealist traces remained visible. Wynn built a lake that hosted a show. Every thirty minutes the lake would bubble, appearing to boil, with multicolored lights swirling on the surface in erotic-abstract patterns. In one performance, a giant fiberglass disembodied woman's head rose from the lake, singing to classical music; in another, a 30-foot-tall frog sang Louis Armstrong's "What a Wonderful World."

To make sure noise from the Strip would not interfere with his spectacle, Wynn planned to build a barrier. "It started out as something to hide the traffic,"[11] a landscape designer said. But Wynn ended up moving 800,000 cubic yards of earth to form a "natural" barrier between the Strip and his resort. No longer would people from the Strip be able to see the lake.

"The hell with the 'wow factor,'" Wynn said. "I've done the volcano. My audience here is my guest in the hotel."[12]

But from the outside, a mound of earth was considerably less exciting than a volcano. Still, it did make the Wynn appear more exclusive. *Time* magazine noted: "The draw isn't glitz; it's buzz."[13]

"No plastic theme-park bullshit ... it's all real,"[14] Wynn said of the $200 million artificial mountain, meaning it was not fiberglass or plastic. Eventually he covered it with 1,500 plum and pistachio trees, and included an interior elevator for maintenance. The mountain was shaped in such a way that it formed five waterfalls and eight gardens, which provided backdrops for restaurants, nightclubs, and lounges.

Instead of designing restaurants themed like Bali at the Mirage, Wynn hired famous interior architects such as Yabu Pushelberg to bring their sleek signature interiors. "Forget the Las Vegas you once knew—a desert town where miles of blinking neon and mirrored ceilings eclipse good taste," *Interior Design* wrote in 2005. The magazine, dedicated to contemporary design, found "hundreds of worthy projects," roughly a dozen of them in Wynn's new venture alone.[15]

Roger Thomas, in charge of designing an upscale casino interior, went in clear violation of conventional wisdom of casino design as codified by gaming consultant Bill Friedman. Friedman, a former gambling addict, argued that "low ceilings beat high ceilings," to keep the focus on games, and "the maze layout beats long, wide, straight passageways and aisles," to get visitors to stray to the tables.[16] Thomas, however, designed high-vaulted corridors around the casino, helping guests to orient themselves. Where Friedman argued "the gambling equipment is the décor,"[17] Thomas stuffed Wynn's casino with art, decadent furniture, and colorful flowers.

7.1 A man-made mountain of 1,500 trees and eight waterfalls shields the Wynn casino from the public realm of the Las Vegas Strip, 2014. Photograph courtesy of Daniel Ramirez, Flickr.

All of this was meant to represent a new design strategy, for which Thomas coined the term "evoca-tecture," intended to elicit an emotional response from the customer. In contrast, for the previous design strategy of themed architecture he coined the term "repli-tecture."[18] To hook into people's emotions, Thomas adopted surrealist aesthetics. He commissioned decorator Jacques Garcia to design the hotel's signature carpets, protozoan patterns of fuchsia-colored sea-life-like creatures. Thomas also hung upside-down from the ceiling eighteen large parasols, which automatically moved up, down, and turned around—inspired by René Magritte's surrealist paintings. And then there was the custom-designed vegetal chandelier, which, to make sure its red glass branches did not block the cameras monitoring the gaming tables, had built-in CCTV cameras hidden in its shiny fruit. The Wynn went deep into its customers' unconscious by disseminating so-called "brandscents," smells patterned so that no other company could smell that way.

Whether or not Wynn's "evoca-tecture" evoked more emotions than the "repli-tecture" of resorts themed after existing places, it did have psychological effects on customers. Recent gaming research claimed that in contrast to Friedman-type casinos, "playground" casinos—high ceilings, decorations, and other whimsical distractions—have a restorative effect on people's psychology.[19] "Gamblers in a playground casino will stay longer, feel better, and bet more," one of the researchers stated. "Although they come away with bigger losses, they're more likely to return."[20]

The Wynn's high-art surrealism, luxury, and all-pervasive sensory design made it the first resort of the Strip's starchitecture phase. But while it would set the tone for new Strip casinos, it also foreshadowed questions about the meaning of art that would make critics deeply uncomfortable. Surrealism, the once avant-garde art movement dedicated to shock us out of the establishment, had been co-opted by a corporation as a high-end phantasmagorical theme for a casino, a way to "hook" into people's subconscious, and to mentally restore gambling addicts.

ASIA'S LAS VEGAS

Wynn Resorts, MGM Mirage, and the Sands Corporation were all eager to export their Las Vegas brands to Macau so that they could tap into its Mainland China hinterland, where 1.3 billion people were deprived of legal gambling. In 2002, China's Communist Party, as they had done for other industries, wanted to encourage innovation, and granted all these Westerners gaming concessions. Little did they know that the Las Vegas developers would reinvent the sleepy colonial backwater within just a few years, and build a full-fledged bustling Strip.

In 2004, Venetian owner Sheldon Adelson opened the Sands Macau, the first Las Vegas-owned casino in China. He beat his rivals by designing and constructing his casino in only two years: a gaudy gold shimmering box, nicknamed the "stadium" casino, its cavernous interior contained a 50-ton chandelier hanging from a 50-foot-high ceiling. Steve Wynn was proud that his casino, Wynn Macau, was more refined. "I took the long-term view and decided not to compromise the brand," he said.[21]

With gaming corporations expanding nationally and globally, no longer confined to only Las Vegas and Atlantic City, designing casinos as brands, rather than on an individual basis, had become increasingly relevant. Having kept its eyes on Macau and Chinese customers early on, the Wynn in Las Vegas was already designed as a Sinocentric brand. Interior designer Roger Thomas had placed a pair of Chinese guardian lions at the entrance, and decorated the interior with a predominantly red tone—the color the Chinese consider to be the luckiest. He also had the elevator skip floors 40 to 49—a consequence of the pronunciation of the number four in Mandarin and Cantonese, which sounds too close to the word "death."

In 2006, the Wynn Macau opened. While it was a close replica of the Wynn Las Vegas, Thomas nevertheless had to tweak the basic design. The lobby had an animatronic dragon that curled into the air every hour, his nostrils puffing smoke.

Most important, constrained by the smaller lots of Macau's downtown, Wynn could not build an exact twin of his copper Wynn Las Vegas tower, built on the large lots of the Strip. He had to scale down the 2,700-room tower to 600 rooms only. This made it hard to build a full-scale Las Vegas casino complex that would give customers not only gambling, but also shows, pools, and large room suites.

But Sheldon Adelson was not going to be confined by this limitation. He persuaded the government to approve a resort development plan in an area that was reclaimed from the South China Sea. He recommended large plots, to be occupied by large resorts, and a wide highway in the middle. In short, he wanted a Las Vegas-style strip. In 2007, Adelson opened the $2.4 billion Venetian Macau on an area to be called the Cotai Strip. A full-fledged resort with 3,000 suites, it was the world's largest casino. But while he brought his canals and Campanile to Macau, he did have to make some adjustments. The Venetian Macau's Grand Canal, unlike the one in Vegas, did not float from the inside to the outside—since water flowing to the outside is bad *feng shui*, a symbol of disappearing wealth, not exactly the message you want to send in a casino.

For Macau, it was a breakthrough. By building the Venetian on the Cotai Strip, Adelson had created an entirely new market for multi-night visitors, to whom he offered Las Vegas-style entertainment—Macau's downtown casinos, on the other hand, were mainly day-trip destinations. Adelson knew he could tap into a market of billions a few hours' flight away, not only in China but in Hong Kong, South Korea, and Japan. To reel them in, he bought his own ferries and even airplanes.

By 2005, Adelson had already recouped the $265 million construction costs of his Sands Macau. By the end of 2006, Macau was the world's number one gambling city at $6.9 billion gaming revenue, compared to $6.5 billion in Las Vegas. By 2008, the city had $13.6 billion in revenue, twice as big as Vegas. The city that named itself "Asia's Las Vegas" not only started to look a whole lot like the city in the Mojave Desert, it even eclipsed the original. Adelson said that Las Vegas should be called "America's Macau."[22]

Las Vegas had exported its main product with such overwhelming success that it was no longer the world's gambling capital. But it was not a matter of money alone. When gaming developers unleashed their suburban casinos into China, they changed the pedestrian city of Macau forever. The mega-casino industry would permanently transform the Macau peninsula—its ocean reclaimed, its hillsides excavated, and glimmering towers tossed into the historic skyline—culminating in a full-fledged, automobile-oriented, Las Vegas-style Strip.

THE MANHATTANIZATION OF LAS VEGAS

Back in Las Vegas, the battle between casino tycoons Steve Wynn and Sheldon Adelson was flaring up. The two had argued over everything from having too few parking spots at the Venetian to the noise of the Mirage's volcano. Adelson planned a second major tower within the original Venetian complex, which was initially going to be 460 feet tall. But when he found out that Wynn's tower was going to be 614 feet, he extended his to 642. It ended up overtaking the Pentagon as the United States's tallest building, taller than three Empire State Buildings, making the combined Palazzo-Venetian the world's largest resort with a total of 7,074 rooms.

Adelson had originally planned to call the new tower the Lido, after the beach town Lido di Venezia. But what could have been an exercise in copying Lido's monuments, such as its Grand Hotel des Bains, turned into something else. In Las Vegas, replica buildings had lost their luster, so Adelson changed the name to the more generic Palazzo. Instead of a classic Venetian style, it was going to be a modern interpretation of Italian Renaissance like the one that was so pervasive in Southern California's high-end shops and McMansions. "The Palazzo won't have a recognizable theme like the Venetian," a Las Vegas Sands spokesman said, "but instead will be an upscale design reminiscent of Bel Air, Rodeo Drive and Beverly Hills."[23]

The Palazzo had even adopted green building design principles. Adelson packed 6.9 million square feet onto only eight acres, including a four-story underground parking garage, in sharp contrast to the vast swaths of surface parking on the Strip two decades earlier. He built an octagonal atrium with a garden and waterfall, bringing natural daylight inside. He built hotel rooms with lighting occupancy sensors and automatic air-conditioning shutoffs. He installed permeable paving outside instead of asphalt, so it could soak up rain, planted fake grass instead of water-hungry natural turf, and powered the swimming pools with solar panels. All of this earned the Palazzo the title of the world's largest "green" building, awarded by the U.S. Green Building Council. But while it made good market sense for Adelson to associate the Palazzo with the sustainability trend, since the government incentivized him with a $27 million tax break, how could a casino complex situated in the dry uninhabitable desert ever make any real sense as a shining example of "green" building?

Wynn also planned a second tower to the Wynn, the $2.3 billion Encore, which opened in 2008. While the fifty-three-story curved bronze glass tower looked exactly like

7.2 Crocodile-embossed leather VIP booths surround a pool surrounding a larger pool at XS, a pool-nightclub hybrid.

the Wynn, it was aimed at a higher-end and younger demographic, with all the rooms built as suites. Encore's centerpiece was a giant pool surrounded by a 40,000-square-foot nightclub called "XS"—referring not to extra small but to excess. VIP tables and cabanas surrounded the prime real estate of the pool, floors were decorated with mirrored mosaics, bar tops were made of brushed brass and gold resin, and couches of gold-crocodile-embossed leather.

By then Adelson had already announced an expansion of his Venetian complex: the St. Regis Residences, a 400-unit condominium tower with prices topping $1 million each. Adelson planned to ride on Las Vegas's condominium boom. Gaming corporations eagerly included condos inside the casino complex, as pioneered by the MGM Grand in 2004. All of the units of the first tower of The Residences at MGM Grand were sold out even before the first spade had hit the ground. By 2007, 72,000 condo units in more than 100 projects were planned in Las Vegas, including by Donald Trump, who built a 620-foot-high slab, gilded in 24-carat gold.

With all the high-rises popping up, some termed this new phase the "Manhattanization" of Las Vegas. Now that Las Vegas had become a complete entertainment destination, with Cirque du Soleil shows, celebrity-chef restaurants, and a vibrant nightlife, retirees and people looking for a second home wanted to buy into it. But whereas they could choose a condo with a sea view in Miami, or a view of Central Park in New York, in Las Vegas their view of choice was the Las Vegas Strip, a highway. It was a unique postmodern view, a glimpse of a reproduction of the Eiffel Tower alone enough to raise real-estate prices.

But this new Manhattan of the Mojave Desert was not like New York City. Few people actually lived in the high-rises, which were too expensive for local residents to rent or buy. Most of the new growth was caused primarily by pure speculation. The careful observer of Las Vegas's postmodern panorama might have noticed that at night, very unlike Manhattan, many of the new condo towers were dark. They were "ghost towers."

THE STRIP STARCHITECTS

In 2004, MGM Mirage announced a multibillion-dollar resort, America's most expensive private development, designed as an "urban metropolis." But the company did not want to duplicate an existing metropolis, as New York New York had with its replica Chrysler Building. It was going to build a "real" city, a casino complex called "CityCenter," with original architecture, designed by star architects.

The architects alone would change the public perception of the Strip, hitherto seen as anti-urban and kitschy. "Las Vegas is always looked down upon," said MGM executive Jim Murren, the visionary behind the project. "CityCenter is a counterpoint to the kitschiness."[24]

Murren assembled an unprecedented powerhouse of star designers, including Daniel Libeskind, César Pelli, and Norman Foster. Only Rockefeller Center in New York in the 1930s, a much-cited reference of CityCenter, came close to this unusual teaming of elite architects. But it was not easy to get the architects on board. An MGM executive described their typical reaction: "I don't do volcanoes so what do you want from me?"[25] However, the advent of the star architects on the Las Vegas Strip was a logical extension of their recent worldwide popularity. In the late 1990s, and throughout the early years of the twenty-first century, city leaders, corporations, and institutions had increasingly tried to attract celebrity architects to design buildings from university campuses to fashion stores. They assumed that the characteristic signatures of such architects would help them establish a brand identity, and allow architectural images to circulate in the image economy. The architects' elevated media status even led to the 2001 neologism "starchitecture," a conjunction of "star" and "architecture."

But "starchitecture" also had a pejorative connotation, typically critiqued as exuberant architectural shapes devoid of a local context, with the sole purpose of being iconic, at the expense of other buildings. This is an architecture of spectacle as opposed to use, obsessed with creating a "wow factor" not too far from the architectural philosophy of Las Vegas. Only when elite architecture in the twenty-first century evolved in ever more exuberant shapes, relying on shock and awe formalism, and after it had seeped into the cultural mainstream, could it come to the Strip as a fierce rival to thematic architecture like the Luxor pyramid.

In Las Vegas, the all-star architect team refused to respond to the context of the Strip. "Everything else around is the un-architecture," Rafael Viñoly commented. "It's a cartoon; it's a horror show."[26]

However, the architects, each charged to design part of the project, did respond to one another's designs—simulating the way in which towers in real city centers are designed. Rafael Viñoly's crescent-shaped hotel tower complemented the arcs of César Pelli's project, and together carved out a large circular space with, at the center, a Nancy Rubins sculpture, a thorny bouquet constructed of more than two hundred aluminum canoes. The sculpture was part of a $40 million "public" art program that scattered art throughout the resort. Some of this art was even reminiscent of critical questions pertaining to Las Vegas, with Maya Lin's silver cast sculpture of the Colorado River above Aria's lobby desk, and Jenny Holzer's 266-foot-wide LED panel scrolling her "truisms" at the valet, including: "It's not good to operate on credit."

César Pelli, known for the Petronas Towers in Kuala Lumpur, designed the Aria, located at the back of the site. He broke down the mass of the 4,000-room tower into two elegant intersecting curvilinear shapes, rising up to sixty-one stories. Pelli also detailed the all-glass energy-saving façade with window reflectors that added texture and deflected the desert sun. It was one of many "green" building strategies, including water-saving measures such as drip irrigation of the landscape and innovative low-flow showerheads, invented by the Aria staff.[27] The gaming process, too, had been "greened":

7.3 *Big Edge*, Nancy Rubins's bouquet of canoes, fronts the energy-saving façade of the César Pelli-designed Aria hotel.

cool air was more efficiently distributed through a base underneath the slot machines, rather than from the ceiling, where it would waste energy on cooling empty space.

CityCenter's most spectacular pieces were closer to the Strip. Sir Norman Foster designed an elliptical tower with a disco-ball façade, with shades of blue- and white-mirrored glass. Helmut Jahn designed two yellow checkerboard towers leaning in opposite directions—as one observer noted, "like a pair of drunken revelers."[28] Only the Mandarin Oriental hotel was more understated, a rectilinear volume with a tranquil bamboo-lined courtyard.

Daniel Libeskind designed the jagged-shaped Crystals mall, CityCenter's most iconic form. In contrast to the casino, which was right at the back of the resort, the mall featured prominently on the Strip, illustrating of how quickly retail had gained importance in the post-industrial mix of the casino complex. By designing the mall in the titanium angular forms that had become his trademark style ever since he designed Berlin's Jewish Museum, Libeskind effectively lent a high-culture aesthetic of memorialization to commercialism: the mall and its grand atrium had the feeling of a museum. Despite the quality of his project, which was arguably one of the world's most spectacular malls, Libeskind attracted the most criticism. "Is this the sort of thing that progressive architects should be involved in?"[29] asked the *Washington Post*. Critics objected to the way architects with high-cultural backgrounds worked increasingly with mainstream developers, and instead of designing cultural institutions and mass housing, now built malls and even casinos. One critic described how Libeskind, who had applied a literary theory called deconstruction to his buildings by designing fractured façades—a technique which worked so well in his Jewish museum—had "delivered decon's angular angst … a hulking shell for Prada and Gucci boutiques."[30]

When he was asked how he reconciled his past idealism with designing a luxury Las Vegas mall, Libeskind described his contribution as a "rich, urbane, cosmopolitan scheme, one you could find in New York or in Paris." In addition, his project attempted "to give a world of simulacra something original and real."[31]

Other critics pointed out that Project CityCenter was not a "real" city, despite its 18 million square feet of hotels, condos, retail and casinos, totaling about the size of six Empire State Buildings. City planners Ehrenkrantz, Eckstut and Kuhn Architects, known for their design of New York's Battery Park City, had attempted to design a number of "public" spaces, including pocket parks and boulevards. But Project CityCenter's "great pedestrian corridors" and "dynamic public spaces"[32] did not live up to their promise. The project's final master plan was fragmented by a large access ramp, more highway than "boulevard," which led to a six-lane traffic roundabout, almost a freeway interchange. Even the monorail that connected parts of the resort was nothing more than an overstated people-mover, a gimmick to conceal the project's suburban nature: a resort designed to move cars, not just pedestrians, around. Project CityCenter revealed the limitations of the transformative effects of star architecture. A cluster of buildings designed by celebrity architects did not automatically make urbanity.

7.4 Daniel Libeskind's titanium-clad Crystals mall outshines Norman Foster's downsized, blue-silver Harmon hotel (right), backed by Helmut Jahn's pair of leaning Veer towers. Photograph courtesy of Jason Mrachina, Flickr.

7.5 A guest scrutinizes Claes Oldenburg and Coosje van Bruggen's "Typewriter Eraser," in front of one of the yellow-checkerboard Veer towers.

But CityCenter's towered skyline did point to a major innovation. The company had outsourced its traditional operations by bringing in different hotel companies that could each focus on a key demographic. By commissioning a different architect for each hotel tower, these brands could differentiate themselves from each other within one complex. It was symptomatic of how increasingly individual operators defined the aesthetics of multiple parts of the resort, including bars, nightclubs, restaurants, and now even entire hotel towers. Rather than being entirely designed by the gaming company, the resort had become almost a structural carcass, filled in with different styles according to the taste of the operators—not unlike a real city.

Nevertheless, from a distance, Project CityCenter looked out of place. Much denser than other projects around it—about six times as dense as the Bellagio—it stood out in the midst of sprawl. And while the buildings were magnificent individually, they looked somewhat tame compared with the Luxor's black glass pyramid. Finally, in the context of a replica Paris, Project CityCenter seemed to have appropriated another theme: that of celebrity architecture, copied from the world's financial districts.

CASINOPOLITANISM

In sharp contrast to "the cluttered landscape of extraneous themes that dictate the architecture of neighboring casinos,"[33] architect Bernardo Fort-Brescia described his design for Las Vegas's latest casino as a "purely abstract architectural expression."[34] He designed two fifty-story glass-finned towers, one a zigzagging slab, the other a tall monolith. Unlike the typical casinos that had been set back from the street, his project engaged "the energy of the Strip"[35] with an undulating façade built right up to the sidewalk. Where previously casinos were dark, he designed his casino with floor-to-ceiling windows.

"I think people will enjoy knowing what time of day it is,"[36] said the casino's chief executive, in a statement that would have been laughed at only a decade before. Where previously elevators were placed to force guests to walk through the casino, the so-called "cattle shoot," now they could avoid the casino altogether to get to their rooms.

In 2005, right next to the construction site of Project CityCenter, The Las Vegas Cosmopolitan broke ground. It packed 6.5 million square feet of condos, hotel rooms, and retail on a parcel of just 8.7 acres, more than ten times denser than the Bellagio next door. Developer Ian Bruce Eichner said: "We will redefine the city's skyline with a vertical design that contrasts sharply with the horizontally developed, replicated cities. … The sheer 'verticality' of this development as it towers 600 feet above The Strip is more akin to the urban terrain of Manhattan, or other cosmopolitan cities around the world."[37]

Going against the Las Vegas belief that tourists don't like to leave ground level, the resort's celebrity-chef restaurants and edgy shops were placed on the second and third floors. Even the lobby's Chandelier Bar covered three stories, and was tucked inside a giant chandelier containing two million crystals. And deviating from the surface

7.6 Four miles of gently pulsating LED lighting accentuates The Cosmopolitan's undulating ground façade and two towers, 2010.

7.7 Where Paris Las Vegas once took pride in being a replica, The Cosmopolitan (right) is an "original," 2014.

parking lot, the resort had a four-story underground garage, the walls spray-painted with graffiti by one of the casino's rotating artists-in-residence.

The Cosmopolitan targeted a demographic similar to the W Hotel, the successful luxury hotel chain that took its cool factor from its urban locations, contemporary design, and nightclubs. Instead of typical high-roller villas in garden grounds, The Cosmopolitan had three-story penthouses overlooking the Marquee nightclub. This 62,000-square-foot nightclub was built around a swimming pool rimmed with cabanas, each with a private infinity pool—a swimming pool designed so that it seems to merge into the surrounding landscape: the dance floor, in this case.

"It defines the new Las Vegas of this century, urban, sophisticated, and cosmopolitan,"[38] Fort-Brescia said of his design. That statement summed up the key to Las Vegas's casino complexes of the twenty-first century and their global spread. By incorporating high-level design, contemporary art, high-end retail, and luxury hotels, the Las Vegas casino complex was able to charge higher rates. At the same time, however, this model also helped the complex to become more cosmopolitan. It facilitated the global export of Strip resorts.

Thanks to its fusion of urban gambling, retail, entertainment, and contemporary architecture, the Las Vegas Strip had become highly successful in attracting urban sophisticates to the city—so successful that the city even became a global urban development model. The Philippines planned a Las Vegas-style Entertainment City, South Korea planned a Paradise City, and Vietnam planned a Ho Tram Strip. One researcher even spoke of "casinopolitanism" as "an emergent set of urban development and branding practices, which make the niche industries of casino gambling, music entertainment venues, shopping malls, and resort hotels a key engine for economic growth."[39]

City governments around the world now aspired to boost their economies with a dash of casinopolitanism. Even Singapore, the country that traditionally saw casinos as a moral hazard, now wished to build its new central business district, the Marina Bay, around a Las Vegas-style casino. The government officials found that Las Vegas's latest incarnation of the casino complex, with its higher focus on entertainment, conventions, and its contemporary aesthetic, would be more acceptable to Singaporeans.

In 2006, Sheldon Adelson won the coveted casino license for Singapore's Marina Bay. He deliberately did not propose to plop down another Venetian, which would have been hard to fit into the image of a global financial district. Instead, he proposed a $5.9 billion project designed by star architect Moshe Safdie.

Safdie designed three skyward-curving towers, and topped them with a platform as long as three football fields—at an altitude of 653 feet, it was the world's highest public platform, its north side cantilevering 213 feet. The sky park included restaurants, nightclubs, and a 450-foot-long infinity pool, taking the pool race to global levels. Safdie scattered art throughout the resort and its soaring twenty-three-story atrium, including sculptures by Anish Kapoor. At the base, he laid out a 1.3 million-square-foot convention center, an 800,000-square-foot mall with seven celebrity-chef restaurants, an ice-skating rink, and two theaters including one that premiered the Broadway musical

7.8 Singapore's Marina Bay Sands casino features a 1,115-foot-long sky park at an altitude of 653 feet, and a lotus-shaped museum, 2014. Photograph courtesy of Leonid Iaitskyi, Wikimedia Commons.

The Lion King. He even built a complete 50,000-square-foot museum, in the shape of a lotus, floating in the Marina Bay, fronted by a musical fountain with lasers projecting holographic mermaids.

In 2012, Sheldon Adelson collected $2.94 billion of gaming revenue from his Marina Bay Sands, the world's highest revenue from a casino. But only because the Las Vegas casino was camouflaged in a cosmopolitan shell, like a Trojan Horse, had it managed to become Singapore's new defining feature. Adelson knew that his casino in Singapore, seen as a model city, was a watershed event for the export of Las Vegas's gaming industry: "Now I see countries who say, 'If it's good enough for Singapore, it's good enough for us.'"[40]

With revenue from Singapore's two casinos alone expected to surpass the revenue of the entire Las Vegas Strip, one thing was clear: in the Strip's cosmopolitan age the most extravagant casinos operated no longer solely in Las Vegas, but had been unleashed into the world.

CASINO CAPITALISM AND THE RISK SOCIETY

By 2007, the Las Vegas Strip had reached a new pinnacle of excess. Star architects had designed America's most expensive buildings, each filled with multimillion-dollar art collections, dozens of luxury shops, and celebrity-chef restaurants. They included the world's highest-grossing nightclubs, making up to a $100 million a year each, thanks to luring revelers to buy champagne with a 1,000 percent markup. Best of all, developers were building tens of thousands more luxury hotel rooms and condominiums. Las Vegas had so many construction cranes on the skyline, some quipped that Nevada's state bird should be changed from the mountain bluebird to the crane.

The starchitecture strategy seemed to work. Elite culture and architecture helped raise the average cost of a night's stay from $97 in 2000 to $146 in 2007 while maintaining occupancy rates over 90 percent, well over the 60 percent national average.[41] Even before completion of Project CityCenter and The Cosmopolitan, two of the United States's largest construction projects, many more projects were announced. In 2007, Boyd Gaming Corporation imploded the Stardust, the resort that had once made Las Vegas affordable to the masses. In its place, it started building the 5,300-room Echelon Palace. Then Turnberry Associates started constructing the 3,889-room Fontainebleau. Glenn Schaeffer, the casino's chief executive, said: "It will blend what's current and what will endure in contemporary art, striking design, world-caliber architecture."[42] Architect Carlos Zapata designed a curved blue glass-clad tower, which would feature chandeliers created by the Chinese artist Ai Weiwei. At 735 feet tall, it was to be the tallest tower in Nevada.

Thanks to all the activity on the Strip, Las Vegas became the country's fastest-growing metropolitan area for two decades: from 854,000 population in 1990 to nearly 2 million in 2007. Historian Hal Rothman claimed that it had become a new example for other cities in the United States. He called it a "triumph of post-industrial capitalism,"[43] shrewd in the selling of the ultimate commodity of the service economy: experience. Thanks to cheap land, low taxes, and high service wages, Las Vegas seemed to be the only place where poorly educated people could still make a middle-class living, and attain the American ideal of a detached single-family home. But the brand of Las Vegas as the last bastion of the American Dream was about to dissolve.

With most of the new architectural icons of the starchitecture phase still in scaffolding, the global financial crisis hit. Fueled by a decade of easy credit and unprecedented debt load, the housing bubble burst, triggering the worst economic crisis since the

Great Depression. Gaming corporations had highly overleveraged themselves. With consumers defaulting on their casino condo mortgages, and capital fleeing away to safer investments, casino stocks plummeted. By early 2009, MGM Mirage stock had fallen 94 percent; Las Vegas Sands dropped 99 percent.

Construction came to a sudden standstill. Project CityCenter was on the verge of bankruptcy. The Norman Foster-designed Harmon tower, pinnacle of the complex, halted its rise at twenty-eight stories only, instead of the planned forty-eight, because of a construction error. When the operator realized that the hotel would never make a profit at its new size, a stump, the tower was demolished. Adding fuel to the fire, the Vdara tower's concave shape and reflective glass façade had an unexpected side effect: they turned the building into a magnifying glass, directing sunlight onto sunbathers in the pool below. This solar convergence, nicknamed the "Death Ray," focused light so intensely that it burned hair and melted cups.

Meanwhile, The Cosmopolitan's developer defaulted on a construction loan, leading Deutsche Bank to foreclose on the casino. Surprisingly, not only did the bank continue construction, it also ended up operating the complex. As odd as it may have seemed for a German bank to run a casino, "given the way banks have operated in this decade," *Time* wrote, "that seems like a logical business extension."[44]

Even worse, some construction projects were canceled completely, like the Echelon Palace, its bare concrete carcass exposed to the elements and the tourist gaze. The condominium tower inside the Venetian, however, had only been stalled. Owner Sheldon Adelson eventually covered it with a million-dollar tarp with printed images of the completed building, to prevent the concrete skeleton from disrupting the tranquil Venetian skyline. The Fontainebleau declared bankruptcy. It had already topped out at sixty-three floors, its blue windows in place. It stood unfinished on Las Vegas's skyline as Nevada's highest building, a hollow shell.

Images of unfinished construction projects, cranes suspended in midair, and empty casino floors made for eerie sights, distributed globally as representations of crisis. They dramatically showed the world the limitations on the transformational ability of architectural icons.

In 2009, the famous "Welcome to Fabulous Las Vegas" sign made the cover of *Time*, with the difference that the sign now said "Less Vegas." The reporter wrote that Las Vegas was "the deepest crater of the recession,"[45] leading the nation in unemployment and foreclosure rates.

The brand of Las Vegas as the last bastion of the American Dream had vanished. Instead, the Las Vegas casino had become a metaphor for a troubled nation led into despair by an economy built on debt financing and increasingly high risk: "Casino Capitalism."[46]

Even before Las Vegas had recovered from the recession, it faced a massive environmental crisis. Fourteen years of drought had caused Lake Mead, the city's main freshwater source, to drop 130 feet. The lake was now at its lowest level in history, and featured a white "bathtub ring" of mineral deposits left by higher water levels. Moreover, empty boat slips now hovered above the cracked sandy desert, where there was water before. If the water level drops another 80 feet, Las Vegas's pipeline will be sucking air—leaving 90 percent of the city gasping for water.

Sociologist Ulrich Beck has argued that the increasing number of industrial accidents, including Chernobyl, as well as the results of man-made climate change, including floods and permanent droughts, were lasting side-effects of our "Risk Society."[47] Las Vegas proved the point. Hedging environmental risk had become part of its fabric. It had already changed turf to fake grass, recycled its water, and started drilling a billion-dollar three-mile tunnel—another straw through which to suck out the lake. But even at its completion, the tunnel dealt only with the symptoms of the problem, not with the source—pools and fountains and lawns don't really belong in the Mojave Desert.

In their continuing effort to grow, Las Vegas developers have pushed the limits, putting their entire population and economy at risk. And where Las Vegas was plagued by droughts, Atlantic City, its sister gambling city, suffered when Hurricane Sandy destroyed much of the Jersey shore. And with casinos opening in neighboring states, four of Atlantic City's twelve closed in 2014.

Ironically, as the recession and the droughts of the American Southwest turned Las Vegas into the poster child of crisis, and its East Coast sister lay in tatters, the city has become more relevant than ever as a desirable model for cosmopolitan urban development worldwide. Cities battered by the Great Recession now look to gambling to bring jobs and revitalize neighborhoods. Even the city of Boston, full of historic landmarks that stand as a testament to the founding of the United States of America, is currently building a Wynn casino.

But back in Las Vegas, the starchitecture phase of megastructures has had its day. Fixer-uppers are the new trend, like the renovation of the Sahara, now branded as "SLS" thanks to fresh white paint covering its sand-colored buildings. Other plans are to make the Strip look more like other cities, with a new concert arena and a vibrant urban park designed by the landscape architecture firm !melk. Meanwhile, Zappos founder Tony Hsieh plans to turn downtown's Glitter Gulch into a Brooklyn-inspired start-up district.

Nevertheless, after the peak of the starchitecture era, the Las Vegas Strip was entirely different from what it was before, with cutting-edge architecture, titanium-jagged buildings, glass-finned towers, and renowned contemporary sculpture. Ironically, in 2010, the same year Project CityCenter opened with its multimillion-dollar art collection inside its casino, Las Vegas's contemporary art museum closed as a result of the economic downturn. Las Vegans could now see art in the casino, rather than the museum, for free.

While the Strip during its starchitecture phase on one hand represented new levels of economic crisis, environmental waste, and the commodification of architecture and art, on the other hand it also led to a surprise. Casino developers were leading the world in "green" building and had become the twenty-first-century Medicis, unlikely patrons of the arts, making privately financed artistic marvels visible, as well as accessible, to the masses.

Conclusion: America as Las Vegas

The Strip began as an exception. But increasingly it has become a rule—in its holistically designed and multisensory environments, in being technologically wired and "smart," in patterns of urban development, in financial practices, and in aesthetic tastes. For decades, Vegas marketed itself as an over-the-top series of urban stunts. But this seemingly outrageous behavior took advantage of fundamental changes in American society. The urbanistic role of Vegas has also taken a turn. The Strip began as essentially anti-urban, with inwardly oriented resorts located outside of the incorporated city of Las Vegas. Today, the Strip is a major pedestrian space with casinos that contribute to a larger urban experience. Vegas has now even become a model for twenty-first-century urbanism that other cities are seeking to emulate. Not only that, the city provides lessons for anyone called upon to create landmarks, attention-getters, fantasy environments, spectacular images or memorable experiences. I personally witnessed the city's impact as an architect when Chinese clients for the world's largest tower, after a visit to the Strip, wanted the Bellagio's musical fountains. They wanted Vegas.

From its inception in 1941, the Strip has mutated beyond even its own wildest dreams. In the 1940s, Strip developers dressed like cowboys, some packing real guns, built hacienda-style casinos that broke ground with moving neon displays as big as windmills. By the 1950s, casino builders replaced the wagon wheels with Cadillac tail-fin forms, and pumped underwater Muzak into exotically shaped pools. The 1960s neon signs, as tall as twenty-story buildings and as long as two football fields, were ripped down in the 1970s when the emphasis shifted to the buildings themselves, and chandeliers the size of trucks. By the next decade, the chandeliers had been replaced by a ten-story, laser-eyed Sphinx and a fiery volcano spewing piña colada scent. Charmed by the world's famous cities in the late 1990s, Las Vegas built replicas, including the

Eiffel Tower, New York skyscrapers, and Venetian canals. But in the new millennium, a mere decade later, replicas were out and serious architectural originals, which housed museum-quality collections of authentic art, were in.

If any city deserves the "Makeover Award" for the most drastic changes to its image, it is Las Vegas.

But as outrageous as the Strip's excesses may seem, it has always been the ultimate manifestation of a quintessentially American practice: marketing. At the peak of the popularity of Western movies, casino builders welcomed guests with cowboy saloons featuring stuffed buffalo heads. On the cusp of the suburbanization of America, they built bungalows with lavish pools and verdant lawns. When the Space Age and nuclear testing enthralled the nation, they enveloped guests with neon planets and plastered a casino with a sign of the atom bomb. Even before Gordon Gekko celebrated unfettered materialism in the movie *Wall Street*, developers built mirror-clad, corporate modernist casinos. When Disney became the world's number one entertainment corporation, Vegas casinos built entire theme parks and a larger-than-life Cinderella castle. As heritage tourism flourished, and Americans became fascinated with design from former eras, developers reciprocated by enhancing their casinos with *Belle Époque* monuments. And when other cities built architectural icons to attract tourists, Las Vegas developers commissioned the world's "Starchitects." The history of the Strip represents the ever-evolving architecture of the American Dream.

Over a period of seventy years, developers have built a more sophisticated "Mousetrap." The casino has come a long way from the original small box with about fifty rooms to thousand-room megastructures, the earth's largest. The Strip's first casinos were low-rise bungalows surrounded by surface parking; the latest incarnations are high-rise towers with underground parking. The first casinos followed the "island" model resort, isolating guests with buildings set back from the Strip, but they now abide by the urban model, fully enmeshed into the sidewalk. Initially the only entertainment was a lounge act; today there are entire arenas, Broadway theaters, and the world's largest nightclubs. At first the revenue came from the gambling hall; now the casino complex generates more from conventions, nightlife, restaurants and retail. Once known for their five-dollar steaks and cheap motels, casinos presently lure guests with celebrity chefs and luxury suites.

There have been times when Las Vegas was considered tacky—and it still is by some. But today the Strip is becoming an authority on art, performance, and architecture, with multimillion-dollar art collections, a lineup of Cirque du Soleil shows, and buildings designed by star architects. Moreover, the Bellagio, a Las Vegas casino, is *the* most popular recent building in America, according to *America's Favorite Architecture*, a poll by the American Institute of Architects. Meanwhile, as public budgets for museums and shared spaces decline, while art collections and streets are being privatized, the Strip is reflective of a world in which the lines between private and public are increasingly blurred. While the distinction between mass consumerism and elite culture continues to fade, with museums run more and more like franchises, Las Vegas already perfected the art of "exit through the gift shop."

The fact that the Strip keeps updating itself to the latest fad in architecture obviously leads to destruction and waste; on the other hand, it has created publicly accessible architectural marvels that attract many to the desert. On the positive side of the Strip's "creative destruction" lay the most holistically and sensually created environments, and unbridled place-making freed from traditional ideas.

To everyone's surprise, despite more relaxed planning regulations, the Las Vegas Strip has become one of the most pedestrian-oriented urban areas in the American West. The great irony was that corporatism, rather than planning theory, caused this shift. As the Strip became denser, as a result of its success, corporations implemented urban design principles to appeal to pedestrians as well as automobilists. Instead of blank concrete walls and asphalt parking lots, they built "active" streets with restaurants, fronted them with pocket parks and landscaped sidewalks, and even arranged terraces and benches. If the postwar Strip was symptomatic of the suburban sprawl of the United States, the twenty-first-century Strip is representative of a nationwide migration from suburbia back to the cities, America's "urban renaissance."

America changed along with Las Vegas.

The Strip adapted to changing trends with such overwhelming financial success that it has even become a global model for urban development. Singapore, despite its moral objections to gambling, has built its new central business district around a Las Vegas-styled casino. Macau has reclaimed hundreds of acres of the South China Sea, only to build a Las Vegas-style Strip. Ironically, with casinos thriving in these and other places, Las Vegas may be eclipsed by the very model it helped create.

Vegas operators are so finely tuned to pleasing their guests that the Strip is a pioneer in the "experience economy," in which companies compete for customers by staging memorable experiences. As creepy as it may be, casinos track their guests, knowing where they have been, or whether they drank coffee or tea. Vegas tracking technology is so advanced that after 9/11, Homeland Security visited Las Vegas to learn about surveillance. As wasteful it may be to have megastructures in the desert, the city now leads the world in water-saving techniques, with casinos even developing their own low-flow showerheads.

Where gambling in the United States used to be contained in the remote Mojave Desert—for the same reason it was a site for nuclear detonations—today hundreds of casinos have entered Indian reservations and American cities. Following the Strip's privately managed sidewalks and plazas that lure tourists to try their luck, public space in other cities has also become increasingly privatized, converting citizens into consumers, one by one. These days, Mob king "Bugsy" Siegel's "build it and they will come" attitude finds its equivalent in cities' desperate attempts to build icons that attract tourists. In a world where every metropolis is a competitor for visitors, cities learn from Las Vegas's continuous reinvention to "fix" their own image. The Strip-style economy, shaken up by high risk-taking and the whims of individuals like casino mogul Sheldon

Adelson, has become the formula for "casino capitalism" worldwide. Built in the middle of the Mojave Desert, Las Vegas has faced a water crisis since its founding, while other cities now face environmental hazards such as floods and droughts resulting from man-made climate change.

When the first casino developers hung cow horns on walls and guns on their hips, critics derided Las Vegas as fake. But billions of dollars of investments and hundreds of thousands of jobs over a century are no desert mirage. Ever since the Hoover and Roosevelt Administrations built the Boulder Dam, the political economy of Las Vegas's development has reflected America as a whole. While Lake Mead still provides the water and the hydroelectric force to power the Strip's bright lights, today American ideology has shifted toward deregulation and neoliberal prioritization of private enterprise, with Las Vegas as the avatar once again. Las Vegas, however, has been more than a mirror of society alone. The city shaped both American and global urbanization, setting a template for practices of city branding, spatial production and control, and high-risk investment in urban spaces. The Strip is both a promoter of hypercapitalism and a paragon of modernity in which "all that is solid melts into air."

In its current incarnation, the Strip continues to lead the charge in innovation and setting the tone. Our cities are affected by an increasing number of casinos, the tourist industry, rampant consumerism, fickle casino capitalism, and environmental crises. That once dusty, potholed road stretching through a barren desert wasteland has grown into one of the world's most visited boulevards, with an impact that is felt worldwide. Today, we all live in Las Vegas.

Notes

INTRODUCTION: LAS VEGAS AS AMERICA

1. Quoted in Kurt Andersen, "Las Vegas U.S.A.," *Time*, January 10, 1994.

2. Joseph A. Schumpeter, *Capitalism, Socialism and Democracy* (London: Routledge, 1994 [orig. pub. 1942]), 83.

3. Joseph Pine and James Gilmore, *The Experience Economy: Work Is Theater and Everyday Business a Stage* (Boston: Harvard Business School Press, 1999).

4. Susan Strange, *Casino Capitalism* (Manchester: Manchester University Press, 1997).

CHAPTER 1: WILD WEST (1941–1946)

1. Las Vegas Chamber of Commerce Monthly Report, April 1939.

2. Quoted in Elizabeth Nelson Patrick, "An Exhibit and Reception Commemorating the Grand Opening of the Last Frontier Hotel," University of Nevada Reno Library, University of Nevada, Las Vegas, Special Collections.

3. Quoted in Sally Denton and Roger Morris, *The Money and the Power: The Making of Las Vegas and Its Hold on America* (New York: Vintage, 2002), 92.

4. John Steele to George A. Smith, July 25, 1855.

5. Remy Jules and Julius Lucius Brenchley, *A Journey to Great Salt Lake City* (London: W. Jeffs, 1861), 412.

6. "John F. Cahlan: Fifty Years in Journalism and Community Development: An Oral History," Oral History Program, University of Nevada, 1987, 79.

7. Quoted in Bruce Barton, "No Rip-Roaring Town a Boulder," *San Bernardino County Sun*, August 4, 1929, 24.

8. "Las Vegas Made Safe," *Time*, June 1, 1931.

9. "California 'Navy' Conquers Armada of Gambling Ships," *Pittsburgh Press*, August 2, 1939, 32.

10. Quoted in Alan Balboni, "Tony Cornero," *Las Vegas Review-Journal*, February 7, 1999.

11. "Wild, Woolly and Wide-Open," *Look*, August 14, 1940, 21.

12. John Findlay, *People of Chance: Gambling in American Society from Jamestown to Las Vegas* (New York: Oxford University Press, 1986), 4.

13. "Helldorado," *Desert Magazine*, May 1940, 28.

14. "Nevada: One Sound State," *Time*, March 8, 1937.

15. Ibid.

16. Las Vegas Chamber of Commerce Monthly Report, April 1939.

17. Richard Gordon Lillard, *Desert Challenge: An Interpretation of Nevada* (New York: Knopf, 1942), 317.

18. "Wild, Woolly and Wide-Open."

19. Katharine Best and Katharine Hillyer, *Las Vegas: Playtown U.S.A.* (New York: David McKay, 1955), 61.

20. For more on this, see Chris Nichols, *The Leisure Architecture of Wayne McAllister* (Layton, Utah: Gibbs Smith, 2007).

21. "John F. Cahlan," 178.

22. Lillard, *Desert Challenge*, 321.

23. El Rancho Promotional and Publicity Collection, UNLV Special Collections.

24. Wesley Stout, "Nevada's New Reno," *Saturday Evening Post*, October 31, 1942.

25. George Stamos Jr., "The Great Resorts of Las Vegas: How They Began. Part 1," *Las Vegas Sun Magazine*, April 1, 1979.

26. Ibid.

27. Ibid.

28. Stout, "Nevada's New Reno."

29. "An Interview with William J. Moore," Oral History Program, University of Nevada Reno Library, 1985, 3.

30. "An Interview with Morton Saiger," Oral History Program, University of Nevada Reno Library, 1985, 8.

31. "An Interview with William J. Moore," 3.

32. Ibid., 15.

33. George Stamos Jr., "The Great Resorts of Las Vegas: How They Began. Part 2," *Las Vegas Sun Magazine*, April 8, 1979.

34. Last Frontier Promotional and Publicity Collection, UNLV Special Collections.

35. "John F. Cahlan," 182.

36. Best and Hillyer, *Las Vegas: Playtown U.S.A.*, 61.

37. Findlay, *People of Chance*, 134.

38. "An Interview with William J. Moore," 2.

39. Gaston Bachelard, *The Poetics of Space* (Boston: Beacon Press, 1994), 150.

40. "An Interview with William J. Moore," 33–34.

41. "Loden Fashions Paper Mache Western Figures," *Las Vegas Review-Journal*, September 3, 1950.

42. "Moore Carries Through Idea of R. E. Griffith, Founder," *Las Vegas Review-Journal*, September 3, 1950.

43. "An Interview with William J. Moore," 19.

44. Richard Erdoes, *Saloons of the Old West* (New York: Knopf, 1979), 37.

45. Nichols, *The Leisure Architecture of Wayne McAllister*, 67.

46. David G. Schwartz, "The El Rancho Vegas and Hotel Last Frontier: Strip Pioneers," *Journal of Gambling Issues* 3 (2001).

CHAPTER 2: SUNBELT MODERN (1946–1958)

1. Julian Halevy, "Disneyland and Las Vegas," *The Nation*, June 7, 1958.

2. Quoted in "Las Vegas: An Unconventional History," PBS American Experience documentary, <http://www.pbs.org/wgbh/amex/lasvegas/filmmore/pt.html> (accessed October 5, 2013).

3. Quoted in Dennis Eisenberg, Uri Dan, and Eli Landau, *Meyer Lansky: Mogul of the Mob* (New York: Paddington Press, 1979), 225.

4. For more on this, see Alan Hess, *Googie Redux: Ultramodern Roadside Architecture* (San Francisco: Chronicle Books, 2004).

5. Bernard DeVoto, "The Anxious West," *Harper's*, December 1946, 485.

6. W. R. Wilkerson, *The Man Who Invented Las Vegas* (Beverly Hills, CA: Ciro's Books, 2000), 47.

7. Eisenberg, Dan, and Landau, *Meyer Lansky*, 226.

8. Wilkerson, *The Man Who Invented Las Vegas*, 76.

9. "Hotel Flamingo Provides Luxury Accommodations in Keeping with Its Slogan," *Las Vegas Review-Journal*, March 1, 1955.

10. Sally Denton and Roger Morris, *The Money and the Power: The Making of Las Vegas and Its Hold on America* (New York: Vintage, 2002), 53.

11. Quoted in Stan Delaplane, "Las Vegas," *San Antonio Express*, April 8, 1969, 12.

12. Susan Berman, "Memoirs of a Gangster's Daughter," *New York* 14, no. 29 (July 27, 1981), 29.

13. "John F. Cahlan: Fifty Years in Journalism and Community Development: An Oral History," Oral History Program, University of Nevada, 182.

14. Strip Historical Site, "The Thunderbird," <http://www.lvstriphistory.com/ie/thun48.htm> (accessed May 1, 2014).

15. Eugene P. Moehring, *Resort City in the Sunbelt: Las Vegas, 1930–1970* (Reno: University of Nevada Press, 1989), 69.

16. Mike Davis, "Las Vegas versus Nature," in Hal K. Rothman, ed., *Reopening the American West* (Tucson: University of Arizona Press, 1998), 61.

17. See Stephen Graham and Simon Marvin, *Splintering Urbanism: Networked Infrastructures, Technological Mobilities and the Urban Condition* (London: Routledge, 2001).

18. Denton and Morris, *The Money and the Power*, 5.

19. Ed Reid and Ovid Demaris, *The Green Felt Jungle* (New York: Trident Press, 1963), 60.

20. A. J. Liebling, "Our Footloose Correspondents: Action in the Desert," *New Yorker*, May 13, 1950, 112–113.

21. Quoted in Richard English, "The Million-Dollar Talent War," *Saturday Evening Post*, October 24, 1953, 73.

22. "An Interview with Morton Saiger," Oral History Program, University of Nevada Reno Library, 1985, 43.

23. Ibid., 27.

24. From "Investigation of Organized Crime in Interstate Commerce: Hearings before the Special Committee to Investigate Organized Crime in Interstate Commerce," U.S. Senate, 81st Cong., 2nd Sess. and 82nd Congress, 1st Sess., Part 10, U.S. Government Printing Office, Washington, D.C., 1950.

25. "An Interview with Morton Saiger," 22.

26. Denton and Morris, *The Money and the Power*, 102.

27. Ibid., 103.

28. Ibid., 131.

29. Quoted in Eisenberg, Dan, and Landau, *Meyer Lansky*, 37.

30. Liebling, "Our Footloose Correspondents: Action in the Desert," 107.

31. "Sahara Interior Design Set Up by Ragnar Qvale, Young Engineer," *Las Vegas Review-Journal*, October 6, 1952.

32. John Findlay, "Suckers and Escapists? Interpreting Las Vegas and Post-War America," *Nevada Historical Society* 33 (1990), 1.

33. Quoted in Steven Bach, *Marlene Dietrich: Life and Legend* (Minneapolis: University of Minnesota Press, 2011), 368.

34. Quoted in Donald Spoto, *Blue Angel: The Life of Marlene Dietrich* (New York: Cooper Square Press, 2000), 198.

35. Gladwin Hill, "Klondike in the Desert," *New York Times Magazine*, June 7, 1953.

36. Phil Patton, "Wayne McAllister, b. 1907: The Guru of Googie," *New York Times*, January 7, 2001.

37. William H. Honan, "Wayne McAllister, Architect for a Car Culture, Dies at 92," *New York Times*, April 3, 2000.

38. Dick Pearce, "Pleasure Palaces," *Harper's*, February 1955.

39. Jeff Witse, *Contested Waters: A Social History of Swimming Pools in America* (Chapel Hill: University of North Carolina Press, 2010), 200.

40. Quoted in George Stamos Jr., "The Great Resorts of Las Vegas: How They Began. Part 7," *Las Vegas Sun Magazine*, June 17, 1979.

41. Quoted in Larry Gragg, "The Risk in Using Gambling to Create 'America's Playground': Las Vegas, 1905–60," in Pauliina Raento and David G. Schwartz, eds., *Gambling, Space, and Time: Shifting Boundaries and Cultures* (Reno: University of Nevada Press, 2011), 157.

42. "Showgirl Shanghri-La," *Life*, June 21, 1954.

43. "Las Vegas: 'It Just Couldn't Happen,'" *Time*, November 23, 1953.

44. David G. Schwartz, "'A Fun Night Out': Shifting Legal and Cultural Constructions of Gambling, the Slot Machine, and the Casino Resort," *Gaming Law Review* 1, no. 4 (1997), 547.

45. Katharine Best and Katharine Hillyer, *Las Vegas: Playtown U.S.A.* (New York: David McKay, 1955), 76.

46. Ibid., 85–86.

47. Ibid., 75.

48. "New Frontier in Premiere Monday Nite," *Las Vegas Review-Journal*, April 3, 1955.

49. Best and Hillyer, *Las Vegas: Playtown U.S.A.*, 106.

50. Findlay, "Suckers and Escapists?," 8.

51. English, "The Million-Dollar Talent War," 73.

52. Quoted in David E. Nye, *American Technological Sublime* (Cambridge, MA: MIT Press, 1996), 284.

53. Best and Hillyer, *Las Vegas: Playtown U.S.A.*, 67.

54. "Heavyweight Star to Make Nightly Show Attractive," *Las Vegas Review-Journal*, April 19, 1995.

55. Michael T. Pavelko, David B. Wood, and Randell J. Laczniak, "Las Vegas, Nevada: Gambling with Water in the Desert," U.S. Geological Survey Circular 1182, Las Vegas, Nevada (1999).

56. Pearce, "Pleasure Palaces," 81.

57. Parry Thomas welcomed casino loan applications "outside of conventional channels," so-called "character loans," approved without collateral. Eisenberg, Dan, and Landau, *Meyer Lansky*, 162.

58. Denton and Morris, *The Money and the Power*, 164.

59. Gladwin Hill, "The 'Sure Thing' Boom at Las Vegas," *New York Times*, January 30, 1955.

60. Quoted in Myrick Land, *A Short History of Las Vegas* (Reno: University of Nevada Press, 2004), 145.

61. Alfred Gottesman to Joe Perrett, July 31, 1954, The Dunes Hotel Collection 93–98, University of Nevada, Las Vegas, Special Collections.

62. Peter Wyden, "How Wicked Is Vegas?," *Saturday Evening Post*, November 11, 1961, 17.

63. Ibid.

64. Quoted in Art Lynch, "Homer Rissman: Casino Master," *Southern Nevada Contractor's Journal*, August 17, 1987.

65. Wyden, "How Wicked Is Vegas?," 20.

66. Gilbert Millstein, "Cloud on Las Vegas' Silver Lining: A Few Bright Lights Have Dimmed," *New York Times*, March 18, 1956.

67. Reyner Banham, "Las Vegas," *Los Angeles Times West Magazine*, November 8, 1970.

68. Millstein, "Cloud on Las Vegas' Silver Lining."

CHAPTER 3: POP CITY (1958–1969)

1. Norman Mailer, *An American Dream* (New York: Vintage Press, 1999), 269.

2. Quoted in Patricia Leigh Brown, "In City of Change, Is 'Las Vegas Landmark' an Oxymoron?," *New York Times*, October 7, 1993.

3. Newspaper accounts of each new sign, including by the *Las Vegas-Review Journal*, typically mentioned the miles of neon.

4. For a detailed account of the chaotic construction process, see Alan Hess, *Viva Las Vegas: After-Hours Architecture* (San Francisco: Chronicle Books, 1993), 69.

5. Dorothy Wright, "Kermit Wayne: Renaissance Designer from the Golden Age of Las Vegas," *Las Vegas*, June 1986, 37.

6. Ibid., 39.

7. "Flashing Color Display Featured in Stardust Sign," *Las Vegas Review-Journal*, July 1, 1958.

8. The city qualified as the core of a Standard Metropolitan Statistical Area. "Clark County Population Growth," CensusSope, <http://www.censusscope.org/us/s32/c3/chart_popl.html> (accessed June 5, 2010).

9. Quoted in Hess, *Viva Las Vegas*, 66.

10. Quoted in Wright, "Kermit Wayne," 37.

11. Ibid., 39–40.

12. Quoted in Tom Wolfe, *The Kandy-Kolored Tangerine-Flake Streamline Baby* (1965; New York: Macmillan, 2009), 8.

13. Ibid., 15.

14. Ibid., 8.

15. Ibid., 7.

16. Ibid., 15.

17. Ibid., 8.

18. Ibid., 11.

19. Ibid., 7.

20. "Oral History of Milton Schwartz: Interview by Harvey M. Choldin," Chicago Architects Oral History Project, Art Institute of Chicago, 2007, 57.

21. Ibid., 58.

22. Ibid., 70.

23. Ibid., 58.

24. Ibid., 59.

25. "Minksy in Vegas: French Flavored Burleycue Sears the Desert Sands," *Playboy*, April 1958, 40–44.

26. Wolfe, *The Kandy-Kolored Tangerine-Flake Streamline Baby*, 16.

27. Ibid.

28. Ibid., 17.

29. Ibid.

30. "Oral History of Milton Schwartz," 79.

31. Ibid., 60.

32. Ibid., 69.

33. Ibid.

34. Ibid.

35. Albert Elsen, "Night Lights," *Art News*, November 1983, 113.

36. Hess, *Viva Las Vegas*.

37. Charles F. Barnard, *The Magic Sign: The Electric Art—Architecture of Las Vegas* (Cincinnati: ST Publications, 1993).

38. Ibid., 97.

39. "The Aladdin Hotel History: The White Knight Arrives," *Classic Las Vegas*, <http://classiclasvegas.squarespace.com/a-brief-history-of-the-strip/2008/4/24/the-aladdin-hotel-history-the-white-knight-arrives.html> (accessed October 5, 2013).

40. Brian O'Doherty, "Highway to Las Vegas," *Art in America* 60, no. 1 (January–February 1972).

41. Barnard, *The Magic Sign*, 104.

42. Elsen, "Night Lights," 113.

43. Wolfe, *The Kandy-Kolored Tangerine-Flake Streamline Baby*, 10–11.

44. Elsen, "Night Lights," 108.

45. "Vegas Glitter Makes Gold," *Sign Business*, April 1987.

46. Reyner Banham, "Las Vegas," *Los Angeles Times*, November 8, 1970.

47. Ibid.

48. Ibid.

49. Ibid.

50. Reyner Banham, *The Architecture of the Well-Tempered Environment* (London: Architectural Press, 1969), 270.

51. Ibid., 269.

52. Peter Cook, Ron Herron, and Dennis Crompton ("Archigram"), "Instant City," *Architectural Design*, May 1969, 280.

53. Ibid.

54. Hunter S. Thompson, *Fear and Loathing in Las Vegas: A Savage Journey to the Heart of the American Dream* (1972; New York: Vintage, 2010), 47.

55. Wolfe, *The Kandy-Kolored Tangerine-Flake Streamline Baby*, 5.

56. Ibid., 6.

57. Ibid.

58. *Electrical West* 129 (1962), 143–161.

59. Mailer, *An American Dream*, 267.

60. "Air Conditioning Is Important Here," *Las Vegas Review-Journal*, March 1, 1955.

61. Pete Earley, *Super Casino: Inside the "New" Las Vegas* (New York: Bantam Books, 2001), 67.

62. Jane Wilson, "A Double Roman Holiday," *Los Angeles Times*, June 18, 1967.

63. For more about the psychological differences between high-ceiling "Kranes-type" and low-ceiling "Friedman-type" casinos, see Karen Finlay, Vinay Kanetkar, Jane Londerville, and Harvey H. C. Marmurek, "The Physical and Psychological Measurement of Gambling Environments," *Environment and Behavior* 38 (July 2006), 570–581.

64. George Stamos Jr., "The Great Resorts of Las Vegas: How They Began. Part 15," *Las Vegas Sun Magazine*, October 14, 1979.

65. Jim Barrows, "The Man Who Dreamed Las Vegas … Jay Sarno," *Las Vegas Style*, May 1994, 11.

66. According to architecture critic Alan Hess, "Caesars was a true popular culture appropriation of high-art forms overtly mixed with historical forms." See Hess, *Viva Las Vegas*.

67. Quoted in Wright, "Kermit Wayne," 37.

68. Barrows, "The Man Who Dreamed Las Vegas," 10.

69. Stamos, "The Great Resorts of Las Vegas. Part 15."

70. Wilson, "A Double Roman Holiday."

71. Quoted in A. D. Hopkins, "Jay Sarno: He Came to Play," in Jack Sheehan, ed., *The Players: The Men Who Made Las Vegas* (Reno: University of Nevada Press, 1997), 95.

72. See Margaret Malamud and Donald T. McGuire, "Living Like Romans in Las Vegas," in Sandra R. Joshel, Margaret Malamud, and Donald T. McGuire, eds., *Imperial Projections: Ancient Rome in Modern Popular Culture* (Baltimore: Johns Hopkins University Press, 2005), 257.

73. "The Talk of the Town," *New Yorker*, August 20, 1966.

74. Quoted in Forrest Duke, "Why Lack of Apostrophe in 'Caesars Palace'?," *Las Vegas Review-Journal*, 1968.

75. David G. Schwartz, *Grandissimo: The First Emperor of Las Vegas* (Las Vegas: Winchester Books, 2013), 69.

76. Quoted in "Gambling on 'the Grind,'" *Service World International*, May 1969, 42.

77. Barrows, "The Man Who Dreamed Las Vegas," 12.

78. Thompson, *Fear and Loathing in Las Vegas*, 47.

79. "Gigantic Circus Circus Opens Friday," *Las Vegas Review-Journal*, August 17, 1968.

80. Ibid.

81. Thompson, *Fear and Loathing in Las Vegas*, 47.

82. John Scott, "Circus Circus Opens on the Vegas Strip," *Los Angeles Times*, October 22, 1968.

83. "Inside Straight," transcript from interview with Burton M. Cohen by MPH Entertainment, 21–22.

84. "Gambling on 'the Grind,'" 46.

85. Thompson, *Fear and Loathing in Las Vegas*, 47.

86. Ibid.

87. Robert Venturi, Denise Scott-Brown, and Steven Izenour, *Learning from Las Vegas: The Forgotten Symbolism of Architectural Form* (1972; Cambridge, MA: MIT Press, 1986).

88. Tom Wolfe, "I Drove Around Los Angeles and It's Crazy! The Art World Is Upside Down," *Los Angeles Times*, December 1, 1968.

89. Kent Lauer, *Las Vegas Review-Journal*, October 27, 1983.

90. Venturi, Scott-Brown, Steven Izenour, *Learning from Las Vegas*, 116.

91. Ibid., 34.

92. Ibid., xvii.

93. Ibid., 119.

94. Ibid., 34.

95. Peter Vandevanter, "Venturi: Controversial Philadelphia Architect," *The Daily Princetonian*, February 26, 1972.

96. Ibid.

97. Fredric Jameson, *Postmodernism, or, the Cultural Logic of Late Capitalism* (Durham: Duke University Press, 1991), 2.

98. Wright, "Kermit Wayne," 41.

99. Kurt Andersen, "Las Vegas U.S.A.," *Time*, January 10, 1994.

100. Adolf Loos, in his 1908 book *Ornament and Crime*, wrote against ornamentation, arguing that it would cause objects to go out of style too quickly.

101. Tom Wolfe, *From Bauhaus to Our House* (New York: Farrar, Straus and Giroux, 1981), 109.

102. George Stamos Jr., "The Great Resorts of Las Vegas: How They Began. Part 18," *Las Vegas Sun Magazine*, December 9, 1979.

CHAPTER 4: CORPORATE MODERN (1969–1985)

1. Dorothy Wright, "Kermit Wayne: Renaissance Designer from the Golden Age of Las Vegas," *Las Vegas Magazine*, June 1986, 40.

2. K. J. Evans, "Howard Hughes," *Las Vegas Review-Journal*, September 12, 1999.

3. Michael Drosnin, *Citizen Hughes* (New York: Henry Holt, 1987), 108.

4. Ibid., 278.

5. Peter Harry Brown and Pat H. Broeske, *Howard Hughes: The Untold Story* (New York: Da Capo Press, 2004), 337.

6. Jack Sheehan, ed., *The Players: The Men Who Made Las Vegas* (Reno: University of Nevada Press, 1997), 148.

7. Quoted in Drosnin, *Citizen Hughes*, 107.

8. Ibid., 118.

9. Ibid., 116.

10. Ibid.

11. Steven M. Lovelady, "The Old Gang: 'Cleanup' of Las Vegas Fails to Oust Hoodlums Who Run the Gambling," *Wall Street Journal*, May 23, 1969.

12. Donald L. Barlett and James B. Steele, *Howard Hughes: His Life and Madness* (New York: W. W. Norton, 2004), 318.

13. See also Reinhold Martin, *The Organizational Complex: Architecture, Media, and Corporate Space* (Cambridge, MA: MIT Press, 2003).

14. David G. Schwartz, *Suburban Xanadu: The Casino Resort on the Las Vegas Strip and Beyond* (New York: Routledge, 2003), 156.

15. Tom Wolfe, *From Bauhaus to Our House* (New York: Farrar, Straus, and Giroux, 1981), 2.

16. The International Promotional and Publicity Collection, University of Nevada, Las Vegas, Special Collections.

17. Drosnin, *Citizen Hughes*, 118.

18. Ibid., 173.

19. Laura Deni, "It Takes a Business Analyst to Know Who Owns What in Vegas," *Billboard*, September 19, 1970.

20. Hal Rothman, *Neon Metropolis: How Las Vegas Shed Its Stigma and Became the First City of the Twenty-First Century* (New York: Routledge, 2003), 22.

21. Ibid., 29.

22. Quoted in "Homer Rissman," Dreaming the Skyline, University of Nevada, Las Vegas, Digital Collection, <http://digital.library.unlv.edu/skyline/architect/homer-rissman> (accessed October 5, 2013).

23. Drosnin, *Citizen Hughes*, 117.

24. Quoted in David A. Cook, *Lost Illusions: American Cinema in the Shadow of Watergate and Vietnam, 1970–1979* (Berkeley: University of California Press, 2000), 303.

25. Hal Lancaster, "Dream Factory: High and Low Rollers Swell Corporate Till at MGM's Vegas Spa," *Wall Street Journal*, September 17, 1975.

26. From a conversation with Martin Stern, Dreaming the Skyline, UNLV Digital Collection, <http://digital.library.unlv.edu/skyline/architect/martin-stern> (accessed October 5, 2013).

27. Lancaster, "Dream Factory."

28. Paul Goldberger, "Las Vegas: Vulgar and Extraordinary," *New York Times*, April 13, 1978.

29. Rem Koolhaas, "Bigness and the Problem of Large," in Rem Koolhaas and Bruce Mau, *S, M, L, XL* (New York: Monacelli Press, 1995), 494–516.

30. Mike Davis, "Fortress Los Angeles: The Militarization of Urban Space," in Michael Sorkin, ed., *Variations on a Theme Park* (New York: Hill and Wang, 1992), 157.

31. Ed Vogel, "LV Glitter: Tiny Cost for Great Publicity," *Las Vegas Review-Journal*, September 2, 1984.

32. Robert Macy, "Neon Wars: Las Vegas Signs Strike a Glow for Brighter Future," *Los Angeles Times*, December 8, 1985.

33. Wright, "Kermit Wayne," 40.

34. Quoted in Rhonda Quagliana, "Artist Uses Neon for Paint, Steel and Plastic to Canvas," *Las Vegas Sun*, August 13, 1983.

35. Albert Elsen, "Night Lights," *Art News*, November 1983, 114.

36. "Vegas Glitter Makes Gold," *Sign Business*, April 23, 1987.

37. Elsen, "Night Lights," 113.

38. Alan Hess, *Viva Las Vegas: After-Hours Architecture* (San Francisco: Chronicle Books, 1993), 93.

39. Bill Johnson, "An Answer at Last: It Takes 40 Nevadans to Change the Bulbs," *Wall Street Journal*, October 15, 1985.

40. Ibid.

41. Quoted in Susan Condon, "The Neon Patrol," *Las Vegas Review-Journal*, November 9, 1986.

42. Ibid.

43. Johnson, "An Answer at Last."

44. Ibid.

45. Condon, "The Neon Patrol."

46. Ibid.

47. Molly Ivins, "Las Vegas Raises Tacky to a Magnificent Level," *New York Times*, November 25, 1979.

48. Kurt Anderson, "Las Vegas USA," *Time*, January 10, 1994.

49. Neal Karlen, "A Stroke of Genius," *New York Times*, April 25, 1993.

50. Iver Peterson, "On the Way Out: Outdoor Neon Signs," *New York Times*, February 10, 1985.

51. Sara Harris, "Leftovers / (G)litter," *Cabinet* 5 (Winter 2002), <http://cabinetmagazine.org/issues/5/glitter.php> (accessed January 15, 2015).

52. Donald Janson, "Financing Casinos," *New York Times*, April 30, 1978.

CHAPTER 5: DISNEYLAND (1985–1995)

1. Quoted in Gabriel Trip, "From Vice to Nice: The Suburbanization of Las Vegas," *New York Times*, December 1, 1991.

2. "Las Vegas Buzzing Over Trop 'Island,'" *Casino Gaming Magazine*, April 1986, 15.

3. Quoted in Amy Caroll, "Step Inside: A Look at Interior Design in the Casino Industry," *Casino Gaming Magazine*, October 1987, 6.

4. "Casinos in America: Then and Now," *Casino Gaming Magazine*, August 1986.

5. "Design/Construction Firms: Providing Return on Casino Investment," *Casino Gaming Magazine*, November 1985, 25.

6. Tom Gorman, "With Castles and Casinos, Pirates and Pyramids, the New Las Vegas Is Betting on High-Stakes Style," *Los Angeles Times*, December 12, 1993.

7. Quoted in Eben Shapiro, "All About/Theme Park Spinoffs; Need a Little Fantasy? A Bevy of New Companies Can Help," *New York Times*, March 10, 1991.

8. Ibid.

9. Gorman, "With Castles and Casinos."

10. David Spanier, *Welcome to the Pleasuredome: Inside Las Vegas* (Reno: University of Nevada Press, 1992), 33.

11. Quoted from Mike Panasitti and Natasha Schull, "A Discipline of Leisure: Engineering the Las Vegas Casino," unpublished thesis, University of California, Berkeley, May 1993.

12. Christina Binkley, *Winner Takes All: Steve Wynn, Kirk Kerkorian, Gary Loveman, and the Race to Own Las Vegas* (New York: Hyperion, 2008), 26.

13. Howard Stutz, "The Mirage to Become a Reality," *Las Vegas Review-Journal*, November 20, 1989.

14. William N. Thompson, "Steve Wynn," in Richard Davies, ed., *The Maverick Spirit: Building the New Nevada* (Reno: University of Nevada Press, 1999), 204.

15. Quoted in Kurt Anderson, "Las Vegas U.S.A.," *Time*, June 24, 2001.

16. Marc Cooper, "Fear and Lava," *Village Voice*, November 30, 1993.

17. Quoted in Tom Furlong, "Gambling on a Mirage," *Los Angeles Times*, November 21, 1989.

18. Binkley, *Winner Takes All*, 28.

19. Ibid., 28–29.

20. 1989 Annual Report, Circus Circus Enterprises.

21. Amy Caroll, "Taking the Theme to the Limit," *Casino Gaming Magazine*, November 1988.

22. Tom Dye, "Excalibur, Mirage Stir Architects' Excitement," *Las Vegas Review-Journal*, June 17, 1990.

23. Tom Furlong, "Vegas Opens a New Castle of Excess," *Los Angeles Times*, June 18, 1990.

24. John L. Smith, *Sharks in the Desert: The Founding Fathers and Current Kings of Las Vegas* (New York: Barricade Books, 2005), 107.

25. Jamie McKee, "New York-New York, Monte Carlo, The Stratosphere," *Casino Journal*, January 1996.

26. Glenn Schaeffer, "Realizing the Masterplan," *Casino Gaming Magazine*, March 1996.

27. Spanier, *Welcome to the Pleasuredome*, 101.

28. John Welbes, "Special Acts Find Stages in Strange Places," *Las Vegas Review-Journal*, June 17, 1990.

29. Quoted in Stacey Welling, "Excalibur Is a Dream Come True," *Las Vegas Review-Journal*, June 17, 1990.

30. Roger Cohen, "Trying to Give Las Vegas a G Rating," *New York Times*, October 2, 1991.

31. Paul Goldberger, "Mickey Mouse Teaches the Architects," *New York Times*, October 22, 1972.

32. Aaron Betsky, quoted in Ada Louise Huxtable, "Living with the Fake, and Liking It," *New York Times*, March 30, 1997.

33. Jeff Burbank, "As the Theming of Las Vegas Becomes Ever More Elaborate, a New Generation of Superstar Designers Is Prized for Its Flair for Weaving Convincing Architectural 'Tales,'" *Casino Journal*, December 1996, 85.

34. Stacy Shoemaker, "Terry Dougall," *Hospitality Design* 25, no. 3 (April 2003), 116.

35. Aaron Betsky, quoted in Huxtable, "Living with the Fake, and Liking It."

36. Burbank, "As the Theming of Las Vegas Becomes Ever More Elaborate," 85.

37. Goldberger, "Mickey Mouse Teaches the Architects."

38. See Jon Goss, "The 'Magic of the Mall': An Analysis of Form, Function, and Meaning in the Contemporary Retail Built Environment," *Annals of the Association of American Geographers* 83, no. 1 (1993), 18–47.

39. Quoted in Alan Bryman, *The Disneyization of Society* (London: Sage, 2004), 58.

40. Shoemaker, "Terry Dougall."

41. Blair Kamin, "Lessons from Las Vegas: Beneath the Gaudy Glamor Is a City that Works," *Chicago Tribune*, May 15, 1994.

42. But the original monuments of Luxor and Giza were of questionable authenticity as well, with restorations to the Sphinx, the displacement of Abu Simbel temple, and a laser show at Giza.

43. Ada Louise Huxtable, *The Unreal America: Architecture and Illusion* (New York: New Press, 1999), 74.

44. Huxtable, "Living with the Fake, and Liking It."

45. Quoted from "Las Vegas Strip History. Luxor," <http://www.lvstriphistory.com/ie/luxor.htm> (accessed October 5, 2014).

46. Karl G. Ruling, "The Light at the Top of the Pyramid," *Theater Crafts International*, May 1994, 28.

47. Richard Wolkomir, "Las Vegas Meets La-La Land," *Smithsonian* 26, no. 7 (1995), 50–59.

48. Ibid.

49. Ibid.

50. Howard Rheingold, "Total Immersion," *Wired* 1.5 (November 1993).

51. Phil Patton, "Now Playing in the Virtual World," *Popular Science*, April 1994, 82.

52. Anderson, "Las Vegas U.S.A."

53. Kamin, "Lessons from Las Vegas."

54. Quoted in Gorman, "With Castles and Casinos."

55. Lynn Waddell, "Fall of Dunes Much Greater Than Its Rise," *Las Vegas Sun*, October 28, 1993.

56. Doug Bailey, "The Crown Prince of Las Vegas Strives to Titillate His Losers," *Boston Globe*, September 28, 1993.

57. Quote from interview with Roger Thomas on *Dream Factory*, radio program, KNPR Radio, Las Vegas, February 17, 2006.

58. Ibid.

59. Mike Weatherford, "Pirate Shows Sends Ship Sinking and Actors Swimming," *Las Vegas Review-Journal*, October 27, 1993.

60. Wolkomir, "Las Vegas Meets La-La Land."

61. Weatherford, "Pirate Shows Sends Ship Sinking and Actors Swimming."

62. Jeff Burbank, "Treasure Island: Fantasy by Design," *International Gaming & Wagering Business*, March 1, 1995.

63. Anne Raver, "Fooling with Nature," *New York Times*, July 11, 1993.

64. Weatherford, "Pirate Shows Sends Ship Sinking and Actors Swimming."

65. David Johnson, "Buccaneer Bay," *Theater Crafts International*, May 1994, 35.

66. Aaron Betsky, "Future World: With Vegas as a Model—Really!—Our Cities Might Not Be So Grim After All," *Los Angeles Times*, December 12, 1993.

67. Burbank, "As the Theming of Las Vegas Becomes Ever More Elaborate," 83.

68. Frances Anderton and John Chase, *Las Vegas: The Success of Excess* (London: Ellipsis, 1997), 52.

69. Kamin, "Lessons from Las Vegas."

70. Ibid.

71. Dave Palermo, "Wynn Skirting High-Seas Risks," *Las Vegas Review-Journal*, October 24, 1993.

72. Jeff Burbank, "Cannons Herald Opening," *Las Vegas Review-Journal*, October 27, 1993.

73. Abby Gardner, "Expansion in Las Vegas: A Building Boom Like No Other," *Casino Gaming Magazine*, December 1991, 12.

74. Lynn Waddell, "MGM Puts On a Really Big Show," *Las Vegas Sun*, December 17, 1993.

75. Cohen, "Trying to Give Las Vegas a G Rating."

76. Laura Evenson, "Las Vegas Putting on the Glitz," *San Francisco Chronicle*, February 8, 1993.

77. Ibid.

78. Cohen, "Trying to Give Las Vegas a G Rating."

79. George McCabe, "Putting On a Brand New Face," *Las Vegas Review-Journal*, October 14, 1993.

80. Anderson, "Las Vegas U.S.A."

81. Ibid.

82. Cooper, "Fear and Lava."

83. Palermo, "Wynn Skirting High-Seas Risks."

84. Calvin Sims, "Family Values as a Las Vegas Smash," *New York Times*, February 3, 1994.

85. Richard Schickel, *The Disney Version: The Life, Times, Art, and Commerce of Walt Disney* (New York: Simon and Schuster, 1968), 225.

86. See Michael Sorkin, ed., *Variations on a Theme Park: The New American City and the End of Public Space* (New York: Hill and Wang, 1992); Sharon Zukin, *The Cultures of Cities* (Cambridge, MA: Wiley-Blackwell, 1995); Bryman, *The Disneyization of Society*.

87. Patricia Leigh Brown, "Fantasy Hotels: Excess Is All," *New York Times*, October 21, 1990.

88. Mark Gottdiener, *The Theming of America: Dreams, Media Fantasies and Themed Environments* (Boulder, CO: Westview Press, 2001), 3.

89. Schickel, *The Disney Version*, 15.

90. Umberto Eco, *Travels in Hyperreality* (New York: Harcourt, 1986), 48.

91. Ibid., 43.

92. Brendan Gill, "The Sky Line: The Death of the Skyscraper?," *New Yorker*, March 4, 1991.

93. Sorkin, *Variations on a Theme Park*, xiv.

94. B. Joseph Pine II and James H. Gilmore, *The Experience Economy: Work Is Theater and Every Business a Stage* (Boston: Harvard Business Review Press, 1999), xxvi.

95. Goldberger, "Mickey Mouse Teaches the Architects."

96. Shapiro, "All About/Theme Park Spinoffs."

97. Anderton and Chase, *Las Vegas: The Success of Excess*, 52.

98. James O'Brien, "Las Vegas Today—Rome in a Day: Corporate Development Practices and the Role of the Professional," *Journal of Architectural Education* 54, no. 2 (November 2000), 71.

99. John Hench, Peggy Van Pelt, and M. A. Sklar, *Designing Disney* (New York: Disney Editions, 2009), 79.

100. Gary S. Cross and John K. Walton, *The Playful Crowd: Pleasure Places in the Twentieth Century* (New York: Columbia University Press, 2005), 295.

101. Steven Izenour and David A. Dashiel III, "Relearning from Las Vegas," *Architecture*, October 1990, 46–51.

CHAPTER 6: SIM CITY (1995–2001)

1. Glenn Schaeffer, "Making It Modern," *Casino Journal*, May 1997, 76.

2. Ada Louise Huxtable, "Living with the Fake, and Liking It," *New York Times*, March 30, 1997.

3. Nezar AlSayyad, ed., *Consuming Tradition, Manufacturing Heritage: Global Norms and Urban Forms in the Age of Tourism* (New York: Routledge, 2001).

4. Umberto Eco, *Travels in Hyperreality* (New York: Harcourt, 1990), 31.

5. University of Nevada, Las Vegas, Center for Gaming Research, Nevada Gaming Revenues, 1984–2013 (2014).

6. Quoted in Pete Earley, *Super Casino: Inside the "New" Las Vegas* (New York: Bantam Books, 2001), 119.

7. Quoted in Dave Berns, "The Big Five," *Las Vegas Review-Journal*, September 22, 1996.

8. John L. Smith, *No Limit: The Rise and Fall of Bob Stupak and Las Vegas' Stratosphere Tower* (Las Vegas: Huntington Press, 1997), 113.

9. Quoted in John L. Smith, "Bob Stupak," *Las Vegas Review-Journal*, September 12, 1999.

10. "Stratosphere," *Casino Journal*, April 1996.

11. Smith, "Bob Stupak," 247.

12. Quoted in Thomas Moore, "Wine Them, Dine Them, Thrill Them: Las Vegas Casinos Have Figured Out that the More You Entertain," *Casino Journal*, September 1997, 59.

13. Ibid.

14. James O'Brien, "Las Vegas Today—Rome in a Day: Corporate Development Practices and the Role of the Professional," *Journal of Architectural Education* 54, no. 2 (November 2000), 73.

15. Quoted in Stacy Shoemaker, "Terry Dougall," *Hospitality Design* 25, no. 3 (April 2003), 116.

16. Coined in Robert Venturi, Denise Scott Brown, and Steven Izenour, *Learning from Las Vegas* (Cambridge, MA: MIT Press, 1972).

17. Quoted in O'Brien, "Las Vegas Today—Rome in a Day," 74.

18. Quoted in James Rutherford, "Tower of Power," *Casino Journal*, August 1995, 64.

19. Quoted in Jeff Burbank, "As the Theming of Las Vegas Becomes Ever More Elaborate, a New Generation of Superstar Designers Is Prized for Its Flair for Leaving Convincing Architectural 'Tales,'" *Casino Journal*, December 1996, 84.

20. Ada Louise Huxtable, *The Unreal America: Architecture and Illusion* (New York: New Press, 1999), 2.

21. Paul Goldberger, "New York New York, It's a Las Vegas Town," *New York Times*, January 15, 1997.

22. Nezar AlSayyad, ed., *The End of Tradition* (London: Routledge, 2004), 25.

23. Quoted in Kim Severson, "This Lady Liberty Is a Las Vegas Teenager," *New York Times*, April 14, 2011.

24. Quoted in Christina Binkley, *Winner Takes All: Steve Wynn, Kirk Kerkorian, Gary Loveman, and the Race to Own Las Vegas* (New York: Hyperion Books, 2008), 85.

25. Bill Friedman, "Designing Casinos to Dominate the Competition: The Friedman International Standards of Casino Design," Institute for the Study of Gambling and Commercial Gaming, 2000, 17.

26. Frances Anderton, "At home with: Jon Jerde; The Global Village Goes Pop Baroque," *New York Times*, October 8, 1998.

27. John Greenwald, "Playing for a Wynn," *Time*, March 6, 2000.

28. James Rutherford, "Gaming's New Fort Knox," *Casino Journal*, August 1998.

29. Quoted in "Wynn Unveils 'Most Extravagant Hotel on Earth,'" *Casino Journal*, April 1996.

30. Schaeffer, "Making It Modern," 67.

31. Quoted in Earley, *Super Casino*, 374.

32. Wilfrido M. Sy, *Feng Shui, Craps, and Superstitions: The Martial Arts Approach to Winning at Craps* (New York: IUniverse, 2004), 22.

33. Quoted in Earley, *Super Casino*, 227.

34. Ibid., 227–228.

35. Quoted in Rik Kirkland, "The Man with the Golden Gut," *Fortune*, October 17, 2005.

36. Quoted in Jamie McKee, "Along the New Rialto," *Casino Journal*, June 1997, 55.

37. Ibid., 52.

38. Ibid.

39. Quoted in Jamie McKee, "Breaking the Rules," *Casino Journal*, June 1999.

40. Quoted in Wayne Curtis, "Belle Epoxy," *Preservation*, May/June 2000.

41. Quoted in Carolyn O'Neil and Greg Phillips, "Big-Dollar Resorts Give Las Vegas an Upscale Look," *CNN*, June 16, 2000.

42. Quoted in Carolyn O'Neil, "Take a Ride Down Sunset Boulevard, Miami's South Beach and the Las Vegas Strip," *CNN*, June 17, 2000.

43. Quoted in Frances Anderton, "Put It on the Ceiling and Call It High Art," *New York Times*, October 14, 1999.

44. Ibid.

45. Ibid.

46. Quoted in Curtis, "Belle Epoxy."

47. Giovanna Franci, *Dreaming of Italy: Las Vegas and the Virtual Grand Tour* (Reno: University of Nevada Press, 2005), 64.

48. Quoted in Carrie Culpepper, "What It Takes to Run the World's Largest Hotel," *AOL Travel*, June 14, 2010.

49. Quoted in Curtis, "Belle Epoxy."

50. Franci, *Dreaming of Italy*, 64.

51. Quoted in Charles Trueheart, "Vive la France? Viva Las Vegas! It's a Faux Paris," *Washington Post*, April 8, 1997.

52. Quoted in Jamie McKee, "Paris Opens Triumphant," *Casino Journal*, October 1999.

53. Quoted in Shawn Tully, "The New King of Casinos Arthur Goldberg, a Former Trucking Operator, Has Built the Country's Biggest Chain of Casinos," *Fortune*, September 18, 2000.

54. Charles Silverman, interview with the author, 2014.

55. Quoted in Moore, "Wine Them, Dine Them, Thrill Them."

56. Charles Silverman, interview with the author, 2014.

57. Quoted in Smith Hubble, "Tower Adds an Eyeful to Skyline," *Las Vegas Review-Journal*, August 30, 1999.

58. Trueheart, "Vive la France? Viva Las Vegas!"

59. Jean Baudrillard, *Simulations* (New York: Semiotext(e), 1983), 2.

60. Bruce Bégout, *Zeropolis: The Experience of Las Vegas* (London: Reaktion, 2003), 85.

61. See Timothy Mitchell, *Colonising Egypt* (Berkeley: University of California Press, 1988).

62. AlSayyad, *Consuming Tradition, Manufacturing Heritage*, 10.

63. Quoted in Rutherford, "Gaming's New Fort Knox."

64. Anderton, "Put It on the Ceiling and Call It High Art."

65. Curtis, "Belle Epoxy."

66. Susan Strange, *Casino Capitalism* (Manchester: Manchester University Press, 1997).

67. Quoted in Monica Caruso, "Designers Want to Offer a Stylized French Feel," *Las Vegas Review-Journal*, August 30, 1999.

CHAPTER 7: STARCHITECTURE (2001–PRESENT)

1. "Vegas' CityCenter Opens Doors to World's Most Spectacular Offerings in One Singular Setting," MGM Mirage press release, September 16, 2009, <http://www.prnewswire.com/mnr/mgm/40097/> (accessed June 5, 2014).

2. Christopher Hawthorne, "In Las Vegas, One Final Echo of the Boom Years," *Los Angeles Times*, December 11, 2009.

3. Quoted in Tom Gorman, "Plans for Guggenheim in Las Vegas Unveiled," *Los Angeles Times*, October 21, 2000.

4. Ibid.

5. Associated Press, "Mandalay Bay Opens Luxury Hotel on the Las Vegas Strip," *USA Today*, December 22, 2003.

6. Guy Trebay, "After Nice, a Return to Vice," *New York Times*, June 8, 2003.

7. Joel Stein, "The Strip is Back," *Time*, July 26, 2004.

8. See Brian McNair, *Striptease Culture: Sex, Media and the Democratization of Desire* (London: Routledge, 2002).

9. Trebay, "After Nice, a Return to Vice."

10. Nina Munk, "Steve Wynn's Biggest Gamble," *Vanity Fair*, June 2005.

11. Howard Stutz, "Mountain Makers: Forum Told How Wynn Structure Came to Rise So High," *Las Vegas Review-Journal*, June 24, 2005.

12. Kitty Yancey, "Won Over by Wynn," *USA Today*, June 9, 2005.

13. Joel Stein, "Steve Wynn," *Time*, May 8, 2006.

14. Munk, "Steve Wynn's Biggest Gamble."

15. Craig Kellogg, "A Full House," *Interior Design*, March 5, 2005.

16. Bill Friedman, "Designing Casinos to Dominate the Competition: The Friedman International Standards of Casino Design," Institute for the Study of Gambling and Commercial Gaming, 2000, 15–16.

17. Ibid., 17.

18. Blair Lyn, "Wynn or Loose," *Casino Design*, 2005, 7.

19. Karen Finlay, Vinay Kanetkar, Jane Londerville, and Harvey H. C. Marmurek, "The Physical and Psychological Measurement of Gambling Environments," *Environment and Behavior* 38, no. 4 (2006), 570–581.

20. Quoted in Jonah Lehrer, "Royal Flush," *New Yorker*, March 26, 2012.

21. Rik Kirkland, "The Man with the Golden Gut," *Fortune*, October 17, 2005.

22. Quoted in "The World's Casino: Macau Overtakes Las Vegas Strip," *Reuters*, February 12, 2007.

23. Tony Illia, "Sizing Up Las Vegas: Palazzo Takes Shape on the Strip," *Southwest Contractor*, July 2006, 52–54.

24. Paul Goldberger, "What Happens in Vegas: Can You Bring Architectural Virtue to Sin City?," *New Yorker,* October 4, 2010.

25. Roger Gros, "MGM Maestro," *Casino Design*, 2010, 21.

26. Quoted in Robin Pogrebin, "Making the Desert Bloom with Architecture," *New York Times*, September 15, 2005.

27. Charles Fishman, *The Big Thirst: The Secret Life and Turbulent Future of Water* (New York: Free Press, 2011).

28. Tony Illia, "Q&A with Veer Towers Architect Helmut Jahn Tilt Perfect Tip-of-the-Hat to Las Vegas," *Las Vegas Business Press*, January 18, 2010.

29. Philip Kennicott, "Architectural Review of Las Vegas CityCenter Hotel-Casino-Shopping Complex," *Washington Post*, December 27, 2009.

30. Hawthorne, "In Las Vegas, One Final Echo of the Boom Years."

31. Justin Davidson, "The Liberation of Daniel Libeskind," *New York Times*, September 30, 2007.

32. "Vegas' CityCenter Opens Doors," MGM Mirage press release.

33. "$1.8 Billion Plus Cosmopolitan Resort and Casino Breaks Ground at Center Strip Location," The Cosmopolitan press release, October 25, 2005, <http://www.prnewswire.com/news-releases/18-billion-plus-cosmopolitan-resort--casino-breaks-ground-at-center-strip-location-55565307.html> (accessed June 5, 2014).

34. Tony Illia, "Tower of Power: New $3 Billion Cosmopolitan Packs a Punch," *Southwest Contractor*, January 2008.

35. Ibid.

36. Jay Jones, "A Cosmopolitan with a Few Surprise Ingredients," *Los Angeles Times*, December 5, 2010.

37. "$1.8 Billion Plus Cosmopolitan Resort & Casino Breaks Ground," The Cosmopolitan press release.

38. Ibid.

39. T. W. Luke, "Casinopolitanism," in George Ritzer, ed., *The Wiley-Blackwell Encyclopedia of Globalization* (Chichester, UK: Wiley-Blackwell, 2012).

40. Quoted in Sonia Kolesnikov-Jessop, "Spotlight: Sheldon Adelson," *New York Times*, March 16, 2007.

41. Las Vegas Visitors and Convention Authority, "Las Vegas Year-to-Date Executive Summary," years 2000 and 2007.

42. Associated Press, "Fontainebleau Resorts LLC Announces Plans for 2.8 Billion Dollars," April 17, 2007.

43. Hal Rothman, *Neon Metropolis: How Las Vegas Started the Twenty-First Century* (New York: Routledge, 2002), xi.

44. Joel Stein, "Less Vegas: The Casino Town Bets on a Comeback," *Time*, August 14, 2009.

45. Ibid.

46. See Susan Strange, *Casino Capitalism* (Manchester: Manchester University Press, 1997).

47. Ulrich Beck, *Risk Society: Toward a New Modernity* (New Delhi: Sage, 1992).

Index